Open Wound, Open Heart, Open Hands

AND THE FREEDOM OF FORGIVENESS

Leta H. Montague

WestBow
PRESS
A DIVISION OF THOMAS NELSON

WestBow Press books may be ordered through booksellers or by contacting:

WestBow Press
A Division of Thomas Nelson
1663 Liberty Drive
Bloomington, IN 47403
www.westbowpress.com
1 (866) 928-1240

ISBN: 978-1-4908-1367-7 (sc)
ISBN: 978-1-4908-1368-4 (hc)
ISBN: 978-1-4908-1369-1 (e)

Library of Congress Control Number: 2013918937

Printed in the United States of America.

WestBow Press rev. date: 1/2/2014

CONTENTS

Section 3—Open Hands

ACKNOWLEDGMENTS

To my children, my grandsons, and my granddaughters, who continue to give me great joy and who let me know how much they love me.

To my siblings and my close circle of friends: thank you for the constant encouragement.

To the women who have spoken to me, I pray God will meet you in your pain. I pray he will continue to walk with you in your journey. I pray also that he will continue to guide you and help you to grow stronger.

Special acknowledgment
To my mom (my mama) …

She is the best! I want to thank her for her faith. She is a woman who has always been faithful to the God she serves. My faith in God grew from the testimony of her life, and my faith is stronger because of her.

Thank you, Mama!

God bless always!
Leta

Life is a tapestry, a series of twists and turns that no one can predict!

The journey of life is a series of vertical and horizontal paths going every which way but straight. The paths seem to go into seemingly uncoordinated and crazy directions. There are paths that stop suddenly, a loose end where once you thought it would lead to a connecting path. There are paths strewn with flowers, some with trees, some with thistles, and others with thorns.

As I reflected on life as a tapestry, I remembered my craft days. I did many forms of needlework, and it always amazed me when I compared the back part of my work to the front. I wasn't always the neatest needle-crafter, so the back of my projects always had lumps, bumps, and loose threads everywhere. If you looked at the front, however, it was always a beautiful tapestry—a work of art.

Sometimes when we look at our life, we see only the discontinuance, the loose ends leading nowhere, the lumps and bumps similar to the back of my needlework projects. But God sees another side of our life. He sees the smooth, seamless side—the complete picture of the tapestry of our life. He doesn't see the loose ends, because loose ends have finality to them and with him, there is no finality. He sees all the paths of our life, tightly woven together and well coordinated as one, because he lovingly and purposefully constructed each thread and each path when he created the blueprint of our life. Therefore, each path has a purpose and each path and each thread of our life is a part of the whole.

Each time we are wounded, it is a part of the whole picture—a bump in our life. When our life takes a different path than we expected— such as when a relationship dies, or when a child goes astray—we may think, *Why did this happen? What's the purpose?* And more important, we may ask, "Where do I go from here? How do I transition from this situation?" Sometimes the answer comes quickly, and sometimes we never get an answer. I know, however, that these bumps, this suffering, and this wounding that represent adversity also present opportunities for growth. Whether our transition out of our adversity is fast or slow, how we make that transition is up to us.

> "Adversity introduces a man to himself."
>
> —Anonymous

According to early twentieth-century evangelist Oswald Chambers, "We all know people who have been made much meaner and more irritable and more intolerable to live with by suffering. It is not right to say that all suffering perfects. It only perfects one type of person … the one who accepts the call of God in Christ Jesus." (www.apprehended. wordpress.com/tag/Oswald-chambers-quotes/).

Everyone faces the adversity of being wounded; it is an emotional or physical condition caused by the hurtful acts of others. We may find ourselves in a wilderness where we have to walk alone. Many times, people are wounded out of anger and unforgiveness. Wounding is propagated by anger, regardless of whether that anger is fueled by jealousy, resentment, a hot temper, blind anger, frustration, inadequacy, hostility, repressed anger, or insult. No matter which word we choose to express those feelings, it is still anger. One of the beginning signs of anger is resentment. Resentment leads to jealousy and wounding, which in turn can lead to unforgiveness. Anger is a disease; unforgiveness is a symptom of that disease. The root cause of all of the above emotions is spiritual; it is sin. On the other hand, although anger is usually viewed negatively, it can be helpful as well as harmful. It depends on how it is expressed.

Anger as a Constructive Force Is Powerful

Let's look at three men in history and the effects of their anger: Abraham Lincoln displayed his anger with slavery and made public his opposition to slavery. Gandhi was angry with people's oppression, and his subsequent action changed a nation. He is believed to have said, "I have learned through bitter experience the one supreme lesson to conserve my anger, and as heat conserved is transmuted into energy, even so our anger controlled can be transmuted into a power which can move the world" (www.thinkexist.com/quotation-i-have-learned-through-bitter-experience-the-one/295935.html.

Dr. Martin Luther King Jr.'s anger at injustice is still bearing fruits in many cultures, decades after he was assassinated. He once said, "The ultimate tragedy is not the oppression and cruelty by the bad people but the silence over that by the good people."

In another of his speeches, Dr. King said, "The ultimate measure of a man is not where he stands in moments of comfort and convenience, but where he stands at times of challenge and controversy" (www.quotationspage.com/quote/wr973.html) .

When Jesus was here on earth, he went to the temple, expecting to worship his Father, but what he saw made him angry. He was angry enough to do something about it; he drove out the money-changers. These examples of anger are expressed as a disciplined, dynamic, potent, and effective force that transformed situations and society.

On the other hand, the anger we most often hear about in the news and in our community is expressed in a more negative light; for example, the high rate of divorce, the abuse of women and children, school shootings, and the many countries at war with each other all come from misdirected anger.

Sometimes critics who want to justify their anger say, "But Jesus was angry." Let us look at Jesus' anger. No one exercised more purposeful anger than Jesus. His anger was concise, controlled, and aptly wielded when he drove the money-changers from the synagogue. He was not mean or vicious, and he did not seek to destroy. He wanted to make a point, and he did.

In Ephesians 4:26 – 27, the apostle Paul talks about anger and how we should channel it. He says, "In your anger do not sin: Do not let the sun go down while you are still angry, and do not give the devil a foothold."

We give a foothold to the enemy when we hold on to our anger. If we are honest with ourselves, many of us can plead guilty to that! The danger of that undisciplined anger is that it makes us vulnerable, we forget about using our common sense, and our ability to reason fails us.

Anger as a Destructive Force

Most wounds are inflicted through undisciplined anger. Resentment builds up, and before we know it, we are caught up in the cycle of anger. Some people delight in hurting others. They seem to think that if they are unhappy, then no one else should be happy. It is always a dangerous sign when a person gains satisfaction from putting down someone or deliberately inflicting wounds. There is an anger issue, but it goes deeper. I would say it is a spiritual matter, as that anger has been allowed to infiltrate the heart and the mind. The mind and the heart are perfect breeding places for negative and destructive emotions. We need to turn over control of those breeding places to the Holy Spirit and allow him to clean them out.

Many relationships, including marriages, have broken down because of anger. In my wilderness experience, during my grief over my divorce, God's revelations and my self-reflections taught me that even though I might have had a right to be angry over the divorce, it was not my right to hold on to my anger. God made it plain that if I held on to my anger, I would not be able to forgive the person who wounded me. Therefore, I had to deal with my anger and forgive.

God reminded me that forgiveness was a choice, and if I wanted him to continue to use me, I could not afford to nurse my anger. Sometimes we feel we have been treated badly, or life has treated us badly, so our reaction is not as kind as it should be. But our reaction is just as important as our action. We all know that wounds carry deep pain. The wounds we suffer impact our life, as well as the lives of our family and our friends. In this deep pain, however, we can find grace and dignity in the Word of God. And that is what we should use to measure our reaction.

The Word of God is powerful. After reading about the collapse of my marriage and my journey in *God's Grace: A Long Night's Journey into Day*, a non-Christian woman told me that her long-term marriage had collapsed too, but after reading the book, she was inspired to look up some of the Scriptures mentioned and read them. I hope this book has the same effect on you if you have been wounded. The goal in dealing with our wounds is to get to a healthy place in our life, where we have no animosity or hatred toward the people who have wounded us, because God has cleansed us and healed us, and we are happy and content in him. Our happiness and our contentment can come only from Christ.

In this book, I will examine several Bible personalities and some specific incidents in their lives. In all the situations, we will see where direct resentment (or an emotion associated with anger) was the cause of the wounding and the ensuing bitterness, unforgiveness, and discord. As a result of the anger, all the lives of the personalities took a left turn. In the midst of this discord, their lives seemed filled with discontinuance and loose ends, but as their lives unfolded, God used all the loose ends to weave a pattern of beauty into the tapestry of a life that glorified him.

As I examine these Bible personalities, I also looked at how we can apply these principles in our life. When God was allowed to intervene, healing occurred, families were reconciled, and broken lives were pieced back together. Not one of the Bible personalities was perfect, and they each inflicted many open wounds. But God made their way straight, not because of who they were but because of who he is. God will do the same for us. If we accept Jesus as Lord and Savior, we have a right standing with God, even when we do not walk as godly as we should. God takes whatever we offer and uses that to mold, remake, and transform us. He doesn't condemn us or throw us out like garbage. Instead, he gently works his work of sanctification in us, because we are his children—although we still have the choice of walking away from him and living carelessly.

Sometime ago, someone criticized me and scoffed at my calling myself a godly woman. I suspect that person, like many you may know, did not experience the true grace of God. That person sat in pharisaic judgment and missed out on the fact that God sees my heart and your heart, takes what is given him, and uses it to transform us daily. *We have to remember that only God is perfect.*

It is to this perfect God that we go with our open wounds, whether these wounds are physical or emotional. An abusive environment, a dysfunctional family background, post-traumatic stress, the death of a loved one, sexual assault, loss of a child, survival of a disaster, the ending of an important relationship, an extra-marital affair, divorce or abandonment, rejection—the list is endless. Someone once said, "Pain is inevitable; suffering is optional." When we have open, gaping wounds, we can couple the pain and suffering with God's heart and his open hands, and allow for his healing powers to transform us.

In this book, I will show how the biblical characters recovered from their wounds and continued to be everything God wanted them to be. It is my belief that if we have an open heart to receive God's healing, he will offer his open hands to heal our wounds and transform us.

Anyone who is living and breathing has received physical and emotional wounds. In addition, if we are living and breathing, we have inflicted some wounds ourselves. The time has come to be realistic: let's not polish our halo, thinking that we have never wounded anyone. Remember: no one is perfect—except Jesus!

Why am I able to write this book? I am not a psychologist or a professional counselor. My primary qualification is that I was wounded and hit rock bottom, emotionally, psychologically, and sometimes physically, yet I have experienced substantial healing. I also have talked with many women and a few men who have been wounded and have found considerable commonality in the pain and suffering. I am a person who has seen decades of life and have seen the evidence of God's healing. I also have proof of his open heart, whether we inflict wounds on someone or others have inflicted wounds on us. I have the evidence of people who have gone through the process of healing and moved on to a better life, but most important, I have God's Word and his promises!

Christian teacher Watchman Nee is credited as saying,

The breaking of the alabaster box and the anointing of the Lord filled the house with the odour, with the sweetest odor. Everyone could smell it. Whenever you meet someone who has really suffered; been limited, gone through things for the Lord, willing to be imprisoned by the Lord, just being satisfied with Him and nothing else, immediately you scent the fragrance. There is a savor of the Lord. Something has been crushed, something has been broken, and there is a resulting odor of sweetness (www.christthetruth.wordpress.com/2009/03/23breaking-the-alabaster-jar-at-christs-feet).

God's healing provides that fragrance. However, healing an open wound is a process. We have to move from that open, stinky wound to that place of healing, that place of fragrance. We have to work on our healing. We also have to participate in our healing because these open wounds are more than skin deep. They pierce the very soul of our beings, and it takes work and a lot of effort to be whole again. But with God's help and his grace, that healing is a viable option. It doesn't matter how deep the wound is or who inflicted it—either way, you are wounded. All wounds, however, need to be treated so that we can be healed—and healing is a spiritual matter. Don't delay your healing. It is Satan's design to destroy you and prevent your healing. He is the enemy of your soul.

The apostle Peter cautions us to be "self-controlled and alert. Your enemy the devil prowls around like a roaring lion looking for someone to devour" (1 Pet. 5:8). We have to identify the enemy and overcome the enemy's plans for our life. Don't give the enemy an inch to get in, but if the enemy has been let into your family already, remain in prayer. It is spiritual warfare, but you have already won the victory through Jesus. You are on your way to higher spiritual ground. Do not let the enemy sideline you.

In this book, I will discuss the Israelites and how they were sidelined as they were headed for the Promised Land. They wanted to go back to Egypt, a proverbial place of slavery and bondage. Like the Israelites, we are on a journey. Our Promised Land is heaven, where we will meet Jesus. We have to leave all the "drama" in Egypt. Let God take care of the things in Egypt. I have made a commitment to praise and thank him during this wilderness season. I will draw strength from him, grow spiritually, and depend only on him for my happiness and well-being. I have taken evangelist Corrie ten Boom's words to heart. She said, "You may never know that Jesus is all you need until Jesus is all you have."

Remember ...

In this life, we will suffer. We will be wounded. We will cause wounding. We will experience pain and adversity, but this should challenge us. How we deal with adversity will define our character. It will also determine our present, past, and future. It is in the pain of adversity that we should pursue a serious walk with God.

The Lord has moved me toward forgiving the people who have wounded me, and I am encouraged by a quote by Mahatma Gandhi: "The weak can never forgive. Forgiveness is the attribute of the strong."

I hope and pray that as you read this book, you too will make the choice to forgive the people who have wounded you. I hope your pain will make you want to draw closer to God. Most of all, I pray you will have an extraordinary encounter with Jesus, the only person who can heal your wounds and love you past your pain. The key to all the above hope and prayers will culminate in healing and a better life only if you *make this time of wounding a divine moment.*

As always, God bless.
Leta

SECTION I—

OPEN WOUNDS

CHAPTER 1

The Board Meeting

"Are they all in the boardroom?"

"Yes, sir. … Sir?"

"Yes?"

"They are very angry that you sent them those résumés."

The man chuckles. "I'm on my way to the boardroom."

All the board members turn angrily and begin to speak in unison as the man enters the boardroom.

"I can't believe that you sent us these résumés!"

"What were you thinking?"

"This is a prestigious firm!"

He tries to interject. "Gentlemen, gentlemen—"

"Criminals, reprobates, miscreants, and—"

"Conspirators, covetous people, and deceivers. We seem to have a few cowards, too. They're all liars!"

"Lord, preserve us! My righteous brother, look at this one. This one is a liar, manipulator, and definitely has trouble staying honest!"

"This old wreck is eighty years old. He probably has one foot in the grave and one on a banana peel! He also has anger issues."

"This one slept with his neighbor's wife and was very happy until the town crier found out. The story finally came out, and when he found out that she was pregnant, he got his employee to kill his lover's husband. He has power, and he sure knows how to abuse it!"

"Oh, God have mercy! This one was a prostitute!"

"We can put her in customer service," one board member snickers.

"She's out for sure," another pipes up.

"Hey, guys. Wait up! Here's the cream of the crop! This one was a fire-breathing dragon. He stood and watched while some people killed an innocent man. He held their clothes and later, he got special orders to kill other people!"

"Can you imagine?"

"Murderer!"

The man keeps on smiling as the board members rage on. "Gentlemen," he finally interjects, "have you considered that there might be another side to some of these stories?"

"Here is another one you missed," a board member interrupts. "She said she wrote in her journal in 1981 that she wanted a new name."

"What new name?"

"Be patient, will you?"

"Apparently, her mother calls her Rits, and she wants to be called a woman after God's own heart."

"Ha!" snorts a board member.

"She seems to be somewhere in the desert now and cannot come for an interview."

"Man! Why bother to waste our precious time if she can't even be here for the interview?"

"Okay, gentlemen, you seem to be quite expressive about the candidates and their wanting positions in the firm," says the gentleman, finally cutting in. "But before we look at the résumés, let's listen in on some stories."

CHAPTER 2

The Early Years

Vignette

Up to the age of eighteen, my lifelong dream was to become a nurse, as I bandaged dolls and other inanimate victims of my passion. Right after high school, I had an appointment to see the matron of the training hospital to begin my nursing career. As I was getting dressed for my interview with the matron, the phone rang.

"Hello."

"Is Rita Montague there?"

"Speaking."

"This is Air Canada calling."

"Yes?"

"We have a ticket from Canada for you. When can you pick it up?"

"Huh! Who sent me the ticket?"

"Lillian Montague."

"Ah … my mother. I will be there in thirty minutes."

Two paths in the road of life—one never to be traveled.

CHAPTER 3

The Journey

I never regretted not showing up for my nurse's interview. I now know, decades later, that had I pursued the path of nursing, my first stint in the emergency room would most likely have resulted in my being on the hospital floor. As I went through the first-aid course, my mind wandered back to the career aspirations of my teenage years—the path not taken and the joy and pain associated with some of the other paths I've been down:

- the path of becoming a Christian after my younger brother's death
- the path of marriage
- the path of childbirth
- the path of divorce and the physical and emotional wounds associated with it
- the path of listening to other women and the physical and emotional pain they go through as their spouses walk away from the marriage
- the path of women sharing the pain of their children who have wandered far from home and far from the God of their parents

Many paths—one road—one journey.

★ ★ ★ ★ ★

As the voice of the first-aid instructor continued to drone on about physical injuries, my mind conjured up the instant imagery of each injury he described: open wound, gaping skin, profusion of blood, skin pallor, life-threatening wounds, abrasions, incisions, lacerations, and punctures. To heal these physical wounds, he advised that we apply first aid; otherwise, infection would set in and cause further physical damage—or death.

My mind then switched to another type of injury: emotional injury. This brought forth the imagery of distress, depression, abuse, dysfunctional behavior, hopelessness, lack of trust, guilt, resentment, anger, sadness, loss of self-esteem, rejection, abandonment, and other trauma.

Physical wounds are easy to see, identify, and treat. The physical body reacts to pain. Emotional wounds, however, are not as clearly evident—but the wounds are there, and your body reacts just as much to this type of wound as to a physical wound. Some emotional wounds may result in depression and anxiety. There is also the excessive behavior of drinking alcohol, using drugs, deviant sexual behavior, gambling, and indulging in foods that are bad for our health. Some people rush into relationships, with all their baggage, right after a traumatic period, only to find out that these outlets give a false sense of coping. These relationships are transitory and may numb the pain for a while, but they don't heal the wounds.

Emotional wounds are not as clear to the physical eye as physical wounds, and they can lie dormant, in our subconscious, and never be tended to or given the opportunity to heal. They can be fresh and new from a recent trauma, or they can be carryovers from childhood and affect the present. Sadly, all of us can inadvertently receive—and in turn, inflict—emotional wounds by the things we say and do.

Obviously, whether the wound is physical or emotional, pain is pain. Pain respects no gender, nationality, ethnicity, or country. It is universal. So what do we do with our pain and the wounds we carry around?

Author C. S. Lewis is credited with saying, "Pain insists upon being attended to. God whispers to us in our pleasures, speaks in our consciences, but shouts in our pains. It is his megaphone to rouse a deaf world."

However we hear God, pain needs to be attended to, or we'll regret it!

CHAPTER 4

In the Beginning

The Painful "What If" and "If Only"

"If only" is one of the saddest phrases in the English language. "If only I had … if only I hadn't …" Then we go on to "What if I had …" and "What if I hadn't …" These questions torture the psyche—but we do that to ourselves, don't we?

What do you do about the pain when someone you love betrays you—betrays the marriage vows, betrays your trust, and the relationship he or she once had with God? You ask yourself, "What if …?"

What do you do when your children have gone mad in a crazy world of "anything goes"? You ask yourself, "What if …?"

What do you do when a friend or relative betrays you? You ask yourself, "What if …?"

These are very difficult questions to answer. We wish we could ponder each question for weeks, months, and years, but time isn't always given to us to do so.

When we are caught in a situation, it is sometimes difficult to see what is happening. Afterward, when the situation is clearer, we feel like fools and say, "What if …?" Sometimes the pain is so great that we inflict wounds and receive wounds, either intentionally or unintentionally. Sometimes we muddle through, make many mistakes, and in the end, we regretfully say, "If only …"

After the "if only" and the "what if," do we wallow in our pools of regret and waste the rest of the God-given years entrusted to us? Well, we can—or we can forgive ourselves and others. It seems simple, doesn't it? Yet forgiveness is the mountain on which some think they will die. It's that unscalable, never-ending Mt. Everest that seems impossible to climb. But we can climb that mountain if we move in the right direction—that is, God's direction.

As a wounded person, you may ask, "What about the person who accuses me of causing emotional and psychological pain, when that person has caused me pain but refuses to acknowledge it? What about the person who, for years, has caused me emotional pain and now blithely smiles at me and says hello in a saccharine voice?"

You may ask, "What about the children I've nurtured who then turn around and say I've never done anything for them?" or "What about the spouse who refuses to acknowledge that I've contributed to the relationship, because to acknowledge this would jeopardize the argument he [or she] used for leaving the relationship?" There are many "what abouts." You go around in a never-ending circle. Each circle leads to pain, wounds, and scars. The question arises, "Do we just grit our teeth, bear it, and wait for the years to pass slowly and painfully?" If you are in this season of your life, I would love to say that the next few months will be easy. The only encouragement I can give is that Jesus promises that he will never leave you or forsake you. However, we need to take this opportunity to learn, grow, and eventually heal.

We learn and grow by looking into God's Word. As part of the human race, we experience pain, but we have choices: endure it, be patient in it, or overcome it and eventually rejoice in it. We also look to God to see why he allowed it. It may be that he allowed it to test our heart; it may be to teach us his will, to teach us patience, or to humble us. We won't know the reason until we begin to communicate with God on a different level.

In order to learn and grow from these life experiences, let's look at Bible personalities to find out what makes them special, and which principles we can learn in the process of healing our wounds. First, we have to acknowledge our wounds, expose them, list them, and then dress them.

CHAPTER 5

Acknowledging, Exposing, Listing, and Dressing the Wounds

Acknowledgment

Wounds can be healed, but first we have to acknowledge that we are wounded or that we have wounded someone. The ostrich mentality does not work at a time like this. Being honest and truthful with ourselves, others, and God will take us down the path toward our healing.

Exposing and Listing the Wounds

The circumstances of life can wound us, and most emotional wounds are caused by someone we loved, someone we trusted, or someone in authority. Sometimes it is an event or a situation that hurts us emotionally. Sometimes it is a relationship or the breaking down of a relationship. It does not matter how these wounds were obtained; they need to be healed. Emotional wounds that don't heal can contaminate every aspect of our life—how we think, how we react to people and events, and even how we live our life after the wounds were inflicted. Some of our wounds could have begun in the early years and manifest themselves in behaviors and attitudes years later. Untreated wounds can destroy us by causing physical, mental, emotional, and spiritual problems.

Let us agree to embark on our healing by exposing and listing all the wounds. Expose them to the light so they can be cleaned and dressed. We have to do an examination of the wounds by laying them bare. Below, list your personal wounds, the specific situation or incident

– both the person's part in the wounding and also your contribution. After you have listed them, pray over them, and give them up. Include all the information you can for each one. *List them honestly.*

Personal wounds	*Situation in detail*	*Wounds - list your contribution also*
_____	_____	_____
_____	_____	_____
_____	_____	_____

If you need more space, use a separate sheet.

Dressing and Taking Care of the Wound

Some common wounds we can discuss are the pain of stress, abandonment, rejection, and abuse. Sometimes, there is so much pain, we ask ourselves why God allows certain situations to develop. We may even reference Job's pain in conjunction with ours. *Why did he allow Job to suffer so much? What did I do to deserve this? When I fasted and prayed, why didn't God answer?* Sometimes, God allows pain, including stress, to help us grow. He sometimes has to prepare us so we can effectively participate in his plan.

The Pain of Stress

Stress seems to play a big factor in the breakdown of relationships. A young person told me once that she was very distressed and had suffered many sleepless nights because a male friend had told her that he was going to leave his wife and children because he could not take the stress. *How much wounding would he cause his family if he left?*

In most relationships, especially marriage, there is stress. It is like any relationship where you have two imperfect human beings. You may have heard the adage, "Smooth sailing does not a sailor make."

Marriage is not smooth sailing, but the trip can be great if you allow for imperfections.

The only people who have no stress are the ones lying in the cemetery. I smiled recently as I heard a pastor say that "marriage is not to make us happy; it's to grow us up." Some very immature people are married to other immature people who cause wounding when they are stressed and are in stressful moments. *Stress is not bad; it is how we handle it that counts.*

Sometimes we are buffeted by storms. Sometimes life is like a roller-coaster ride; sometimes it is smooth sailing; and sometimes it seems we go from crisis to crisis, from one stressful situation to another. At the same time, stress and adversity hone our character, as we are still under construction by the Holy Spirit. Jesus was perfect. He needed no reconstruction, yet he had adversity. He had stress, from Satan's tempting him when he came out of the desert, to his own disciples betraying him and denying him. Jesus had stress on earth. Yet he was not stressed out. How did he handle it? With prayer! How are you handling your stress?

What Is Involved in Dressing a Wound?

Many of us have been wounded by a person whose love was conditional and couldn't go the distance with us. That person might not have heard the proverb, "Love me when I least deserve it, because that's when I really need it." On the other hand, others couldn't go the distance with their partners because the love they expected didn't materialize the way they thought it would. Either way, someone was wounded. That wound, as well as others, can only be dressed through the Word of God. The only way to dress a wound is to put on the entire armor of God. We are at a very vulnerable point of our life when we are stressed out, wounded, and living within our emotions. In Ephesians 6:10–18, the apostle Paul tells us how to be victorious. He says,

Finally, be strong in the Lord and his mighty power. Put on the full armor of God so that you can take your stand against the devil's schemes.

For our struggle is not against flesh and blood, but against the rulers, against the authorities, against the powers of this dark world and against the spiritual forces of evil in the heavenly realms.

Therefore put on the full armor of God, so that when the day of evil comes, you may be able to stand your ground, and after you have done everything, to stand.

Stand firm then, with the belt of truth buckled around your waist, with the breastplate of righteousness in place, and with your feet fitted with the readiness that comes from the gospel of peace.

In addition to all this, take up the shield of faith, with which you can extinguish all the flaming arrows of the evil one Take the helmet of salvation and the sword of the Spirit, which is the word of God.

And pray in the Spirit on all occasions with all kinds of prayers and requests. With this in mind, be alert and always keep on praying for all the saints.

As a Roman citizen, the apostle Paul was very familiar with the kind of armor that the Roman palace guards wore. He wrote to the new believers in Ephesus because he wanted them to stand firm against the old influences, lest old influences contaminate their new life in Christ. As with dressing physical wounds to prevent infection and disease, we have to put on the full armor of God to prevent spiritual infection. Spiritual infection causes us to make wrong choices, which brings about wounding to others. The armor of God gives us spiritual strength and protection, but we can do this *only if we are connected to God.*

SECTION 2—
OPEN HEART

CHAPTER 6
Plugged In

Vignette

"Oh!" I cried in frustration. "I hate technology!"

I had been trying to print two pages for the last hour. First, I sent the document to the printer. That was easy. Then … nothing! No paper being picked up from the printer. No printing. Nothing! I tentatively clicked on the printer icon, quite pleased with myself to have found it. I then opened it, and lo and behold, there were five of the same documents, all queued to be printed. I fiddled with it for another fifteen minutes until I had a brainstorm. "Why don't I pray about this?" I asked myself. "Surely God knows how to fix a printer and print a document. He gave us technology and made the printer, didn't he?"

I prayed for a few minutes, and to my astonishment, after I prayed, it was as if someone held my head and tilted it slightly to the right. What did I see? I burst out laughing, and I imagine that God and the angels in heaven were laughing too and were thoroughly enjoying the joke at my expense. There, staring me in the face was the printer cord, happily resting on the floor—unplugged!

I had to include that story in this section because the Lord actually spoke to my heart as if to say, "You have to be plugged in to access my power."

Your heart has to be opened to access God's power. If your heart is not opened to God's power, his grace, and his mercy through the Holy Spirit, you will need spiritual "open-heart surgery." Are you ready to be plugged in to God's power?

CHAPTER 7

Open-Heart Surgery

Is Your Heart Ready to Accept Surgery on the Open Wounds?

People who have partners often get excited around Valentine's Day because of the focus on love. Everywhere you go there are red hearts and cupids with poised arrows, depicting love. That's all very nice. The heart has always been used in a symbolic way. For example, ancient philosophers used the heart as a symbol of thought, reason, and emotions. Some believed it was the seat of the soul. Other thinkers believed it was the seat of feelings and passions—the symbol of the spiritual, emotional, moral, and intellectual core of the human being. However, when we compare the heart of Valentine's Day to some Bible verses, we see a startling contrast. Here are a few contradictions:

- hardness of heart—Proverbs 28:14, Hebrew 3:7–13
- false values of the heart—Matthew 6:21; Philippians 3:8
- pride of heart—2 Chronicles 25:2; Psalm 86:11; James 1:6–8
- bitterness of heart—Psalm 73:21; Proverbs 14:10; James 3:14
- stubbornness of heart—Exodus 7:14; Psalm 78:8; Jeremiah 3:17

It is not all doom and gloom, however. The heart is also the place of praise and worship, but it needs to be centered on God. Psalm 111:11 says, "Praise the Lord. I will extol the Lord with all my heart."

"I will praise you, O Lord, with all my heart" (Ps. 9:1).

We are told many times in Scriptures to worship God. Worship is love, obedience, and service, which means the total involvement of our heart—mind, emotions, and will. Therefore, in order to eliminate hardness, pride, bitterness, and stubbornness from our heart and replace it with the right emotions, our heart needs to be purified. It needs to be open to the Lord's X-ray eyes. We have to trust him to do the work that needs to be done. Psalm 62:8 says, "Trust in him at all times, O people; pour out your hearts to him, for God is our refuge." This is based on God's promise that not only does he care for his children, but he wants to hear from them. He wants our whole heart centered on him. God should never be an afterthought! We need to keep his truth on center stage in our hearts. If it isn't, then all the cares, stress, and sinful desires will intrude and push aside God's desires. In our heart will be our desires, rather than God's, which, as we know from the beginning of humankind with Adam and Eve to our present day, has never worked in our favor. Proverbs 4:21 reminds us to keep God's words and his desires as our focus. It says, "Do not let them depart from your sight, keep them within your heart; for they are life to those who find them and health to a man's whole body."

"I have hidden your word in my heart that I might not sin against you" (Ps. 119:11).

The contents of our heart are very important to God. What is in your heart? Are you ready for a heart transplant?

In our modern times, it is very common for a person to survive triple-bypass heart surgery. Physical open-heart surgery is usually performed by a skilled physician, but spiritual open-heart surgery can only be done by the Great Physician. Since the heart is the seat of emotions, will, behavior, and morals, we have to regularly do open-heart surgery. First, we have to contact the Great Physician. Through prayer and his Word, we receive all we need to change our heart for cleansing and for healing. In 1 Peter 2:24, Peter talks about Jehovah Rapha, the God who heals. He says,

"He himself bore our sins in his body on the tree, so that we might die to sins and live for righteousness; by his wounds you have been healed."

And in Exodus 15:26:

"If you listen carefully to the voice of the lord your God and do what is right in his eyes, if you pay attention to his commands and keep all his decrees, I will not bring on you any of the diseases I brought on the Egyptians, for I am the Lord, who heals you."

Jeremiah 29:11–13 tells us,

For I know the plans I have for you, declares the Lord, plans to prosper you and not to harm you, plans to give you hope and a future. Then you will call upon me and come and pray to me, and I will listen to you. You will seek me and find me when you seek me with all your heart. I will be found by you, declares the Lord.

Most physical wounds need medical attention or else the person will suffer or possibly die. Spiritual wounds require the same treatment. Sometimes we limp along for years with emotional and spiritual wounds so wide that even a blind man could see them. There's the wounding of self-esteem. There's the wounding and betrayal by a spouse having an affair. There are so many wounds we carry around that need healing. How can we attend to them?

By biblical standards, we have to do several things:

1. With an open heart, we have to contact the Great Physician for healing.
2. We have to participate in our healing.
3. We have to prepare for our method of healing.

In order to access God's power, our heart has to be plugged into God's heart.

In the human body, the heart is a life-maintaining organ that pumps and circulates oxygenated blood to all the cells in the body. Several risk factors can cause heart disease: age, gender, the environment and lifestyle. Preventive measures against heart disease include exercise, healthy eating, and avoidance of smoking. Without a healthy heart, the body gets diseased and dies.

In the spiritual realm, the heart is just as important to our well-being. Proverbs 4:23 admonishes: "Above all else, guard your heart, for it is the wellspring of life."

The heart is a prominent concept in the Bible, representing the inner person and the spiritual life in all its various aspects. Like the human heart, the spiritual heart is central and vital to our existence. If we do not nourish this spiritual part of our being and care for it, it too will die.

What is in your heart?

We live in a consumer-oriented society, focused on the pleasing of self. We enjoy many luxuries not afforded to those in third-world or developing countries. With this comes the idea that we deserve to enjoy the fruits of our labor. If we acquire a better house, a better job, add more material possessions, we will be happy. We fail to recognize, however, that this notion is promoted by Satan.

This worldview of seeking happiness in material possessions at any cost, even to the detriment of the family structure, is spiritual warfare. It is my belief that Satan doesn't like us; he doesn't care about us. His one and only aim is to hurt God; and because the family is close to God's heart, Satan will aim his cannons dead center at it.

The media constantly bombards us to buy things, to have more than the neighbors and friends, or to buy a better or bigger "thing." Sadly enough, many Christians fall into the trap laid by the enemy. Jeremiah 17:9 says, "The heart is deceitful above all things and beyond cure. Who can understand it?" The heart is easily influenced by the world's standards, but God reminds us that he searches the heart and "examines the mind, to reward a man according to his conduct, according to what his deeds deserve."

Right from the beginning of our history with God, we see his deep concern for the inner person and the condition of the heart. He does not want the condition of our heart to be like a backed-up sink that spews out stagnant water and debris that only a professional can unclog. He can unclog it, but he wants us to be just as concerned and protective of our heart as he is. We too have to constantly examine our heart to see what we are allowing in it. In 1 Samuel 16:7, Samuel was on God's mission to choose a king for the people of Israel. Samuel saw Jesse's tall, strapping sons and would have chosen one of them. However, God said to him, "Do not consider his appearance or his height, for I have rejected him. The Lord does not look at the things man looks at. Man looks at the outward appearance, but the Lord looks at the heart."

In Matthew 12:33–37, the Sermon on the Mount, Jesus was very harsh in his criticism of the Pharisees. He said,

Make the tree good and its fruit will be good, or make a tree bad and its fruit will be bad, for a tree is recognized by its fruit. You brood of vipers, how can you who are evil say anything good? For out of the overflow of the heart the mouth speaks. The good man brings good things out of the good stored up in him, and the evil man brings evil things out of the evil stored up in him.

Several other passages that make reference to God's concern for the condition of our heart are as follows:

"For where your treasure is, there your heart will be also" (Matt. 6:21).

Jesus had talked about being clean and unclean. When Peter wanted an expansion on the parable, Jesus said to him,

"Are you still so dull? Don't you see that whatever enters the mouth goes into the stomach and then out of the body? But the things that come out of the mouth come from the heart, and these make a man unclean. For out of the heart come evil thoughts, murder, adultery, sexual immorality, theft, false testimony, slander. These are what make a man unclean." (Matt.15:18)

These passages teach us that God is more interested in what is internal than what is external. Why? Because the issues of life come out of the heart. Our thoughts, ideas, activities, and all our moral precepts come from the heart.

The matters of the heart are so serious to God that when Jesus addresses adultery in Matthew 5:28, he said that even when you look at a woman with lust, you've already committed that sin in your heart. God knows that if the inside is clean, the outside will be also. What is in the heart of a person who decides to abandon the family? What is in the heart of a person who sells drugs to children? What is in the heart of a person who commits any of the many other atrocities currently active in our society? What is a person's heart condition when that person cruelly, and with deliberate intent, wounds someone? The character of a man is wrapped in the inner being of the heart. Proverbs 27:19 says, "A man's heart reflects the man."

In Jeremiah 4:14, the prophet talked about washing the evil from the heart. He proclaimed many nations, including Israel, as "uncircumcised" in heart. The challenge to us is to open our heart to the light of the Holy Spirit so our open heart will become "circumcised" as the Spirit of God washes away the debris. It will also be a receptacle ready to receive what God wants to put into it, not what the world wants to put in it.

Food for Thought

Is your heart filled with anger, unforgiveness, and cruelty toward someone who might have wounded you?

The modern worldview is uncircumcised in heart, morals, and behavior. We need to ask two questions:

- As Christians, are many areas of our life uncircumcised in heart?
- How much of these worldviews have we allowed into our heart?

If the answer to the first question above is yes, then we have to use the scalpel of the Word of God to surgically remove the debris from our heart. Psalm 51 is a good psalm to begin. We can start by confessing what's in our heart and asking for forgiveness. The key verse is "Create in me a pure heart."

In Ezekiel 18:31, God promises to circumcise our heart by giving us a new heart and a new spirit. As such, we only have to want it and ask for it to receive it. Begin by contacting the only person who can cleanse and heal the heart. To whom do you turn for healing?

CHAPTER 8

The Physician

Before we contact the healer of our wounds, we have to know whom to contact.

First, examine your circle of friends. Is there anyone in that circle who has a perfect life, with no problems, no difficulties, and no challenges? Is there a priest, a pastor, a rabbi, or a religious leader without problems who can help you effectively heal the wounds made to your soul? There isn't such a person, is there?

Let me introduce you to Jesus. This has nothing to do with religion but everything to do with a relationship. If you are skeptical about whom Jesus is, take the time to look at the historical records of Jesus. In my earlier years, I believed in God, but I had no time for him. I always thought when I was old and had a few years left on this earth, I would make time for him—fire insurance, so to speak. My fire insurance came due very quickly when my younger brother was killed at the age of twenty-five, and I realized that had that been me, I could not have faced God confidently, because I did not a have a personal relationship with him. The fact is that you or I cannot face someone or contact someone we don't know!

Jesus is that someone, and we have to contact him with an open heart.

Contacting the Healer with an Open Heart

1. Psalm 145:18 tells us, "The Lord is near to those who call on him, to all who call on him in truth."
2. The Holy Spirit enables us to draw near.

3. The Father draws us to him. As humans, it is not in us to draw near to God on our own initiative. God the Father has to draw us. In John 6:44, Jesus rebuked the Jews about their grumbling and informed them that no one could come to him "unless the Father who sent me draws him."

4. Ephesians 3:12 tells us, "In him [Jesus Christ] and through faith in him we may approach God with freedom and confidence."

Jesus refers to himself as the Great Physician. In Mark 2:17, Jesus' opponents accused him of hobnobbing with unsavory characters, such as sinners and tax collectors. Jesus responded, "It is not those who are healthy who need a physician, but those who are sick; I did not come to call the righteous, but sinners."

Throughout Jesus' ministry, he healed the demon-possessed and all who were ill. This, Matthew maintained, was to fulfill the prophecy that Isaiah the prophet prophesied: "He himself took our infirmities and carried away our disease" (Matt. 8:17).

You might not be sure about this Jesus as yet. You might even have denied his existence in the past. But if you have faith, even as small as a mustard seed, it should force you to say, "Nothing is impossible for God."

James 1:17 tells us, "Every good thing given and every perfect gift is from above, coming down from the Father of Lights, with whom there is no variation or shifting shadow. God proved, in the giving of his only Son, that he keeps his word."

Let me assure you that God does exist! Do not be fooled by the enemy of your soul. Jesus ministered and healed the leper (Luke 5:12–15). He healed the withered hand and a crippled woman (Luke 13:11–13). He healed the deaf (Mark 7:31–37). He raised the dead (John 11:1–46).

Why would he change now? Contact him and begin to participate in your healing!

His number is P-R-A-Y-E-R.

Call him!

CHAPTER 9

Participate in Your Healing with an Open Heart

Several stories come to mind when I think of participating in healing. Matthew tells the story of two blind men, sitting by the road, who heard that Jesus was passing by. As he passed, they cried out to him, saying, "Lord, Son of David, have mercy on us!" Then Jesus asked them a curious question: "What do you want Me to do for you?"

I noticed for the first time that in the Bible translation I was reading, the M in the word "me" was capitalized. I was curious why there seemed to be emphasis on the "Me." What message was Jesus conveying? There were several other rabbis in Jerusalem at that time, preaching and teaching. In comparison to the other rabbis, did it mean that Jesus was different? Nobody else had been able to do what the blind men expected Jesus to do. Did the blind men recognized Jesus' power, and believed in his ability to heal them. Although Jesus healed them, why did they ask him for mercy instead of healing?

Another story that intrigues me is the healing of the man at the pool of Bethesda. In John 5:2–6, we're told that the man had been lying there sick for thirty-eight years. John picks up the story in verse 3 to say that at the pool, called Bethesda, there were people who were sick, blind, lame, and paralyzed. They waited for the moving of the waters, because at certain seasons, an angel came down and stirred up the waters. The first person to step in after the stirring of the water would be healed. This man had been lying there for thirty-eight years.

I would not have been able to lie passively and wait for someone to put me in the waters. If there was any life in me and if there was any chance of my being healed, I would have inched my way slowly, little by little, toward the edge, and right after the stirring, I would have said, "Okay, boys, move over. My turn! Coming through!"

So then, thirty-eight or so years later, Jesus came along and asked the man, "What do you want me to do? Do you want to get well?" You might think this was a dumb question, considering how long the man had been waiting for someone to assist him. The question Jesus asked the paralyzed man, however, tells me that God wants us to be active participants in our healing.

What do you want God to do? The pains of your wounds, whatever they might be, might seem overwhelming; but it's up to you to purposely deal with the pain. Just like the blind men and the man at the pool of Bethesda, we can influence our journey, based on our participation. Again, I ask, what do you want God to do?

God has offered to heal our wounds. Are we going to sit and wait, moan and groan, and blame the person who wounded us? The person who wounded me and the person who wounded you have probably forgotten about us and the incidents, so let's begin to move to claim our healing.

Jesus wasn't just a man preaching and teaching; he was sent by God. Although there were probably as many self-elevated preachers and teachers as we have in modern times, Jesus wasn't a self-fulfilling prophet. His birth, life, and death were predicted years before he was born. Jesus asked the question, "What do you want me to do?"—he knew he was different; the blind men knew he was different. The blind men could have asked for money, alms, or other things to salve their physical needs; but they asked in faith for their sight. The gospel of Matthew tells us that Jesus had compassion on them and healed them.

Get to know Jesus and answer in faith the questions he still asks: "What do you want me to do? Do you want to get well?"

Another way of participating in your healing is by making a conscious choice to forgive the person who wounded you. Open your heart to the Holy Spirit and let him minister to it. Don't be afraid! Forgiving someone doesn't mean you don't have a wound. But through the Holy Spirit, you can experience freedom. Mark Twain once said, "Holding on to unforgiveness is similar to drinking poison and expecting the other person to die." Offering forgiveness frees you to begin your healing.

One of the most effective ways of participating in your healing is through prayer. Jesus' disciples came to him and said, "Master, teach us to pray."

He said, "When you pray, do not be like the hypocrites, for they love to pray standing in the synagogues and on the street corners to be seen by men. This, then, is how you should pray":

Our Father in heaven, hallowed be your name
Your kingdom come, your will be done
On earth as it is in heaven
Give us today our daily bread
Forgive us our debts as we also have forgiven our debtors.
And lead us not into temptation, but deliver us from the evil one.
For thine is the kingdom and the power and the glory
For ever
Amen (Matt. 6:9)

The key to this prayer is that if we don't forgive the person who wronged us, God won't forgive us. That seems straightforward enough! There's an old saying that goes, "Doing an injury puts you below your enemy; revenging an injury makes you but even; forgiving it sets you above."

I have gotten into the habit of praying the Lord's Prayer as soon as I wake up and several times during the day, especially when negative thoughts about the person who wounded me enter my thoughts. Once I've finished the Lord's Prayer, I find my heart has softened, and I am at peace. This brings to mind the adage, "God is in his heaven, and all is well with the world."

It is important to note that the healing power of Jesus goes beyond curing the physical. He heals emotionally and mentally too—if, like the psalmist, you say, "Be gracious to me, Oh Lord, for I am pining away; Heal me, O Lord, for my bones are dismayed and my soul is greatly dismayed (Ps. 6:2–3).

My experience taught me that some of my open, gaping wounds

were inflicted deliberately. Some were unintentional; and there were times when my soul was greatly dismayed. However, I had to forgive, because forgiving the people who wounded me helped me to focus on my healing. It is a process, and we have to actively participate in building up our physical, mental, psychological, and emotional strength. *No one can do it for us!*

Make a conscious choice to participate in your healing. God wants to heal us; he wants us to be plugged in; he wants us to participate. He wants us to be proactive. He wants us to be prepared.

Prepare for Your Method of Healing

We are so out-of-step with God when we try to box him into our way of doing things. We always want God to heal us by using the softest method or the method we prescribe or envision. But be careful! We might be heading for a wilderness experience, the likes of which we have never seen. We have neither the right nor the qualifications to tell God how to heal us. God is the ultimate healer. Jesus healed as many people as he could, with as many methods as he wanted. We should not be presumptuous to tell God what to do, or we will get ourselves in trouble. If we get our "self" in the way, self can increase our troubles.

We need to access God's power with an open heart. As an example, over the years I had been praying fervently and asking, in faith, for various requests. Then one day, this changed! I was praying the many requests on my heart when, as clear as anything, I heard in my spirit, *"You haven't asked me what I want."* I stopped in horror! All along, I had been telling God all I would like to see happen, not asking him what he wanted. I had to ask his forgiveness. I did, and said to him, "Lord, whatever you want is what I want. I will accept your decision. I will not fight—I lay my weapons down. I will only pray, praise, and listen."

I then made a commitment to prayer, praising, interceding, and listening. I said, "Lord, my heart is open to you. I want your heart to be my heart and my heart to be your heart."

Psalm 34:4–6 says, "Delight yourself in the Lord and he will give you the desires of your heart. Commit your way to the Lord; trust in him and he will do this: He will make your righteousness shine like the dawn, the justice of your cause like the noonday sun."

Several things have transpired since that moment:

1. I have taken my eyes off my circumstances and the people who wounded me. My eyes are on the Lord. I trust him.
2. I know that one day, he will bring forth my righteousness.
3. I have committed my life, which is my journey through this life, to him. Wherever and whatever paths my feet travel, it will be good and for my good as, according to Proverbs 20:24, "A man's steps are directed by the Lord. How can anyone understand his own way?"

The elements of our participation are, therefore, prayer, intercession, and faith. There is no telling or supervising God.

The human heart controls our emotions, our thoughts, and our mind. We can choose to be angry. We can choose in our heart to be malicious or evil. Yet we can also choose in our heart to be compassionate, like Jesus; to be humble or to be glad that our happiness is tied up in him. Make a choice in your heart to lock your heart to God's. Here's how to begin:

1. Cry out to God.

Psalm 84:1 says, "My soul yearns, even faints, for the courts of the Lord; my heart and my flesh cry out for the living God."

2. Seek God

"Blessed are they who keep his statues and seek him with all their heart" (Ps. 119:2).

3. Hide his Word in your heart.

"I have hidden your Word in my heart that I might not sin against you" (Ps. 119:11).

4. Meditate on God and his Word.

"May the words of my mouth and the meditation of my heart be pleasing in your sight, O Lord, my Rock and my Redeemer" (Ps. 19:14).

Every morning when you wake up, before your thoughts wander to your job, your situation, your wounds, or anything that will distract you from God, say like the psalmist:

"As the deer pants for streams of water, so my soul pants for you, O God. My soul thirsts for God, for the living God. When can I go and meet with God?" (Ps. 42:2).

It is of no consequence which path your life has taken. Hold onto your faith in God. Think about the following quote, attributed to Dr. Martin Luther King Jr.:

"Faith is taking the first step, even when you don't see the whole staircase."

CHAPTER 10

Rushing to Meet God

Vignette—a Childhood Memory:

As a child I was very athletic. I remember racing down the field on track-and-field day on short, stubby legs, just enjoying the speed of running. As the years went by, God gave me a special talent for sports. I lived for sports.

One day when I was around twelve years old, some of my friends and I had a netball game at the national stadium. My friends and I were all skipping along, walking, talking, laughing, enjoying ourselves, and anticipating winning the game as usual, when suddenly, a huge Rolls-Royce stopped inches from us, with a flourish and a bit of a screech of tires, as if to get our attention. *It did!* As if in one accord, my friends and I all jumped back and pasted ourselves against the fence behind us. From out of the darkened interior of the Rolls-Royce, I heard a voice say, "Where are you girls going?" We were silent, backed against the wall like the proverbial sardines in a can. Again, the voice, "Do you want a ride?" No answer from us.

Finally, knowing better but letting curiosity get the better of me, as I was wont to do at that age, I glanced at the chauffeur, who looked back at me stoically. Tentatively peeling myself off the fence, I took one step toward the Rolls-Royce and peered inside. To the surprise of my friends, I squealed and jumped inside the Rolls-Royce. I heard a concerted gasp behind me as I disappeared into the Rolls-Royce. My friends on the outside didn't know that I had found someone inside the Rolls who usually was inaccessible. It was unusual that this person was willing to take the time to talk to us. Inside the Rolls-Royce was the prime minister of Jamaica, the Honorable Alexander Bustamante.

As I recalled this treasured memory and the many times my friends and I discussed this incident, I thought of our heavenly Father. How often we hear his voice in the darkness of our situation, but we are too afraid to respond. We see only the darkness around us and feel only our pain. Seeing through our own lens, we are afraid to take one step forward, even out of curiosity, to sit someplace quiet and peaceful with him, just to talk.

It seems that often, when someone says, "Can I talk to you?" that's exactly what the person does—talk. It's more a monologue than a dialogue. However, when we talk to God, his expectation is that it will be a dialogue. I told you of my experience of asking God to do something in a difficult situation, but not asking him what his will was in the situation. When we converse with God, it's communicating with him. "Communication" is defined as the "imparting or interchange of thoughts, or opinions, or information by speech, writing or signs" (Dictionary.com).

Therefore, communication requires a sender, a message, and a receiver. It means to share. The percentage of talk time between the talker and listener varies at times, but it is a sharing. It has been my experience that at the beginning of my wounding and difficult situation, I was doing more of the talking than God, as I poured out my heart to him. I knew he was listening to every word I said. God, in his love, lets us talk before he talks. We have to pour out what is in our heart before he can fill and replace it with what he has to offer. Once we have finished pouring out our heart, we must begin to listen to his heart. Instead of just asking him to do something, ask him what he wants to do.

When our children are hurt, we don't say, "Quit your whining and sniveling. Had you listened to me the first time I cautioned you, you wouldn't have hurt yourself." No! We gather them in our arms, lovingly wipe away their tears, and hug and comfort them. It is only after we bestow love and hugs that we administer discipline, if necessary. Discipline is usually a wilderness experience. As children, when we needed to be disciplined, we may have been sent to stand in a corner with our face to the wall, sent to our room, grounded, or even spanked.

We had no contact with other family members or familiar objects until our parents deemed we had been suitably chastised.

In like manner, when we are hurt and cry to our Father, he sends the Holy Spirit to comfort us. He disciplines us too; and sometimes his discipline is a wilderness period—a time of "aloneness," a time where it is just us and him.

In his sovereign wisdom, he knows our heart, and he knows what we need. Our wilderness experience is always a necessity for spiritual growth. So instead of gritting our teeth and fighting, we can embrace the experience and see what God has in store for us. We should also plan to survive it by having an open heart. Do not worry if he seems silent in the darkness and the "aloneness" of our time out, for in our wilderness of pain, he is there, and he is listening. God is in the dark places with us. He will talk when he is ready. *Just be patient!*

The twists and turns of the paths of your journey will eventually make sense as you commune with him in the wilderness. Even if things do not make sense, he is there with you, and that should be sufficient.

CHAPTER 11

Sojourn in the Wilderness

Surviving the Wilderness Experience

The most common emotion in a wilderness is confusion. The most common feeling is pain. Pain is a directional force. It goes many ways. It's an arrow that knows no boundary and has no respect for gender, age, or religion. When we are wounded and in pain, we hurt others and vice versa. This puts us in a place that requires God's intervention. When he intervenes, we like to tell him how to conduct this process, but God's method of dealing with our pain, our hurts, and our wounds is his business. He has years of experience in tending wounds and in healing—he doesn't need our help. What he needs is our cooperation, not our advice.

Many of us would prefer to sit and nurse our wounds instead of rushing to God for healing. We would rather stay in a state of anger and unforgiveness than to take responsibility for our part in the debacle of the difficult situation or in the downward spiral of our children. In many cases, God has to stop us to get our attention, and one of his methods is to send us into the wilderness.

What can the wilderness do for us? It can help us to develop our faith, acquire spiritual maturity, and develop perseverance. The wilderness breeds character and humility. It's a great teacher! For example, Moses was described as the humblest of men. Do you think he learned that humility in the royal household in Egypt? I think not! I surmise that he learned humility during his wilderness years. Take time to read Acts 7:23–37, which tells the story of Moses' entering his wilderness experience. Verse 35 says, "This is the same Moses whom they had rejected with words, who made you ruler and judge?"

33

The same people who rejected him and caused him to flee from his life of comfort in Egypt and into the wilderness were the same people to whom God sent him as their ruler and deliverer. When they rejected him, he was not prepared to be a deliverer. But forty years later, traveling through that same wilderness, he was very well prepared. You too might have been hurt with words, acts, or deeds. You might not understand your pain and rejection now, but God works out his plan for your life during this period in the wilderness. Years from now, it might make more sense.

The wilderness is a lonely place from which many of us try to escape, but it is a refining place, as 1 Peter 1:7 describes it. It softens and tenderizes our hearts. It affects us and makes us more effective for ministry. In the wilderness, we find out that Jesus is the bread of life (John 6:35). He is a gift that refreshes and nourishes (John 4:10).

He says, "If anyone is thirsty, let him come to me and drink. Whoever believes in me, as the Scripture has said, streams of living water will flow from within him" (John 7:37).

The psalmist says, "My soul thirsts for God, for the living God. When can I go and meet him?"

Let us look at some defining aspects of a wilderness.

A wilderness is considered an area with the following criteria:

- natural, intact, undisturbed (not modified by human hands)
- minimal human imprint (no human activity or human interference)
- educational value
- cultural, spiritual, moral, aesthetic benefits
- no roads or developed roads

When you're in the wilderness, it is very difficult to survive if you have no experience and no survival skills and if are there by yourself. Isaiah 41:17–20 describes the condition of a person in the wilderness, especially in the phrase, *"Their tongues are parched with thirst."* However, in the midst of this wilderness, God promises to be there, like an oasis in the desert.

The poor and needy search for water, but there is none; their tongues are parched with thirst. But I the Lord will answer them; I the God of Israel, will not forsake them. I will make rivers flow on barren heights, and springs within the valleys. I will turn the desert into pools of water, and the parched ground into springs. I will put in the desert the cedar and the acacia, the myrtle and the olive. I will set pines in the wasteland, the fir and the cypress together, so that people may see and know, may consider and understand that the hand of the Lord has done this, that the Holy One of Israel has created it. (Is. 41:17–20)

Jesus said in the Sermon on the Mount, "Blessed are they which do hunger and thirst after righteousness for they shall be filled" (Matt. 5:6). That hunger and thirst should be the heart condition of the person in the desert. It should be the condition of the heart that wants more from God. This is the open heart that is prepared to receive what God has to offer. This heart should be hungry and thirsty and ready to seek God's purpose, accept his preparation and be ready for transformation.

CHAPTER 12

The Wilderness as Purpose, Preparation, and Transformation

The wilderness helps to clear our senses and draw us closer to God. It provides purpose, preparation, transformation, and a new future. How does this happen?

The Wilderness as Purpose

God has a purpose for all things in the life of a believer, especially the experience of being in the wilderness. Although it may not seem like it, God does great things in our lives during these times, even when it seems like he's not doing anything at all. At times in our pain, we ask, "Why did God allow this?" In our less painful moments, we know that God didn't cause any of our pain. He knew in advance of all the difficult situations in which we would find ourselves, but he allowed each to happen, according to his sovereign purpose.

Think ahead. Get a vision of the glory God can get if you "pass the test" of your suffering and can testify of how God sustained you through the journey. So do not grumble, complain, or wimp out on God. Let him prepare you for what his plan requires!

The Wilderness as Preparation

Every great or sustainable ministry began in the wilderness. Every great work done for God and every great leader began in the wilderness. If you have your doubts, just read the Bible or think of a great saint of God. For each leader, it was a time of getting down to the nitty-gritty—a time of peeling, like an onion, the outer layers until there was nothing left but the core; a time of preparation. God established this pattern throughout biblical history, as we will see when we examine the lives of the Bible personalities.

Preparation in the wildernesses is "training season" with God. There is almost always a period of training and waiting between the time you receive a promise of God in your heart and the time of its fulfillment. He therefore trains us and works with us to be the kind of people who can slay giants and be giants of faith for him. This only happens in the wilderness. We will enjoy God's blessings far greater than we could ever know in the world when we put ourselves in his care and trust in him. But before we get to the blessings, we will be tested—often severely and often in the wilderness. So trust him in this situation. His knowledge is more far-reaching than ours. When God prepares us for a mission, we don't dare to ask why. Isaiah 29:16 says, "You turn things upside down, as if the potter were thought to be like the clay! Shall what is formed say to him who formed it, he did not make me? Can the pot say of the potter, He knows nothing?"

The apostle Paul says, "But who are you, o man, to talk back to God? Shall what is formed say to him who formed it, 'why did you make me like this?' Does not the potter have the right to make out of the same lump of clay some pottery for noble purposes and some for common uses?" (Rom. 9:20–21).

Our attitude toward God should not be rebellious, impenitent, or defiant. It should be reverentially trusting in his sovereign freedom in dealing with his people and knowing exactly what is right for each person. Our attitude is crucial. Do not allow your attitude to become an obstacle that hinders you.

Satan does not want us to go into the wilderness with God, because it is in the wilderness that all major decisions about life are made. It is in the wilderness that we learn to listen to God. It is in the wilderness that our faith is strengthened. It is the wilderness experience that allows God to powerfully use the man or woman, who then leaves with a deeper faith. This wilderness experience allows God to display his power, his sovereignty, and his totality as the only one in control of the destiny of our soul. Are you willing to access God's transforming power!

The Wilderness as Transformation

In the transformational stage of our wilderness experience, we undergo psychological changes, but first, we have a choice to make. Do we want to turn to self-pity and bitterness, complaining like the Israelites during these hard times, or do we want to bow to God's divine knowledge of what is best for us? Once we make the right choice—to give God his place in our life and give him the right to choose for us—we will get to the place he wants us to go.

We will only reach the place God has built for us by surviving the wilderness. However, just like Israel, we can disobey God and remain in the wilderness longer than we have to. Clearly, if we trust him to help us to survive the wilderness times, we have to trust him totally. We cannot trust him when he provides manna but complain when he doesn't provide what we think he should. God cannot help us survive the wilderness if we don't trust him enough to hand over the reins of our life to him. When we do this, he will bless us and use us beyond our imagination. But first, we have to let go and trust!

The Wilderness Relevant to Our Future

In Philippians 4:11–12, Paul is convinced that we will gain new confidence and trust in God if we are content in all situations. He believes it is the love of money that is the root of all evil. In our society, it is the love of money, riches, and the pursuit of happiness that is bankrupting and robbing families of parents and propelling people into drugs and other destructive substances. Paul maintains that since he brought nothing into the world and will leave with the same, he can be content. This is a difficult characteristic to master, because it demands a trust in God that puts him at the center of our environment. This can be difficult, as we are enmeshed in the "me generation." However, it is not an impossible task to accomplish if we do not allow the pain of our wounds to temporarily blind our vision.

Each pain, wound, and trial is an opportunity to get closer to God and to make him the center of our future. As we are tried and tested, God sees what is in our heart. He already knows. But in our testing, we become more aware of how far we are willing to trust him to walk the valley with us. It is then we have to make another choice. Can we trust him with our future? Should we trust him to work out our problems—the spouse who dishonors the marriage vows, the children on drugs, the ungodly boss, the loose women who invade the marriage relationship, the spouse with a hardened heart, the financial problems, and so many other challenging situations? Can God intervene and work in these situations? Of course he can! Are you ready to trust your future to him?

The future outcome of our wilderness experience depends upon our attitude of heart. The length of our wilderness experience may vary from one person to another. Therefore, our responses to God will determine how quickly we get out of the wilderness phase of our life and into the Promised Land phase. The Israelites could have been out of the wilderness in less than a week if they had only believed God's promises to them at the time the spies returned from Kadesh Barnea. However, from the time they left Egypt, their attitude stunk like the leeks and onions of Egypt that they craved. Their discontent and mistrust of God led to their downfall. They misunderstood the situation completely. They reported that the land was filled with "giants."

So what? Was conquering the giants of the land too hard for God? The Israelites certainly thought so. On a personal level, like the Israelites and like David, we will always have to face giants in our life. We have the history of the Israelites to learn from, so we ought to learn from their mistakes. Our faith in God should not be shaken by stress and the pressures of life. When God allows us to go through the valley and be put under pressure, it is only then that we will find out what's in our heart and how strong our faith is. That is why the psalmist warns us: "Keep thy heart with all diligence; for out of it are the issues of life" (Prov. 4:23).

Similar to the wilderness experience of the Bible personalities, when we go through the wilderness, we get to know God's purpose for our life. We train under his guiding hand, we are prepared for future use by God himself, and we are transformed by his sovereign hand. As we study the various Bible personalities, we will learn about their call, their purpose, their preparation, and their transformational changes, as Abram became Abraham, Jacob became Israel, and Saul became Paul. Their name change signified a complete metamorphosis. Their names changed along with their attitude, personality, and character. Abram changed from a childless man to the father of many nations (Gen. 17:5). Jacob's name changed from deceiver to Israel, one who wrestles with God (Gen. 35:10). Saul of Tarsus changed from the persecutor to the persecuted by becoming Paul, the apostle to the Gentiles (Acts 13:9).

Let us now examine the call, the purpose, the preparation, and the transformation of some of the heroes of the Bible and see how God, in his sovereignty, directed their path.

CHAPTER 13

Abraham

The Call of Abraham

God always had a plan for mankind, and with the call of Abraham, he activated his plan of love for the human race.

Sometime into his journey, Abraham was asked a most challenging question (Gen. 18:14). God had promised Abraham and Sarah a son. From this son, God told them, they would have numberless generations. They had now passed the childbearing age, and the son had not made an appearance. On this day, God reiterated his promise to them, but Sarah laughed in disbelief. God asked Sarah and Abraham a crucial question: "Is anything too hard for the Lord?"

Let us begin at the beginning.

At the end of Genesis 11, we get acquainted with Terah, Abraham's father, who started on a journey from Ur of the Chaldees to Canaan. Instead of going to the "land flowing with milk and honey" (Ex. 3:8, 17; 13:5; 33:3) and receiving all of God's blessings, he dies short of his destination.

Now the Lord said to Abram:

Leave your country, your people and your father's household and go to the land I will show you. I will make you into a great nation and I will bless you; I will make your name great, and you will be a blessing. I will bless those who bless you, and whoever curses you I will curse; and all peoples on earth will be blessed through you. (Gen. 12:1–3)

The covenant between God and Abraham was for Abraham to leave his current home, leave his extended family, and go to an unspecified area. God's part of the covenant was that he would direct Abraham to the unspecified area, make Abraham's descendants into a great nation, make his name great, make him a blessing, protect him, and bring worldwide blessings to him. Right after God finished speaking are the words, *"So Abraham left as the Lord had told him."*

The Significance of Abraham's Call

- Abraham knew nothing about God. Prior to hearing God's voice, he worshipped idols (Josh. 24:2).
- He had to abandon the security of his culture.
- He had to leave a civilized area and go into the unknown.
- His idols had never spoken to him, and now he heard a voice telling him that he was God.

If I were Abraham, I would probably have been frightened. Many of us, put in the same situation, would think we were going crazy, that we were hearing voices. Many people must have thought that Abraham was crazy.

Questions to Ponder

1. Do you think Abraham made the decision lightly?
2. Do you think he was excited about the voice and the move?
3. Was he frightened?
4. How would you react, were you in his place?
5. How long would you have to think about obeying the new God?
6. How much trust would you put in this new God?

In this present age, the gods of the world—happiness, money, and excitement, among others—beckon. Have you heard, like Abraham, that voice saying, "Leave"? The call of Abraham is synonymous to the call to each of us as followers of Christ.

We are called:

- to leave the pleasures of the world.
- to leave familiar territory and set out on a pilgrimage to "find" God.
- to trust the "real" God.
- to promptly obey God's instruction.

Would you have acted differently from Abraham if you were told to leave the comforts of your home or even your comfort zone? Would you feel too vulnerable to obey? Abraham and Sarah were vulnerable to the times. As the husband of a beautiful woman, Abraham could have been captured and killed and Sarah taken against her will. His "failure," as some would call it, when he told Sarah to lie and say that she was his sister, must have been a very difficult decision. It was partly due to the vulnerability of his situation. He wanted to trust the new god, but his self-protection got in the way.

As indicated in Genesis, his new life was very stressful, compared to his past life. He had to choose between the certainty of his idols and the uncertainty of his new God; security of family and culture versus a nomadic existence; stress-free life versus the stress of his new wilderness life. However, Abraham's decisions, choices, and his wilderness experience determined the source and the strength of his faith. His call, his prompt obedience, and his heart were centered on God, and his faith was intact.

When I think of Abraham packing up and leaving, I have to laugh at myself. I don't travel lightly! I take house and home with me when I travel. I tend to take three to four times the clothes I need, just so I can choose what I want to wear according to my mood. I also take several pairs of shoes—dress shoes, runners, and sandals. Then there's all the hair goop, the jewelry, reading material, listening devices—a home away from home. Once I was stopped at the airport when going through security. I had so much jewelry in my carry-on that they thought all that metal was something other than what it was. The female security officer asked rhetorically, "Who travels with all that jewelry?" I looked at her and thought, *Not you, obviously.* Since then,

I've cut back on the jewelry but not on my other travel accoutrements. I'm working on that!

Food for Thought

What would you have chosen to take?

Are you willing to just pack up and go, when, where, and how God wants you to?

Has God called you to leave your place of comfort, to trustingly place your hand in his, and go on a road trip, with no directions and no road map—just your faith and his promises? What is your answer?

The question still stands: Is anything too hard for the Lord?

Jeremiah, the prophet, gives an answer to Abraham's question that should resonate in our mind, heart, and spirit:

"Ah sovereign Lord, you have made the heavens and earth by your great power and outstretched arm. Nothing is too hard for you" (Jer. 32:17).

God challenges you and me to answer the question!

- When he took the millions of Israelites through the Red Sea, was it too hard for him?
- When Jesus turned water into wine, was it too hard for him?
- When Jesus stilled the storm, was it too hard for him?
- When he fed the five thousand, was it too hard for him?
- When he raised the dead, was it too hard for him?

What miracles has God performed in your life? Was it too hard for him?

Be a Jeremiah in your response!

CHAPTER 14

Hagar

Hagar, the Invisible

Genesis 16:1-14 gives us the account of Hagar, a slave to Sarah and Abraham. In her culture, Hagar's value was less than a donkey. Her plight was similar to many women of her time—she was a slave, she was usable, and she was disposable.

God had promised Abraham and Sarah that they would be parents to a nation. So they waited for twenty-five years, and still God did not fulfill his promise. Sarah then took it upon herself to misinterpret God's promise and concoct her own plan to produce children.

Although I don't condone it, I can understand Sarah's impatience, because in biblical times, being without a child was not only a misfortune, but it was also a stigma. However, in this instant, she was doubtful, disobedient, and impatient. She advised Abraham to sleep with Hagar in order to produce children. Abraham listened to her bad advice and as a consequence, he was drawn into her sin, when he should have said, "Woman! Shuttest thy lips! Trust God's promise!

To add insult to injury, when the plan began to unravel, Sarah did not own up to her responsibility, as the now-pregnant Hagar began to disrespect and lord it over her. We could say, "Serves her right. She deserved what she got." Hagar was never supposed to be Abraham's wife. God made a covenant with Abraham and Sarah to bear children, to be a nation, and to glorify his name. It wasn't supposed to be a threesome. They broke the covenant when Hagar was added to the mix. However, God, in his mercy, honored the covenant made to Abraham and provided for Hagar later, when she was forced into the wilderness, but he was very firm about with whom he had made the covenant—Abraham and Sarah.

God chooses who will be part of our families. As a matter of fact, he ordains it before we are born. When we try, by human means, to overrule God's plan, we set in motion events that can be detrimental to many lives. Sarah's action to circumvent God's plan produced Ishmael, a nation that is still at war with Israel several centuries later. In fact, some critics may ask, "What was the purpose in letting Ishmael be born? Didn't God know that his descendants would be a thorn in Israel's side?"

In Isaiah 55:8, God says, "For my thoughts are not your thoughts, neither are your ways my ways."

Psalm 33:11 says, "But the plans of the Lord stand firm forever, the purposes of his heart through all generations."

"The Lord Almighty has sworn, surely as I have planned, so it will be, and as I purposed, so it will stand" (Isa. 14:24).

Hagar's plight began when Sarah took it upon herself to misinterpret God's promise to her and Abraham for a child. First, she doubted God's ability to keep his promise. She then got impatient and became outrightly disobedient. She gave Abraham bad advice, and he was drawn into disobedience with her. Sarah's action, however, demonstrated doubt, impatience, and lack of trust in God promise.

What about you? Have you been railing against God's lack of action in providing the things you want him to do?

Does it seem as if he's sitting on his throne, doing nothing?

Obviously, as Sarah's plans went awry, she accused Abraham of causing her grief—she got angry when the outcome was not as she envisioned it. She said, "You are responsible for the wrong I am suffering. I put my servant in your arms, and now that she knows she is pregnant, she despises me. May the Lord judge between and me" (Gen. 16:5).

You might say that Sarah tried to help God. Although she knew the promise God had made to her husband—that he would have "many descendants"—in all reality, she knew that their biological time clocks were ticking away. She had all the obvious facts correct, but her focus was on what she could see through finite eyes—her and Abraham's physical stage, their age, their situation. She could not see through God's infinite eyes or what he could do.

When we fail to see our situation from God's perspective, we tend to jump ahead of God and make a lot of bad choices. I have found that jumping the gun does not work. There were times when I knew in my spirit that God wanted me to wait patiently, yet I would get anxious and impatient. Sometimes I have found, to my cost, that God doesn't need my help in accomplishing his will. I have also learned, the hard way, that I need to allow him to do what he needs to do. Here are some home truths we need to take to heart:

- Be careful what you wish for—you might just get it.
- God has a perfect plan.
- God is more than capable of accomplishing his promises, but he accomplishes everything in his way and in his own time.

Whenever I reflect on my own journey and my past feelings of despair during a dark season of my life, I recall God assuring me—as he assures me now—that he indeed cares for me, just as he cared for Hagar thousands of years ago. It doesn't matter how long he seems to be taking in showing up or accomplishing his promises. He hasn't changed. He will keep every promise he makes, but it will be in his perfect time.

We are told that when Hagar realized that she was going to have a child, she then began to despise her mistress, and that made Sarah angry. When Sarah complained to Abraham, he told Sarah to do whatever she thought was best. Sarah then became very unkind to Hagar, and Hagar had no choice but to flee from Sarah's presence. Remember, Hagar was disposable property of very little value. Sometimes the people who wound us treat us like disposable property. Spouses who walk away leave behind what they believe is disposable property. Fathers or mothers who abuse children treat them like disposable property. But if someone has treated you like disposable property, look at God's treatment of Hagar and take courage!

In the continuing story, Abraham wimped out and decided to do what Sarah asked. He sent Hagar and Ishmael into the wilderness with only a skin of water and some bread. It didn't take long for the food to run out, which placed mother and son near the point of death.

In the wilderness, Hagar was worried about what was going to happen to her and her child. In the midst of her despair and darkness, she heard a voice. It is in this haze of alienation—this unfriendly seemingly godless environment of pain—that she encountered God. Can you imagine her fright as her cries of despair reverberated in the desert, bouncing from rock to rock, shrub to shrub? Then, out of nowhere, an angel of the Lord spoke and asked her two very important questions:

1. "Hagar, where have you come from?"
2. "Where are you going?"

Hagar responded, "I'm running away from my mistress." Hagar did not say where she was going because she probably didn't know. When we face similar situations, God knows where we're coming from, because he is there with us. He also knows where we're going, because he is the only one who knows what is ahead of us and can lead us there. Most important, he knows where we're going, because he is going with us. Hagar was in the same position as some us are. But God had an answer for her. As a slave, she was invisible and disposable. On the day God spoke to her, Hagar was no longer invisible.

The Lord told her that he had heard her misery. "You are the God who sees me, for she said, I have now seen the One who sees me" (Gen. 16:13).

Remember: we are not invisible to God!

After Hagar answered the question the angel had asked her, he told her to go back to her position and to submit to Sarah. He also told her that her descendants would also be too numerous to count. He told her that she too would bear a son and that she was to name him Ishmael, for the Lord had heard of her misery.

Although going back must have been painful to Hagar, she was obedient and returned to Sarah.

Painful situations help us to grow. Sometimes if the pain is great, we beg God to stop the pain. We say we are so stressed out! However, if the pain stops from our hand and not from God's hands, our spiritual growth is retarded—nipped in the bud! Remember: nothing is too hard for the Lord, not even painful situations.

Our difficult situations do not stump God, but we need to stay and grow spiritually. If you have already run away from a difficult situation or are thinking of running away, and you hear the voice of God telling you to go back, do not resist. You probably will miss out on immense spiritual growth and blessings if you resist.

Hagar recognized that the only way she would survive her difficult situation was to reconcile with Sarah. So although going back must have been painful to Hagar, she was obedient and returned. She trusted God and obeyed, and soon Ishmael was born. God caused a great miracle to happen in the wilderness that day. He still causes miracles to happen and will answer us in our wilderness times, if we call out to him. This should be an encouragement for us as Christians. Even in a seemingly hopeless situation, God is Jehovah Jireh. He provides what we need.

Psalm 46 tells us, "God is our refuge and strength, a very present help in trouble."

I love this part of the story, because it tells how this young slave girl actually recognized who God was, even to giving him a name. That day in the wilderness, Hagar learned that God indeed saw her and knew her needs. She also realized that there was someone watching over her and her child. She was no longer invisible! Most important, God was not invisible either. She had found and was now connected to the one true God.

Unfortunately, it was not all cozy for Hagar when she went back to camp. Things didn't get better miraculously. In fact, Hagar and her son were the proverbial thorns in Sarah's side. Thirteen years went by, and then Sarah decided that she had had enough of Hagar and her son. By that time, Sarah had seen God's promise come to pass in her own life and had a son of her own, whom she named Isaac. She did not need Hagar as a surrogate any longer. Once again, Hagar was at

Sarah's mercy. Scripture tells us that Abraham held a feast to celebrate the day Isaac, the son of the covenant, was weaned:

"But Sarah saw the son whom Hagar the Egyptian had born to Abraham was mocking and she said get rid of that slave woman and her son, for that slave woman's son will never share the inheritance with my son Isaac" (Gen. 21:9–10).

Once again, Hagar was disposed of. She was given some food and a skin of water and sent away, where she and her son wandered in the desert of Beersheba. They eventually finished the food and water and just waited to die. It would be an unbearable sight to watch your child die before your eyes. It was no different for Hagar. She put him under a shrub and sat a little distance away. Here began her second encounter with God.

As a mother, I can imagine the heart-wrenching, gut-clenching sounds that emanated from her belly up to her throat, echoing around in the desert as she watched her son slowly began to fade away. I imagine she was not only crying at the imminent death of her son, but she was also crying at the realization that she was a slave and had no value. She was crying for the times she was mistreated and could not retaliate, the times when she had no choice but to be a wife to Abraham. She had been invisible her whole life—a nobody, disposable property, at the whim of her mistress. At this moment, she was no longer a wife, and in a little while, she would no longer be a mother—important components of that culture. She had lost her identity, even that of being a slave to a prominent man. She had lost everything! She was a castaway! Hagar had lost all hope.

It is in this state that God found her and said compassionately, "What is the matter, Hagar? Do not be afraid; God has heard the boy crying as he lies there. Lift the boy up and take him by the hand, for I will make him into a great nation" (Gen. 21:17-18).

Once again, God rescued Hagar. Suddenly, Hagar opened her eyes and saw a well of water right in front of her. Hagar then went to fill the skin of water and gave the life-giving refreshment to her son. God had mercy on Hagar in her pain and anguish of spirit. He provided for her and her son. A key verse in this Scripture is verse 20 that says, "God was with the boy as he grew up." Not only did God show them mercy, but he continued to watch over Ishmael and take care of him. This is a reminder to us that God loved Ishmael, and he loves his descendants. Ishmael was not a coincidence, and neither are his descendants.

Nothing happens to us by coincidence. At this point, your wounds might seem crippling. You might even feel that you have been tossed out like a disposable nonentity. You might be tempted to feel that what you are going through is useless and unprofitable. Remember: God does not make mistakes! There are benefits to this pain that you cannot see or understand right now. You might feel that you are in an emotional prison, but if you put your full trust in God, you will discover that he is ever present, ever listening, and ever caring.

I see a correlation between in Hagar's story and my own, as we both walked through a wilderness. Like Hagar, I felt rejected and abandoned when I was set adrift like disposable property. In the same manner, we both had a great need, and God provided for both of us. When I was filled with despair, I experienced the loving care and tenderness of the Lord, as he looked after me, loved me more than I could have imagined, and carried me during my wilderness experience—just as he will carry you.

The beautiful part to this story is that although Hagar had no input in the situation, God extended his mercy to her and made her promises that have been fulfilled up to this present day.

I found an amazing portion of Scripture, one that I hadn't seen previously in the years I have been a Christian. With all the animosity and hatred between Abraham, Sarah, Hagar, and their offspring, Isaac and Ishmael, there must have been reconciliation of sorts, at some point, because Genesis 25:7–9 tells us "when Abraham breathed his last and died at a good old age, an old man and full of years; and he was gathered to his people, his sons Isaac and Ishmael buried him in the cave of Machpelah near Mamre."

Most times we are so busy concentrating on the feuds, the gossip, and the he said/she said that we miss God's intervention and the result of his intervention. In this case, it was the relationship between Ishmael and Isaac and God's continued promise to a nation.

CHAPTER 15

Jacob

Jacob: a Man Who Struggled with God and Humans and Overcame

Jacob is one of the great patriarchs of the Old Testament. The biblical record shows that at times, he was also a schemer, liar, and manipulator; he also was sly and deceitful. Many times he caused a lot of pain. But God established his covenant with Jacob's grandfather Abraham, and the blessings continued from Abraham through Jacob's father, Isaac, and then to Jacob and his descendants. As a result, Jacob's sons became leaders of the twelve tribes of Israel. (Gen. 25:29–34; 27:1–29; 30:25–43).

From the beginning, we saw where Jacob would be different. Before he was born, he fought with his brother. Genesis 25:19 tells us that when Rebekah inquired of the Lord, she was told, "Two nations are in your womb, and two peoples within you will be separated; One people will be stronger than the other, and the older will serve the younger."

When Jacob was born, instead of coming into the world in the usual fashion of any newborn baby, he came out grasping the heel of his brother. It was a foreshadowing of his life and things to come. He was not willing to take second place but would grasp at whatever he wanted, even if it meant wounding others in the process.

The third time we see Jacob, he is scheming to get an advantage over Esau, his brother. Jacob liked to stay home and cook. Esau was the hunter, the outdoorsman. One day, Esau came home famished and asked Jacob for some of his stew. Jacob, ever the opportunist, said, "First, sell me your birthright." One's birthright in modern times might not be as significant as in ancient times. In ancient times, the firstborn inherited the major portion of the father's estate. Jacob was the second twin of Isaac and Rebekah. The birthright did not belong to him, yet he coveted this.

A desperate man will sometimes sell his soul to find relief, and Jacob knew that. So when Esau said, "I am famished," Jacob took the opportunity to put into effect the plan that he had probably been hatching in his mind for years. The result of his deception fostered the hostility that brewed between them for over twenty years. In all probability, every time the mention of the birthright came up, Jacob's envy would increase. This envy developed into full-blown deceit when he and his mother deceived Isaac into giving Esau's blessing to Jacob.

Jacob voiced the risks involved if Isaac were to discover them, but the risks were not enough to deter him from the plan. Like the tasty stew he was good at cooking, he and his mother cooked up another dish—a dish of deceit, ready to be served, and he could almost taste the victory of getting the blessings that went with the birthright of a firstborn.

Their plot brings to mind a quote from Sir Walter Scott: "Oh, what a tangled web we weave when first we practice to deceive."

The plots and deception emanating from the hearts of Jacob and Rebekah were successful, because it deprived Esau of what was legally his. Esau lost his birthright and the blessings that went with it. In this situation, it was no wonder that Esau became resentful and bitter. He held his grudge against Jacob for a long time because of the family deception and the stolen blessing. It was at that moment of loss that a thought was born in Esau's heart.

He said to himself, "The days of mourning for my father are near; then I will kill my brother Jacob" (Gen. 27:41).

Sometime ago, someone said to me, "You don't know what's in my heart." I do not scare easily, but when I heard those words and the tone of voice in which they were spoken, I knew fear. It was one of the few times that I was afraid for my life.

Jesus himself said, in Mark 7:2,

What comes out of a man is what makes him unclean: For from within, out of men's heart, come evil thoughts, sexual immorality, theft, murder, adultery, greed, malice, deceit, lewdness, envy, slander, arrogance and folly. All these evils come from inside and make a man unclean.

When we examine the life of Jacob, we see that he was very unclean, based on Jesus' assessment of the human heart. But before we indict Jacob, let us look at the pivotal points of his life—what we can call "God moments."

In light of Jacob's behavior, his subsequent actions, and Jesus' debate with the Pharisees, how can we relate this to modern times? When a spouse says he or she is leaving, when a child admits to taking drugs, or a child is involved in illegal or other ungodly activities, it is not a sudden decision. This plan was hatched and fertilized in the mind a long time ago, and the behavior enacted is the result of what was in the heart. That is why the psalmist reminds us to guard our mind and heart, because the wellsprings of life lie in the heart (Ps. 26:2).

After the deception of the stolen blessing, it would be an understatement to say that Isaac's household was in a total mess. Imagine Isaac's regret and his sense of betrayal; Esau's grudge against Jacob; Esau's anger, regrets, and sense of loss; Jacob's fear for his life; and Rebekah's irresponsibility as a parent. Yes, she played favorites, as do so many parents, and did not take responsibility, up to this point, because she advised Jacob to take refuge with her brother Laban in Haran. She said, "When your brother is no longer angry with you and forgets what you did to him …" She seems to minimize everything—the betrayals, the various losses, and even her part in the deception.

Genesis 27:5 tells us that Rebekah eavesdropped on the conversation between Isaac and Esau and later was the instigator who devised the plot to deceive Isaac. Every time I read Rebekah's words, "what you did," I always shake my head and say, "Rebekah, Rebekah, take responsibility. Don't shift the blame."

The dysfunction continued in the home, as afterwards, Rebekah then compounded her bad behavior and traipsed off to complain to

Isaac about the Hittite women, "one of the ungodly heathen nations" that Esau had married into. It would seem that Jacob learned how to manipulate from a master manipulator—his mother. However, the advice she gave Jacob to flee to Haran was, for once, sound advice, and Jacob took it; he was away for twenty years.

There was so much bad blood among everyone in Isaac's household that it would have been tempting to give up hope that issues would be resolved and relationships would be restored. It is similar to the bad blood and dysfunctional behavior in many modern families. But when God is allowed to intervene and help us to resolve the issues in his way, everything works out perfectly. In fact, this is what God did as Jacob was on his way to Haran.

According to Genesis 28:12–15,

He had a dream in which he saw a stairway resting on the earth, with its top reaching to heaven, and the angels of God were ascending and descending on it. There above it stood the LORD, and he said: "I am the LORD, the God of your father Abraham and the God of Isaac. I will give you and your descendants the land on which you are lying. Your descendants will be like the dust of the earth, and you will spread out to the west and to the east, to the north and to the south. All peoples on earth will be blessed through you and your offspring. I am with you and will watch over you wherever you go, and I will bring you back to this land. I will not leave you until I have done what I have promised you.

CHAPTER 16

Jacob's Conditional Trust in God

Then Jacob made a vow saying,

> If God will be with me and will watch over me on this journey
> I am taking and will give me food to eat and clothes to wear so
> that I return safely to my father's household, then the LORD
> will be my God and this stone that I have set up as a pillar will
> be God's house, and of all that you give me I will give you a
> tenth. (Gen. 28:20–22)

If—that same word pops up again, that little word that carries
big consequences! In this case, Jacob used it as a conditional to God's
protection. As Christians, we do that too. "God, if you give me more
money, I will tithe. If you give me a new spouse, I will be happy. If ...
if ... if ..."

When are we going trust God unconditionally and stop testing
him? We should be content with what we have.

The fact that God called us, saved us, loves us, protects us, and
provides for us should have us deleting the word "if" from our
vocabulary and have us basking in his love, instead of complaining
and putting conditions on him. We are so fortunate that God's heart is
not like the heart of men. God's ears are open to our sorrow, our pain,
and our wounds, but do you ever think that God is tired of hearing our
complaints about our spouse, our children, and our difficult situation?
Sometimes we seem to have a sense of entitlement—we are entitled
to food, happiness, and more of everything. When we don't get it, we
go wild. The Israelites had a sense of entitlement. They complained
about all they did not have and failed to see the blessings they had.
What do you think would happen if we put the principle of trusting
God unconditionally and being content in all situations into practice?

The apostle Paul said, "Contentment is great gain."

When we complain, become dissatisfied, and forget to count our blessings, as a wise old hymn writer wrote years ago, we blame God for our situation. We blame him for not giving us what we think we should have. One of my mother's frequent phrases when she heard complaining was, "You're spitting in God's face." Do you want to be accused of spitting in God's face? We should always say, "God forbid that God gives me what I want or deserve. I would rather he gives me what I need."

Let us pick up the story of Jacob once more.

He fled to Haran and eventually fell in love with Rachel, Laban's daughter. The next part of the story always makes me smile. Rather than being his usual deceitful self, Jacob now was the one who was deceived. Jacob worked out an agreement with Laban to serve him for seven years and after that, Jacob would get Rachel as his wife. After seven years and a wedding night, Jacob woke up to find himself married to the wrong woman. His father-in-law, Laban, intentionally gave him the wrong bride, and from then on, there were plays and counterplays of deceit among members of that household. This continued until Jacob decided to flee from Laban's house.

However, in fleeing from a hostile Uncle Laban, Jacob had to pass through Esau's hostile territory. Prior to his meeting with Esau after twenty years of uncertainty and fear of Esau's wrath, Jacob began to plot again. This time it was how to outwit Esau once again and to save his life. It was then that Jacob finally came face-to-face with God, and that encounter with God changed his life forever.

Up to this point in Jacob's life, he had gained everything by deception. By the time we encounter Jacob again in Genesis 31, he was on the run, like a common criminal, and his uncle was in hot pursuit of him in order to recover some stolen idols. This was, of course, after Jacob had increased his wealth through deception by countering Laban's method of deception against him. As Jacob was fleeing, he must have finally realized that he was between the proverbial devil and the deep blue sea. In his case, he was between a present devil and a past devil—and his past and his present were about to collide.

Genesis 32 tells us of how Jacob, as usual, tried to accomplish things through his own efforts. Jacob put his plans into action by sending his least favorite wife, maidservants, and sons ahead of him, prior to meeting Esau. It was one of the few moments that he was alone, and in this "God moment," we read, "So Jacob was left alone, and a man wrestled with him till daybreak."

The Bible says, "When the man saw that he could not overpower him, he, touched the socket of Jacob's hips so that his hip was wrenched as he wrestled with the man. Then the man said, Let me go for it is daybreak. But Jacob replied, I will not let you go unless you bless me" (Gen. 32:25–26).

Oh, to be so desperate to hear from God! So desperate for a blessing, so desperate when we face the impossibilities of our life that we hang on to God for all we are worth; so desperate to use our strength to wrestle with him for our family, our children, our spouse. Oh, to be so desperate! We give up too easily when situations become difficult. Oh, that we would get that spirit of determination of Jacob and say:

"I will not give up!"

"I will not give in!"

"I will not give out!"

My heart's prayer is that you and I won't give up too early or too easily. I pray that we will be persistent in our struggles against the challenges that threaten our family, because our blessings will surely come. Jacob's blessings came eventually, when he used his strong persistence and his desperation to gain what he needed from God.

God had already blessed Jacob financially—he was persistent in his pursuits, and he was a hard worker. This characteristic helped him to build wealth for his family. But his weakness of deception and dishonesty wounded many. However, God knew Jacob as he knows us. He did not see what Jacob was; he saw what he could become. God worked with Jacob and the strengths and weaknesses he had to offer.

He sees what others cannot see or just refuse to see. Despite Jacob's faults and imperfections, his scheming, his lying, and all his other misdeeds, God blessed him for his persistence. "Your name will no longer be Jacob but Israel, because you have struggled with God and with men and have overcome" (Gen. 32:28).

God worked with Jacob as he works with us. He works with the wounds, the bad decisions, the scars, the lies, the hurts, and the mistakes we make. Our mistakes never make us discards in God's eyes. If we let him, God is always ready to heal and restore us when we are simply too carnal-minded to behave the way we should. He always sees the potential in us!

When I read the story of Jacob, it reminds me of the song, "The Touch of the Master's Hand," from an original poem by Myra B. Welch. It was originally recorded by Wayne Watson and since has been recorded by many. The message in this song is a beautiful concept of what happens when God, the Father, takes control of our lives, as he did with Jacob. Here is a portion of the song.

The Touch of the Master's Hand

'Twas battered and scarred, and the auctioneer
thought it scarcely worth his while
To waste much time on the old violin,
But held it up with a smile.
"What am I bidden, good folks," he cried.
"Who'll start the bidding for me?
A dollar, a dollar, then, two! Only two?
Two dollars, and who'll make it three?
Three dollars, once; three dollars, twice;
Going for three ..."

(Myra B. Welch, 1877–1959)

No one wanted to buy the old violin for even three dollars. However, the song continues to describe the change that occurred when an old man in the audience came, took the violin, adjusted it and began to play beautifully. The astonished auctioneer then began his bidding again; but this time, he began at three thousand dollars. The crowd asked "What made the difference in the value? Why are you now asking three thousand dollars for the violin?" The old man had the answer. He said, "It was the touch of the Master's hand."

You might feel like that old battered violin. You've been wounded. You've been discarded. You feel worthless. But can you say the Master has you in his hand? Has your dependence upon God become greater than before? Have you experienced the touch of the Master's hand?

Jacob was wounded by the angel with whom he wrestled, but he persisted in fighting for what he desired, and he experienced the touch of the Master's hand. He changed that night, and he never reverted to his old deceitful self. He finally learned to give control of himself and his life to God. Jacob's story demonstrates how God can effect changes after we have been wounded and have wounded others. It also shows that even though Jacob was one of the most imperfect of men, God blessed him and continued his promises through his line of descendants.

Many people might have written off Jacob, similar to what so-called friends and relatives might have done to you. God does not see us as the old violin; he sees us as the violin after he adds his touch to our lives. Because Jacob met God that night and was touched by him, his name is frequently associated as part of a trio—Abraham, Isaac, and Jacob. God can do the same for us. We might not necessarily be the patriarch of a nation, but God can bless other people through us, if we use our misery to minister to a hurting world. We are imperfect human beings. We wound, and we are wounded, but if we give control to God, he will change us and use us by the touch of his hand.

See if you can find a recording of that old song I mentioned and listen to it. Being wounded is not the end of the world, even though it may feel so now. God has great plans for your life.

So many times in the past few years when things were not going the way I had hoped, I would cry to the Lord, "Enough! Lord, I've had enough!" But this is when I would surrender, turn my plans over to him, and embrace his plans. Instead of waiting for the Lord to bring me to my knees or where the Lord has to "touch the socket of my hip," I will gladly embrace God's plan for my life and allow the Holy Spirit to transform me into his image. Jacob's new birth and his transformation came in Genesis 32:27, in this dialogue:

The man asked him, "What is your name?"

"Jacob," he answered.

Then the man said, "Your name will no longer be Jacob, but Israel, because you have struggled with God and with men and have overcome."

Jacob said, "Please tell me your name."

But he replied, "Why do you ask my name?" Then he blessed him there.

Then Jacob called the place Peniel, saying, "It is because I saw God face-to-face, yet my life was spared."

The culmination of Jacob's transformation is in Genesis 35:9–12.

"After Jacob returned from Paddan Aram, God appeared to him again and blessed him. God said to him, Your name is Jacob, but you will no longer be called Jacob; your name will be Israel, so he named him Israel. And God said to him, I am God Almighty, be fruitful and increase in number. A nation and a community of nations will come from you and kings will come from your body."

God's next words sealed the covenant and relationship with Jacob as he said, "The land I gave to Abraham and Isaac I also give to you, and I will give this land to your descendants after you."

Jacob's story teaches us how imperfect people can be greatly blessed by God, not because of who we are but because of who God is.

Remember, when someone wounds us, we make the choice as to how we will act, react, and behave thereafter. From then on, it is a choice how we live. We can either get bitter at the world and everyone in it, or we can become better—better people, better citizens, better human beings, and better children of God. It is not impossible to accomplish, if we have faith. For example, Joseph faced the worse challenges imaginable. Yet he was able to rise above his circumstances through his faith in God.

CHAPTER 17

Joseph

Betrayed by His Siblings

As he lost his footing and fell headlong into the pit, his cries echoed across the barren land. "Brothers!" he pleaded. "Please have mercy. Please don't do this to me. Oh God, please help me, help me."

As the last sound faded slowly into the air, nature stood still and for a moment, the brothers paused their chewing; then they continued, as they passed around the bread and callously ignored their brother's fearful cries.

Chapters 37 to 46 of Genesis have been the subject of many movies and plays for decades. These chapters portray the story of Joseph, who was betrayed by his siblings. They illustrate how God helped Joseph to overcome the many obstacles he faced, and his subsequent rise to power in Egypt after his brothers sold him into slavery.

Young, spoiled, and the favorite son of Jacob, Joseph received a special coat from his father. As the heir apparent to his father's estate, his brothers were jealous of him. This jealousy and sibling rivalry finally culminated in the evil act of selling Joseph to slave traders on their way to Egypt. This was after throwing him in a well to die. In the hardness of their hearts, the brothers did not hear Joseph's fear as he cried in the well. Not even as he was being dragged unwillingly into the wilderness by the slave traders did they consider the brotherly blood flowing between them and Joseph. They were so eaten up with jealously and hate that the evil in them spilled over to commit a crime so heinous that the consequences lasted for generations. They were ruthless and merciless in exacting vengeance on Joseph for Jacob's preferential treatment of Joseph. Betrayal of a blood brother! It seemed that Joseph had hit rock bottom. However, even though Joseph's situation seemed hopeless, God still had a plan for Joseph.

The story began in Genesis, when Joseph brought a bad report about his brothers to Jacob. Then Jacob made a "richly ornamented" robe for Joseph, which funneled their hatred even further. Their hatred was exacerbated when Joseph told them about his dreams, in which their sheaves of grain bowed down to him, signifying his headship over them. In another of his dreams, he related that the sun, moon, and eleven stars bowed down to him (Gen. 37:5–11). After hearing the dreams, the brothers became more incensed. They were totally unaware that God had given Joseph a glimpse into his future and that this was a foreshadowing of things to come.

The brothers' jealousy, anger, and hatred came to a head one day as Joseph was approaching to check on them at his father's request. "They saw him in the distance, and before he reached them, they plotted to kill him …" (Gen. 37:18). In that moment, their evil thoughts came to fruition and these thoughts became a deed that would follow them for years to come.

It must have given them pleasure to get rid of the object that reminded them that they were not at the center of their father's love and affections. Having convinced themselves that Joseph had to go, they stripped Joseph of his robe, threw him in the well, and then callously "sat down to eat their meal" (Gen. 37:25). Joseph must have been petrified! At this point in the story, you might be able to relate to Joseph. He had done no wrong, but he had been deeply wounded. Can you imagine his sense of betrayal? He was betrayed by his own blood; betrayed by people who should have loved and protected him. He was disposed of like yesterday's garbage.

After the brothers disposed of Joseph, or so they thought, they told their father that a wild animal had killed him. I doubt that they ever forgot that tragic day that they lied to Jacob because Jacob, on hearing of the tragedy of his son's death, tore his clothes, put on sackcloth, and mourned for many days. In addition, he did not allow his children to comfort him or to forget, because as he said, "In mourning will I go down to the grave to my son. So his father wept for him" (Gen. 37:35).

Jacob's Grief to Assuage; Joseph's Pit to Conquer

Sometimes God allows us to fall into the pit of pain, into uncertainty, to starve and to suffer deep wounds, and to die to ourselves, only to bring us back to a place where his sovereign plan can be exacted. There are times when God sends us to the wilderness because of our disobedience. However, Joseph's wilderness experience was not through disobedience. It was because of his brothers' sinful hearts and actions.

It does not matter how the wounding takes place; we are always sent into the wilderness to work out God's sovereign plan. Even though the brothers had sent Joseph to the slave pit of Egypt, his physical, emotional, and psychological pain could only hone his character and grow his faith even more. Moreover, his slavery experience was all a part of God's plan.

Recently, an acquaintance and I were talking about the pain of being wounded. Not only had he suffered pain, but he had also caused much pain. He said to me, "Don't worry; the world is round. What goes around comes around." As the conversation progressed, I gathered that he was now reaping what he had sowed so indiscriminately many years before. He freely did what he wanted to do in the past, and in hindsight he could say, "What goes around comes around." He is learning, like Joseph's brothers, that free will carries responsibilities and consequences.

Trusted Chains—a Sovereign Plan

Joseph's next appearance takes us to Egypt, where we encounter him as a man. Although he was still a slave, his status had been elevated. He was now attendant to Potiphar, one of the pharaoh's officials. Potiphar had bought Joseph off the slave block. In no time, he recognized Joseph's talents and made him head of his household. This was also a part of God's plan, and he was positioning Joseph for future events as they unfolded. Genesis 39:5 tells us:

"From the time he put him in charge of his household and of all that he owned the Lord blessed the household of the Egyptian because of Joseph."

Also, "The blessing of the Lord was on everything Potiphar had, both in the house and in the field. So he left in Joseph's care everything he had; with Joseph in charge, he did not concern himself with anything except the food he ate" (Gen. 39:6).

It would appear that Joseph was comfortable—as comfortable as he could be, considering that he was enslaved in a foreign land and away from his home and family. Yet even in his apparently desolate and hopeless situation, God was going to use him to administer to the entire nation of Egypt. But first, it was necessary for Joseph to learn the culture and exercise his administrative skills. He did, in the hardship of slavery. But despite his difficult situation, Joseph remained hopeful and faithful to God.

In Potiphar's house, he bloomed, as the adage goes, where he was planted. Then, what did God do next? He took Joseph out of his "comfort zone" again and allowed him to be framed for a crime he hadn't committed; he was subsequently thrown into prison. This must have been discouraging for Joseph, but little did he know what God had in store for him.

At times, we get discouraged and sometimes angry when we continue to pray for our own situation and instead of it getting better, it gets worse. Despite the many prayers, the children rebel, the in-laws are more like outlaws, the spouse and the boss at work both seem to be on another planet. The more we pray, the worse it seems to get.

Joseph could have railed against his circumstances, against the pain, against the people who caused his discomfort, and even against God. He could have become bitter at the injustices meted out to him, but he did not. When his life took a left turn, he gave God first place in his life and kept himself pure in his singleness, and God moved him along toward the plan he had for him.

As Joseph waited on God and trusted him to work out his plan for his life, another important event occurred. Two of Pharaoh's officials were sent to Joseph's prison in disgrace. It was because of Joseph's presence and his prison experience that the cupbearer would later remember him to Pharaoh.

You may feel like you are also in a prison. It was in Potiphar's house and later in the prison that Joseph learned the skills of administration. It was because he was in prison that he was able to rise to his position, where he was able to spare his family from the famine. Remember that God used Joseph's time in prison to teach him the skills he would need for the future. Perhaps God can use your prison too. Are you willing to wait for God's timing, to wait for him to intervene in your circumstances, and to wait with a purpose? What do you think would happen if we let go of what we want and wait for God's direction as to what he wants?

Psalm 27:14 says, "Wait for the Lord; be strong and take heart and wait for the Lord."

"No one whose hope is in you will be put to shame, but they will be put to shame who are treacherous without excuse" (Ps. 25:3).

"Wait for the Lord and keep his way. He will exalt you to inherit the land; when the wicked are cut off, you will see it" (Ps. 37:34).

Even if we have had to leave the comforts of a home or a relationship, suffer failing health, or suffer from depression and stress, among all the other things that can occur in our human world, we have to wait upon the Lord. He has a perfect plan for each of us. It is natural to want to accept the world's standards and principles and try to remedy the situations by the world's standards but *do not give in to the temptation.*

Principle to learn: Joseph feared the unknown of Egypt but trusted the known—his God.

Betrayal by the World's Principles

When a man and a woman stand before God in marriage, it is a covenant. One part of this covenant is our human sexuality. Every time you come together as a couple, you give away a part of yourself. When one partner takes this intimate part of the relationship and gives it to another, this causes great wounding. I have heard this scenario related to me so often and, sadly, this type of Hollywood-style relationship has pervaded the Christian Church. Joseph's story is the opposite of the current modus operandi of many Christian spouses.

Joseph had suffered deep distress at the hands of his brothers. As he was living in exile in a foreign land, he could have adopted the foreign customs. Genesis 39:6 tells the story of Joseph's encounter with Mrs. Potiphar.

"Now Joseph was well built and handsome, and after a while his master's wife took notice of Joseph and said, come to bed with me."

Joseph refused Mrs. Potiphar's overtures, which incensed her. Joseph said to her,

> With me in charge my master does not concern himself with anything in the house; everything he owns he has entrusted to my care. No one is greater in this house than I am. My master has withheld nothing from me except you, because you are his wife. How then could I do such a wicked thing and sin against God. (Gen. 39:8–9)

When Potiphar's wife said to him, "Come lie with me," Joseph could have slept with her, and no one would have known, but Joseph knew that God would have known. There is an adage that I like: "Hidden secret on earth; open scandal in heaven."

God is never fooled! No matter how people sneak around, hide, and commit sexual sins, God knows.

With this perspective in mind, Joseph said no to sin. He understood the concept of living in purity and the concept of human sexuality. He was wise in discerning the effect of sleeping with Potiphar's wife. Most of all, he understood that it was God he was hurting, and the physical pleasures he would experience would be short-lived compared to the long-term effect on him, the woman, Potiphar, and God. It would have been easy for Joseph to drift from God's standards.

It is easy for someone to drift from God's standards when the convenience and comforts of this world and promises of happiness beckon. We should treasure God's precepts and regard his standard in high esteem. If we put God's standards ahead of the world's, our moral absolutes will not be violated. Joseph's brand of morality was accountable, not just as a single man but as a man of integrity.

Joseph's high standards were a testament to God. He was more or less comfortable in his job, he was doing a good job, and God blessed him, but as usual, there is always a snake in Eden. This time, it was Mrs. Potiphar. Mrs. Potiphar never gave a thought to sexual harassment in the workplace. Neither did Joseph. When she invited him to sleep with her, his thought was not of sexual harassment and loyalty to his master. His most telling statement was, "How then can I do such a wicked thing and sin against God?"

This demonstrates Joseph's spiritual and moral integrity of character. If he had slept with her, it would not have been broadcast over the airwaves, glorified, or talked about, as the media is wont to do in our modern times. Mrs. Potiphar certainly would not have spilled her dirty little secret. However, if Joseph had slept with Potiphar's wife and sinned against God, he would have derailed his eternal destiny. Conversely, he would have had to pay too high a price for a moment's pleasure, and there would have been justice and consequences to face. In all probability, he would have asked for forgiveness, and God would have granted it, but the consequences would have remained. He was fully aware that man's justice is a probability, but God's justice is a certainty.

There are similarities and differences between Joseph's and David's knowledge of sin. Joseph said the sin of sleeping with Mrs. Potiphar would be a sin against God, and David acknowledged the same thing with regard to sleeping with another man's wife. However, it was only after the fact of sleeping with Bathsheba and being publicly accosted by Nathan the prophet that David confessed his sin.

He said, "For I know my transgressions, and my sin is always before me. Against you, only you have I sinned and done what is evil in your sight, so that you are proved right when you speak and justified when you judge" (Ps. 51:3–4).

Here is the key verse: "Against you, you only, have I sinned and done what is evil in your sight."

The difference between Joseph and David is that Joseph fingered the sin prior to sinning, and David sinned and then was fingered. While David succumbed to the temptation of sleeping with Bathsheba, Joseph constantly refused Mrs. Potiphar's wiles and kept himself pure. Nonetheless, as long as we, like David, acknowledge that when we sin, it is against God, and then ask for forgiveness (as in David's case), God will grant us forgiveness.

As we continue to examine Joseph's life, we see where he demonstrated a brand of faithfulness and commitment to God that served him well and is a principle that needs to be adopted. Mrs. Potiphar gave no thought to her marriage or to Potiphar. When we hear stories of marriages breaking up, we sometimes act surprised. Mrs. Potiphar—and others before and after her—did exactly what we hear of on the news and through the grapevine in our society and at our churches. However, we rarely hear and celebrate the stories of the "Josephs" of the world, who resist the temptations placed in their paths. There are still men and women of integrity who will honor God's covenants and stick with their spouses and God through thick and thin. There are still single men and women who will stand pure before God, despite the temptations thrown their way. The media does not celebrate these people, because these stories do not sell well.

After reading of the high divorce rate among Christians, I was curious as to the reason. We have the truth of Jesus Christ, so why weren't more spouses depending on God to fix the problems they face, rather than depending on their emotions and advice from friends. I researched the topic of why some long-term marriages end in divorce. It took months of poring over documents and web pages to make sense of this phenomenon that seems to have invaded the Christian world.

At the time I was doing the research, government officials, sports figures, and other celebrities were having scandalous affairs. However, there were just as many Christians as non-Christians walking out of their marriages. A continuous theme that ran through most of the stories was that spouses left and then concocted stories to enhance their image. Another theme was that illicit relationships began with family friends or people close to the couple. The spouses who left always tried to put the ex-spouses in the worst possible light to justify their actions. In all the stories, one fact was glaringly apparent: the person who left focused on himself or herself. One man, after accusing his then-wife of many untrue things, said, "It is the way I see it." The question is, "Are those the facts? How does God see it?"

As imperfect human beings, we see what we want to see. Jeremiah 17:9 tells us that the human heart is deceitful above all things. Many people see and judge a situation from the evil in their heart. However, God's vision is 20/20, and his judgment is pure! He not only sees the action, but he also sees the motives, and he sees what is in the heart. We are privy to Joseph's story. Joseph was a man of integrity; Mrs. Potiphar was all about "self." *We can learn from them!*

We know that God's sovereign hand was involved in the plan for Joseph's life. When Joseph rejected Mrs. Potiphar's advances, her pride was hurt. How dare a slave, especially a Jewish slave, refuse her advances? She was angry—and Joseph was going to pay!

So she broadcast a sordid trumped-up tale to anyone who would listen. She accused Joseph of trying to sexually assault her. To his credit, when Potiphar heard the tale, he saw what he wanted to see. He had grown to know Joseph and had seen the hand of God in his life. There were so many loose ends of truths and untruths in the story that the only truth he could see clearly was God's sovereign hand in Joseph's life. There were also many sides to the story that he needed to understand—Joseph's, Mrs. Potiphar's, and the slaves. And don't forget that there was God's version. It seemed that only Joseph—and to some extent, Potiphar—knew God's side of this tale. Potiphar's wife re-created the events of the story to the slaves and her husband. She wanted to paint Joseph, a foreign slave who had the audacity to spurn her sexual advances, in the worst light possible. If he were put to death, that would be her delight. Eventually, the events unfolded as follows:

> Joseph's master took him and put him in prison, the place where the king's prisoners were confined. But while Joseph was there in the prison, the Lord was with him; he showed him kindness and granted him favor in the eyes of the prison warden. So the warden put Joseph in charge of all those held in

the prison, and he was made responsible for all that was done there. The warden paid no attention to anything under Joseph's care, because the Lord was with Joseph and gave him success in whatever he did (Gen. 39:20-23).

What a calamity—an innocent man accused of a crime he did not commit. Sound familiar?

Joseph was thrown in prison and now had to wrap his head around the hurt, the pain, and the injustices of his situation again. But God still had a plan!

It was in prison that Joseph met the pharaoh's cupbearer and subsequently interpreted his dreams. This act brought him to Pharaoh's attention. But he had to wait two years for this to transpire. Finally, the hand of a sovereign God very nicely tied together the loose ends. When Joseph was in prison, he learned the skills that allowed him to administer the grain storage for the king. It was because Joseph was in prison that he was able to spare his family from the famine.

You may feel like you are in a prison, trapped in a situation or a relationship, or you may feel like you are in an emotional prison. Remember, that God used Joseph's time in prison for Joseph to learn the skills he needed to minister to a nation and to his family! God is using your prison too.

When Joseph was thrown into prison (Gen. 39:20–40:23), God was with him. In our finite eyes, Joseph's situation had deteriorated. The lies told about Joseph made his situation seem impossible. But we can only see things from our own perspective. God, however, not only sees but knows the truth, and this comes from his infinite perspective. He knew that Joseph had been living in purity as a single person and was not guilty of the crime of which he was accused. There is always the temptation to live by the world's standards, but Joseph proved that it was possible to live by God's standards.

There are several parts of the Bible that leave me very curious. The story of Mrs. Potiphar and Joseph leaves me very much so. I hope that I will see her in heaven, so I can say to her, "Hey! Mrs. P. How was life after you told all those lies about Joseph, scandalized his name all around the community, and he became the second most powerful man on earth? How did you feel?"

I might not be able to ask Mrs. Potiphar that question, but I am sure I will be able to commend Joseph for standing up for the principles he believed in, even though it made him unpopular. When we take a stand on thorny issues, we often become unpopular. People will lie about us and try to ruin our reputations. They will scandalize our name for their own nefarious purposes. Look at what Joseph had to face.

Moreover, look at what Jesus had to face in his day. You and I will probably face people like Potiphar's wife with their lies, but I have recently learned to trust my reputation to God when people try to tarnish it. God knows the truth—that Joseph didn't sleep with Potiphar's wife. If someone has lied about you, God knows the truth and that is all that matters. If someone's lies have placed you in a "prison," God is with you, just like he was with Joseph. His sovereign hands still have control of the cords of your life and he is busy crafting them into his sovereign handiwork.

Three Principles to Learn

- Living in purity as a single person glorifies God.
- The world offers many pleasures, but they are only ephemeral pleasures.
- We must try to see things as God sees them, not as we want to see them.

CHAPTER 18

Joseph's Wilderness Years

A Quick Recap of Joseph's Life

Joseph's situation became desperate the moment he was forced out of his family. He could have spent his years in slavery, stewing over the injustices done to him—taken from his beloved father, Jacob, and unjustly accused of assaulting Mrs. Potiphar. He could have built up a cauldron of anger or seething resentment, bitterness, and unforgiveness. He could have spent the time begging and beseeching God to get him out of slavery. He could have become angry with God for not protecting him and for getting him into such a predicament in the first place. Most of all, Joseph could have been angry with his brothers, who had callously sold him into slavery. But Joseph recognized that God was sovereign. He remembered that God had been with him in his sufferings and that was what gave him the faith to persevere in the hard places of his life. It was a winning combination: God's faithfulness and Joseph's faith.

So many behaviors were open to Joseph, yet in the final analysis, there was only one—trust. He trusted God to protect him. He trusted God to walk with him every step of the way. He trusted God and watched him work out his design for his life. And God honored that trust that Joseph placed in him.

At this point, I have to ask—How are you handling your wilderness experience?

The principles that Joseph learned and that we have to learn are:

- God is sovereign.
- God is just.
- God is faithful.
- God will never leave you nor forsake you, especially in your most challenging times.

CHAPTER 19

Joseph: Pit, Prison, and Palace

An overview of events tells us that Joseph had to learn to trust God

- with the wilderness of his slavery;
- with the relationships with Mr. and Mrs. Potiphar; and
- with the relationship with his brothers.

The high point of Joseph's relationship with his brothers takes place in Genesis 45,; for it is here that they reconcile. This was made possible on the brothers' part by their genuine repentance and remorse for their sin with regard to Joseph, and reversing their actions when a similar situation was presented with regard to Benjamin. And on Joseph's part, reconciliation was achieved through his sincere and total forgiveness of his brothers for the evil they had committed against him.

Although Joseph was thrown in jail because of Mrs. Potiphar's lies, Potiphar had a fair knowledge of Joseph's character and his integrity. He had also seen how God had made everything flourish under Joseph's hands, and despite all the circumstantial evidence stacked against Joseph, Potiphar put Joseph in prison with the king's prisoners instead of having him killed. Subsequently, Joseph gained favor with the warden and was put in charge of the prison. Here are several key verses to note.

But while Joseph was there in the prison, the Lord was with him; he showed him kindness and granted him favor in the eyes of the prison warden. So the warden put Joseph in charge of all those held in the prison, and he was made responsible for all that was done there. The warden paid no attention to anything under Joseph's care, because the Lord was with Joseph and gave him success in whatever he did. (Gen. 39:20–23)

It would appear that the brothers and Mrs. Potiphar had miscalculated in their desire to destroy Joseph. Their schemes had come to naught. The more they tried to destroy Joseph, the more God blessed him. Sometimes when bad situations arise, it seems as if people's hands manipulate our lives, but it is God's sovereign hand that leads the events, not human hands. If we look at Joseph's life and take time to inspect ours, we will see that it is God's sovereign hand that allows events to unfold.

Why did Potiphar put Joseph, a common slave, in with Pharaoh's prisoners? It is because God directed Potiphar—not that Potiphar knew it. God strategically placed Joseph in the position he needed to be for the next stage of God's plan, and soon enough, God began to reveal his hand. While Joseph was in Pharaoh's prison, two of Pharaoh's top men offended Pharaoh and were placed in Joseph's prison.

Sometime later, the cupbearer and the baker of the king of Egypt offended their master, the King of Egypt. Pharaoh was angry with his two officials, the chief cupbearer and the chief baker, and put them in custody in the house of the captain of the guard, in the same prison where Joseph was confined. The captain of the guard assigned them to Joseph, and he attended them. (Gen. 40:1–4)

Scripture tells us that sometime later, the two officials had a dream on the same night. These were very disquieting dreams, and we are told that they were "dejected" because of the dreams and because no one could interpret the dreams for them. However, they told Joseph the dreams, and he was able to use his gift of interpreting dreams to convey the meaning to the baker and the chief cupbearer. The baker was to lose his life, and the chief cupbearer was to be reinstated to his position in the king's household. Joseph's only request of the cupbearer was that when he was restored to his position, as the dream indicated, he should remember him. He said,

But when all goes well with you, remember me and show me kindness; mention me to Pharaoh and get me out of this prison. For I was forcibly carried off from the land of the Hebrews, and even here I have done nothing to deserve being put in a dungeon. (Gen.40:14–15)

The cupbearer promised to remember Joseph to Pharaoh and went merrily on his way. Unfortunately, he forgot him for two years, until Pharaoh himself had two dreams that not even his magicians and sorcerers could interpret. Joseph was then brought to Pharaoh to interpret the dreams. Pharaoh said to him, "I have heard it said of you that when you hear a dream, you can interpret it" (Gen. 41:15).

Joseph replied, "I cannot do it, but God will give Pharaoh the answer he desires" (Gen. 41:16).

Joseph subsequently interpreted Pharaoh's dreams and gave credit to God and honored him. Genesis 41 tells that Joseph was raised from the prison to the palace in a moment. God gave him the knowledge of the coming famine in the land and the wisdom to convey that information to Pharaoh.

Joseph said, "The reason the dream was given to Pharaoh in two forms is that the matter has been firmly decided by God, and God will do it soon" (Gen. 41:32).

Pharaoh said, "Can we find anyone like this man, one in whom is the spirit of God?" Then Pharaoh said, "Since God has made all this known to you, there is no one so discerning and wise as you. You shall be in charge of my palace, and all my people are to submit to your orders. Only with respect to the throne will I be greater than you … I hereby put you in charge of the whole land of Egypt." (Gen. 41:38–40)

Pharaoh then took his signet ring, put it on Joseph's finger, dressed him in fine linen, put a gold chain around his neck, and had him ride in a chariot as his second in command. Joseph was given a position of power and all the symbols and trappings of power that came with his new position. Pharaoh even gave him a wife. Joseph's rise to power is a clear illustration of how perfectly God coordinates the events in our lives if we give him control. For this reason, we have to wait on God's timing, because when God does things, he does them well!

Joseph learned the lesson of his wilderness years well. He served his entire time in slavery as an administrator; first, as an administrator of Potiphar's household affairs, and second, as an administrator of the warden's affairs in the prison. Not only did he hone his administrative skills, but he learned about the prison system, the Egyptian system, and I imagine that in all the years of slavery, he learned as much as he could about the culture from different perspectives. His life was fraught with kidnapping, prison time, attempted assault charges, administrator duties, and now as a governor—what a résumé and what a roller-coaster ride. But isn't it just like God to place us in positions that will train us for the next stage of his plan?

Once again, we see God's providential hand, weaving together the strands of Joseph's path of upward mobility toward the next highest position to Pharaoh's. Now, the second most powerful man in Egypt, Joseph had successfully overcome all the obstacles placed in his life and all the challenges of his situation. How did he achieve this, and why was Joseph so successful in everything he did? First, he trusted God completely. Second, he completely surrendered himself and his situation to God. Third, he did not take any credit for himself. If there's a theme to Joseph's life, it's what he says in Genesis 41:16—"I cannot do it but God can."

Joseph's story is one in which his character, his integrity, and his faith were tested, and he came out like pure gold. It should be noted that problems prove our integrity. Joseph's story parallel's Job's, another Bible personality who had to face many challenges and injustices, even though he was a righteous man. Job was not tested because of any sin he committed. Neither was Joseph tested because of sins committed. But sometimes we fail to remember that we have an enemy of our soul who would like to see us destroyed. God knew both men were righteous men and would come out as pure gold. How about you and me?

Here are some questions to ponder:

- Will we come out like pure gold from the fire of our wounding?
- How is your faith? Has it gotten stronger through the challenges and obstacles?
- Have you grown spiritually through the testing you faced or are facing?
- If you are now in this wilderness, this place of wounding, are you learning the skills that God wants you to learn, or are you "kicking against the pricks," as Paul the apostle was said to have done?

Here is a probing question to ask ourselves: Are we as committed to God's standards as Joseph was? In Psalm 119:9, the psalmist asks a critical question of his readers: "How can a man keep his way pure?"

His response is, "By living according to your word. I seek you with all my heart; do not let me stray from your commands. I have hidden your word in my heart that I might not sin against you."

The Chickens Have Come Home to Roost

Joseph's faith was tested, and it was apparent that there was no sin in his life. His path was now cleared of obstacles, and his integrity of character was a testimony to God. Let us now turn the spotlight on the brothers for a moment. Joseph was now the second most powerful man in the country, and it came to pass, as he had prophesied, that the seven years of abundance were finished, and the seven years of famine began. His life came full circle one momentous day, when he saw his ten brothers bowing down before him.

> Now Joseph was the governor of the land, the one who sold grain to all its people. So when Joseph's brothers arrived, they bowed down to him with their faces to the ground. As soon as Joseph saw his brothers, he recognized them, but he pretended to be a stranger and spoke harshly to them. (Gen. 42:6–7)

I would not want to be in the sandals of those brothers. Their food had almost run out, and they found it more and more difficult to feed their families. They had a family meeting and decided to go to Egypt to buy food. Little did they know that the events they had set into motion twenty years earlier would come to fruition the moment they got on their donkeys and set out for Egypt.

I've heard this saying since I was a child: "Man plans, and God wipes out." In other words, do not make plans out of God's will, because they will not be successful. In the case of the brothers, they planned and executed Joseph's demise. They thought they had succeeded in ridding themselves of the "pesky little dreamer"—the one who told them they would bow down before him. Yet here they were, twenty years later, "bowed down to him with their faces to the ground." God had blessed Joseph and healed his wounds to the extent that even though he recognized his brothers, "he had to bring back to his memory his dreams." Genesis 42:9 says, "Then he remembered his dreams about them and said to them, you are spies!"

At the onset, they had accused Joseph of being a spy for Jacob, their father. So now Joseph accused them of being spies. If they hadn't had anything to hide twenty years ago, they wouldn't have felt the need to accuse him of spying on them. Their behavior was dirty; they had a guilty conscience and as we know, "a guilty conscience needs no accuser." When Joseph accused them of being spies, the chickens had come home to roost. They were getting a taste of their own medicine, and a bitter tasting medicine it was. They were now the accused. The dialogue between Joseph and his siblings is similar to the one between them prior to his being sold into slavery—but now the roles were reversed.

The center of power was in Joseph's hand. Twenty years prior, it was ten of them against one—Joseph. Now, it was one against ten, but now the one—Joseph—had more power than all ten of them together. The irony of the situation is almost laughable. They were between the proverbial rock and a hard place. As events unfolded, and they were finally cornered, it seemed as if the light suddenly shone in their hardened hearts and seared conscience, because they said to each other, "Surely, we are being punished because of our brother. We saw how distressed he was when he pleaded with us for his life, but we would not listen; that's why this distress has come upon us."

Reuben, the oldest of the brothers, said to them, "Didn't I tell you not to sin against the boy? But you wouldn't listen! Now we must give an accounting for his blood" (Gen. 42:21).

The brothers did not realize that Joseph understood them. As modern readers of this story, there is a lesson we can learn from this dialogue. First, God was ready to balance the scales of justice. In addition, God isn't sleeping! He understands injustices; he understands wounding and scarring. He also understands that to heal wounds and to mend relationships, there needs to be forgiveness. Continue to read Genesis 45, where, amid much testing of the brothers to reveal even a semblance of a changed heart, Joseph disclosed his identity.

Genesis 45:3 continues as Joseph said, "I am Joseph! Is my father still alive?"

His brothers could not answer him, for they were dismayed at his presence. Then Joseph said to his brothers, "Please come closer to me." And they came closer. And he said,

"I am your brother Joseph, whom you sold into Egypt. And now do not be grieved or angry with yourselves, because you sold me here; for God sent me before you to preserve life. For the famine has been in the land these two years, and there are still five years in which there will be neither plowing nor harvesting.

And God sent me before you to preserve for you a remnant in the earth, and to keep you alive by a great deliverance. Now, therefore, it was not you who sent me here, but God; and He has made me a father to Pharaoh and lord of all his household and ruler over all the land of Egypt. Hurry and go up to my father, and say to him, 'Thus says your son Joseph, "God has made me lord of all Egypt; come down to me, do not delay. And you shall live in the land of Goshen, and you shall be near me, you and your children and your children's children and your flocks and your herds and all that you have.

There I will also provide for you, for there are still five years of famine to come, lest you and your household and all that you have be impoverished. And behold, your eyes see, and the eyes of my brother Benjamin see, that it is my mouth which is speaking to you. Now you must tell my father of all my splendor in Egypt, and all that you have seen; and you must hurry and bring my father down here."

Then he fell on his brother Benjamin's neck and wept; and Benjamin wept on his neck. And he kissed all his brothers and wept on them, and afterward his brothers talked with him. (Genesis 45:3–15)

I've always found the following dialogue between Joseph and his brothers hilarious, maybe because I've never been in their shoes. Initially, I believe the brothers felt some guilt at the crime they committed against Joseph. But I believe that as the years went by, they got comfortable in their sin. They figured that their secret was safe. Their father had not found out and disinherited them. The community did not know what they had done and so they began to believe their own lies.

Can you imagine when the most powerful person in Egypt, next to Pharaoh, said to them, "I am your brother"? This is the brother they had sold into slavery and believed to be dead. I always visualize the eyebrows flying up their foreheads, the eyes bugging out, and the jaws dropping, amid the chorused groans of horror. It was a ghost sighting! I imagine they could have been knocked over with the lightest feather.

Path of Freedom or Slavery?

The brothers might have thought the worst was over when they explained away the previous occurrences, including the stolen cup, until the Egyptian blurted out in their own tongue, "I am Joseph!" That was the worst news they ever could have heard. It was bad enough to stand before the powerful Egyptian governor who was angered by the theft of a cup, but to realize that he was their brother, whom they had sold into slavery twenty years ago—the tables had been turned dramatically! How could they expect mercy when they had offered none?

Their conscience finally awakened as they stood in silence, with fear and guilt written all over their faces. They had nothing more to say—no defense, no more appeals, no hope for mercy because they had given none. It was not until Joseph demonstrated that he had totally forgiven them and loved them that they were able to speak. The brothers finally came to realize that their past action was a sin (Gen. 42:21) and repented of it (Gen. 44). Joseph then reassured them that it had been God's plan that he be in Egypt.

Joseph said, "It was not you who sent me here, but God. He made me father to Pharaoh, lord of his entire household and ruler of all Egypt" (Gen. 45:8).

Put yourself in the sandals of these brothers for a moment. Joseph has been hospitable to them by inviting them into his home and to his table, despite the fact that they had been stopped, searched, and accused of theft. They were relieved and jubilant—until they remembered their father, Jacob. It would be quite an interesting story to tell their father back home—until they got to the part of them selling Joseph into slavery!

The spotlight of truth now shone, not on the crime the brothers had committed, but on the totality of the forgiveness Joseph offered them and the fulfillment of God's plan. Joseph says, "What you meant for evil, God meant for good." Fueled by anger and jealousy, their action was meant to eliminate him, but God's presence in Egypt, his blessings on Joseph, and his protection during Joseph's wilderness of alienation in Egypt proved that God's plan is always greater and more powerful than man's machinations.

It was a red-letter day when the brothers realized that they had to give an accounting of their cruel act. They had never acknowledged their guilt until Joseph, the once-hated object, stood before them. Some people never acknowledge the pain and chaos done to a child, a spouse that is left behind, or a community that upheld them as moral lanterns.

However, a principle to learn from the brothers is that personal guilt has to be acknowledged for an awakening of conscience to begin.

Food for Thought

To awaken an anesthetized conscience is first to admit personal guilt.

CHAPTER 20

Joseph and His Brand of Forgiveness

Sometimes we get so angry when we are wounded. We say, "I will never forgive that person." Yes, we are hurt; we have been lied about, gossiped about, or betrayed by family, friends, and loved ones. Yet when I compare Joseph's life to mine, I was not torn from family and friends and sent into isolation at an early age. I was not put in prison for crimes I did not commit. Joseph was, and he was able to forgive his brothers completely. Joseph's story reminds me of the saying, "I complained because I had no shoes until I saw a man with no feet." It is all about perspective!

We have to offer forgiveness to those who wound us, regardless of whether it is accepted or rejected. I know how difficult this can be. However, in order to forgive the person, we have to separate what the person did from who the person is. That takes a lot of conscious effort! Although the person has done you wrong, there is more to that person than what he or she has done.

Joseph's brothers were hypocrites. They accused Joseph of evil behavior when they themselves had evil intentions in their heart. With their false accusations, they impinged their own evil motives on Joseph, based on their own hardened hearts. They even allowed themselves to play God. Their thinking was off kilter—we cannot play God, because God does not relinquish his position to anyone! When they sought to destroy Joseph, they thought he would become a victim of his circumstances. He was not!

Are you willing to see the person who wounded you through God's eyes?

I've made a major decision to never to be a victim. I have my mother's faith to believe that God is always looking out for me. No matter what happens to me, I will always come out on top and be a winner, because I have my God fighting my battles. So when I walk tall, it is not pride but the strength of the Lord holding me up and allowing me to hold my head high. Unfortunately, there will always be people like Joseph's brothers, who will do anything to crush other people. But if we remember who we serve, we can stand strong when we are treated unfairly or when we experience spiritual testing.

Just remember that Jesus had his share of "brothers." The people of his day certainly did everything they could to hurt him or crush him. They finally crucified him, thinking they had gotten rid of him. But years later, we have the Christian faith growing exponentially. People are set free from the slavery of sin; people are healed, and they are witness to the goodness of God. My question is, why would we be exempt from having trials? What gives us special status that we will not be wounded? I believe that how we react in and to a difficult situation is more important than our trials and tribulations. What is your perspective on these matters?

Years ago, I listened to a radio broadcast of Corrie ten Boom, and in recent months, the Lord has led me to read her book, *The Hiding Place*. On the radio broadcast and in the book, she talked about her experiences in the concentration camp. She talked about the indignities of having to strip before the guards as a young girl. She also talked about her young sister and the indignities she had to face. As I listened to her thick accent, I remember tearing up as she talked about the murder of the rest of her family. As I continued to listen, she talked about the love of Jesus.

Here is an excerpt of the key point of her message I heard on the radio broadcast:

"It was at a church service in Munich that I saw him, the former S. S. man who had stood guard at the shower room door in the processing center at Ravensbruck. He was the first of our actual jailers that I had seen since that time. And suddenly it was all there—the roomful of mocking men, the heaps of clothing, Betsie's pain-blanched face."

The guard was now a born-again Christian. He did not recognize Corrie so he thrust out his hand to shake her hand but she found it difficult to shake it. As she struggled to forgive this man, she said she prayed and asked God to give her his forgiveness. He did and she was able to shake the hand of the guard who had hurt her and her family so badly. She reminded her listeners that healing is hinged on who God is not who we are.

In the broadcast, Corrie ten Boom also made another point about forgiveness. She said that those survivors of the Nazi brutality who nursed their bitterness remained invalids. Those who were able to forgive their enemies were able to rebuild their lives and function in society. Her attitude was this: Forgiveness is not an emotion. It is an act of the will.

Forgiveness Is Also a Process

Peter asked Jesus how many times he should forgive someone who had hurt him. Jesus told him that he should forgive the person seventy times seven. Jesus' response to Peter's inquiry tells us two things:
1. Forgiveness is not an option.
2. Forgiveness is a process.

It involves forgiving the person who has wounded us and forgiving numerous times—as many times as necessary. When we tabulate wounds and offenses in our heart and allow the wounds to fester over time, without forgiving and letting go, we allow a root of bitterness to grow in us. We also set ourselves up for future disaster. As Jesus said, we need to forgive seventy times seven—daily or each time injury or injustice raises its ugly head. Keeping a list of wrongs is unbiblical!

The Practice of Forgiveness and Releasing the Past

We have to forgive and release the past in order to release the pain. If we do not release our past, we will become our past. We might have to remind ourselves—several times a day, say, "I am not my past." When we spend time with God, it allows us to repent of the past, change, and turn away from old patterns of behavior. When someone throws our past actions in our face—and believe me, someone will—just say, "I am not my past. I will not allow my past into my future!"

We probably will not walk perfectly at all times. Remember, only Jesus walked perfectly. However, even when we mess up, God's sovereignty assures us that while we may do the wrong thing for the wrong reasons, he can cause that to accomplish his good and perfect purposes. Even when other people set out to deliberately hurt you and do outright evil to you, God can use that for his good. Just keep on loving him and trying daily to walk in his light.

According to Romans 8:28, "And we know that in all things God works for the good of those who love him, who have been called according to his purpose."

While God did not sanction the means or the motive of Joseph's brothers, he used their act of betrayal in his plan to raise up Joseph. God is omniscient. He knew what the brothers would do. Joseph's arrival in Egypt was not a surprise to God. Joseph was destined to go to Egypt, where he would be the instrument that God would use to bring about the fulfillment of the plan he had for the Israelites.

The final analysis is that people do not have the final say on our destiny. Joseph's brothers were not responsible for sending Joseph to Egypt; it was God. Joseph was in the wilderness of slavery for a long time, but so were they. The difference was that Joseph thrived and, as the story unfolded, the brothers barely survived. They barely managed to feed their families.

At the beginning, it all seemed hopeless for Joseph. It seemed as if his destiny was in the hands of the brothers, but Joseph's destiny was never at stake!

The brothers' destiny, however, was at stake. Their hearts needed to be cleansed. Their guilt held them in the wilderness for twenty years. They thought that since their sin was hidden and they had managed to fool their father, they had managed to fool God too. But as Christians, we know that God sees everything. Proverb 15:3 reminds us: "The eyes of the Lord are everywhere, keeping watch on the wicked and the good."

We also know: "The eyes of the Lord range throughout the earth to strengthen those whose hearts are fully committed to him" (2 Chron. 16:9).

We have to remember also that "God cannot be mocked; a man reaps what he sows" (Gal. 6:7), and that Bible verse became a reality as the brothers stood before Joseph.

If someone devises an evil plan to destroy you or your family, remember that God sees your tears. He counts every drop. He sees your wounds and promises, "I will turn [your] mourning into gladness" (Jer. 31:13). Once more, forgive that person who has hurt you. Forgiving and releasing the past is to release the pain.

Joseph's Motive in Forgiving His Brothers

Do you think it was difficult for Joseph to forgive his brothers? I don't think it was. He had spent years in his wilderness experience, and he had had time to see the will of God during his time spent in Egypt. As he watched the events of his life unfold and experienced his elevation to power, Joseph's perspective became more focused and developed. In the beginning, it was natural to be unhappy, anxious, and fearful, along with all the emotions that go with a betrayal. However, as the years went by, his thoughts were more centered on God and the destiny God was working out for him. By the time Joseph's first son was born, Joseph named him, Manasseh, meaning "God has caused me to forget."

Joseph's heart was so in tune with God's plan that by the time he saw his brothers again, his desire was only to save his family, rather than to seek revenge. God's plan was now his plan. Written in God's blueprint of Joseph's life, God had ordained it that Joseph would save his family.

Joseph virtually insisted that his brothers leave Egypt quickly and bring Jacob and the entire family to Egypt. By the time the brothers arrived in Egypt, Joseph had already taken his eyes off his situation and problems and moved on with his life. After all the wounds, betrayal, hurt, and pain, Joseph was fully cognizant of God's plans for his life.

He realized that he was in his present situation only because God had allowed it. So as the years went by, he was able to quickly forgive his brothers, forget the misery they had caused, and leave the consequences to God.

It was probably a long time before the brothers could fully grasp the fullness and grace of forgiveness that Joseph granted them. All the events had been under God's watchful eyes. God's care of Joseph through the incredible blessings and favor he had poured out on him was confirmed by none other than Pharaoh himself, as he offered the hospitality of Egypt to Joseph's kin. This demonstrates that even Pharaoh, an ungodly king, was under God's watchful eye. He is Jehovah Roi. He is our shepherd.

God had everything under control. As our Shepherd, he sees us, his children, and when we are wounded, he works it out for his own good. We are always under his watchful eye. We just have to line up our heart with his plan and "lean not to our own understanding," as Scripture advises. It was Jehovah Roi who elevated Joseph to his position of power and prominence, advisor to Pharaoh and ruler over all of Egypt. We might not be next in line to a throne, but God has a great plan for us, if we allow him to walk, talk, and work with us in the wilderness and not rage against our situation. It is only then that we will come out of the wilderness in full power of the Holy Spirit.

There is a noticeable emphasis on all of Joseph's successes and achievements that he attained in Egypt. The evil act of selling him as a slave was precisely the means to his prison promotion and power. Look what his brothers' sin brought about in Joseph's life! He was now the "savior" of their family and the world, as his new name indicated. Sometimes the very means that people use to try to destroy us is the same means God uses to bless us. We have to surrender our will to God.

It is only when we totally surrender our will that we will come out of the wilderness in full power of the Holy Spirit. Joseph's character was not altered by his adversity. Rather, he was fully conscious of God and recognized that while the evil was temporary, God's presence was permanent. Throughout his adversity and suffering, God strengthened him and prepared his heart for his ministry in Egypt.

This might be an appropriate time to let go of the baggage that we are holding so God can do his work.

God used Joseph's adversities to put him in a place of usefulness. Can he use you too?

One of my Chinese students told me the following story:

There were two brothers. The first brother had a beautiful horse that the second brother envied. The second brother begged and begged the first brother to give him this horse. The first brother finally capitulated and gave his brother the horse, even though he knew the second brother did not have the ability to ride this horse. The second brother was very happy and rode off on the horse. He later came back very angry, because the horse had thrown him, and he had broken his leg. The first brother then gleefully took back his horse and rode away. Sometime later, the war came, and the first brother was sent off to war because he was physically fit. The second brother was not sent to war because he had the disability of a limp from the broken leg. The story goes that the first brother was later killed in the war, and the second brother reclaimed the horse.

This story of open motives, hidden motives, and things people do are open to many interpretations.

What do you think?

CHAPTER 21

Final Overview of Joseph's Purpose, Preparation, and Transformation

The story of Joseph and his brothers offers lessons of progression, learning, purpose, preparation, and transformation. God prepares us for each and every step of our journey, so we can complete his plans for us. Sadly, though, many Christians bail out on God when life gets tough. Therefore, their spiritual journey is interrupted, and their spiritual maturity is never completed. Only the enemy wins this one!

Joseph, however, did not bail out on God when life seemed hopeless, and we are privileged to walk through Joseph's journey with him and watch him overcome the obstacles in his path. He had to learn some very tough lessons. Before he was sold into slavery, his dependence was on Jacob. In slavery, his dependence had to be totally on God. In exchange for his pride in his coat of many colors, he wore his slavery loincloth of humility. The unknown, alienated world of Egypt became his solace, as it was just him and God in this wilderness. The unknown language of his wilderness experience became a prayer language that honed his spirit and his heart to meld with God's. His unknown future was fully known to God and the angels and was broadcast in heaven. Enslaved in an unknown world, unknown language, and an unknown future, Joseph still clung to God. Therefore, Joseph won—not the wilderness! Not Egypt! Not the enemy!

How is your journey going?

In the culmination of this season of his life, Joseph parted from his brothers and gave them one last word of instruction: "Do not quarrel on the journey." Joseph knew his brothers well. Quarreling, among many things, was a part of the bad report that he had given his father many years before (Gen. 37:2). Being sons of four mothers and jockeying for position, sibling rivalry would have been common. Probably the only thing they ever agreed upon completely was getting rid of Joseph and his annoying coat of favoritism and power. Joseph knew them well enough that they would quarrel among themselves as he recalled their conversation.

> Then they said to one another, "Truly we are guilty concerning our brother, because we saw the distress of his soul when he pleaded with us, yet we would not listen; therefore this distress has come upon us." And Reuben answered them, saying, "Did I not tell you, 'Do not sin against the boy'; and you would not listen? Now comes the reckoning for his blood." (Gen. 42:21–22)

He also knew them well enough that as they headed home, they would try to lay the blame somewhere, as they still had to give an accounting of Joseph's "death" to Jacob, and although the brothers were forgiven, they would probably be tempted to revert to their previous behavior. This would be a fruitless exercise, as a heated argument would ensue, and the lesson of true forgiveness would be lost in the squabble. Joseph, in his wisdom, knew that it would be a more constructive journey if the brothers spent their time rejoicing at the brightness of the future, rather than quarreling. In fact, their trip home would be a happier one if they focused more on unlimited grain to stem their hunger, getting prime land in Goshen, God's grace, and Joseph's graciousness, rather than finding a scapegoat.

My hope in this demonstration of Joseph's total forgiveness is that this lesson is not lost on us modern-day readers, because this reiterates what Jesus said in Mathew 6:14–15: "For if you forgive men for their transgressions, your heavenly Father will also forgive you. But if you do not forgive men, then your Father will not forgive your transgressions."

The brothers' wicked act of selling Joseph into slavery displayed the hardness and evil of their hearts. So God allowed them in their evil for twenty years, and he used it for his honor and glory. Joseph, on the other hand, allowed the Holy Spirit to transform him. Let's make the choice to allow the Holy Spirit to transform us by first letting him prepare us.

The Holy Spirit sees our heart and transforms our heart.

We are encouraged to walk in the light, as he is in the light (1 John 1:7). Two incidents occurred over the last six months that warned me that there is no place for pride when we are in the process of transformation. One day, I heard that a relative of an acquaintance had passed away. My first thought after hearing the news was not a godly one. But instantly, in my spirit I heard, *"Call her and offer your condolences."* Over the years, this woman had spread gossip about me and had tried to seriously damage my reputation. So when I heard in my spirit to call her, I knew it was the Holy Spirit. Left to my own devices, I wouldn't have picked up that phone.

However, since I am determined to allow God to transform me, I had to be obedient. So I called her. It was almost laughable, because from her reaction, she seemed to wonder why I was calling her. But I was pleasant and offered my condolences, chit-chatted a few minutes, offered my services, and hung up. I felt such a sense of release, freedom, and self-power—first, for being obedient to the leading of the Holy Spirit; and second, by refusing to engage someone who was bent on hurting me.

Remember, it is spiritual warfare, and your faith and obedience will be tested.

Ephesians 6:12 reminds us: "For our struggle is not against flesh and blood, but against the rulers, against the authorities, against the powers of this dark world and against the spiritual forces of evil in the heavenly realms."

The following incident is also a reminder that the enemy is actively working to bring down believers. Several months ago, I contacted someone to say I was sorry for some things that had happened between us. The person's response was deliberately vindictive and cruel. I had only contacted the person because I believed—and still believe—that the Holy Spirit had prompted me to do so. This person tore my character apart, made cruel comments about the work I had done for the Lord, mocked and twisted everything possible, and even added lies to the diatribe. I was horribly hurt that a human being could be so vindictive. I could so easily have said, "I'm not going to forgive that person." But I did what the Lord wanted me to do, and there was nothing I could do but cry before him and hand it over to him.

Even though those cruel barbs tore into my heart, I refused to let those wounds fester. It has taken me a while, but I'm finally allowing God to take care of his own business. The person who wounds us is God's business! When we withhold forgiveness, we interfere in God's business, and we limit God's use of us.

Joseph's forgiveness of his brothers was exactly what Jesus taught Peter to do. Therefore, our attitude should reflect Joseph's, and it should also reflect Proverbs 10:12: "Hatred stirs up dissention but love covers over all wrongs." In 1 Corinthians 13:4–8, Paul the apostle teaches us that we should reflect godly love:

> Love is patient, love is kind. It does not envy, it does not boast, it is not proud. It is not rude, it is not self-seeking, it is not easily angered, it keeps no record of wrongs. Love does not delight in evil but rejoices with the truth. It always protects, always trusts, always hopes, always perseveres. Love never fails.

We are not able to love the people who wound us in our own strength, but we can love them through Christ, if we can only begin to look at them from another perspective—God's perspective!

The apostle Paul says: "Let all bitterness and wrath and anger and clamor and slander be put away from you, along with all malice. And be kind to one another, tender-hearted, forgiving each other, just as God in Christ also has forgiven you" (Eph. 4:31–32).

Life Principle

God requires us to forgive, regardless of how many times we have been wounded. We have to work on its offering. It is God's job to work on the accepting.

CHAPTER 23

Moses

There was no humbler and more forgiving person than Moses, a very interesting biblical personality. He was a man of contrasts. On one hand, he was a prince of Egypt. On the other hand, he was a slave, sent into the wilderness because he murdered an Egyptian. There was the time he argued with God, as he was reluctant to take up the leadership of the Israelites' delivery out of Egypt. Yet he confidently obeyed God as the ten plagues were rained upon the nation of Egypt. On one occasion, he thundered to the water of the Red Sea to separate; in the next, he disobeyed God and struck the rock instead of speaking to it. What a man of contrasts—reluctant deliverer, complaining minister, or just an ordinary man? To the Jews, he was their greatest leader and prophet. He was courageous yet humble (Exodus 2:15–17; 5:1–3; 33:12–23; Numbers 12:3). We can call this man any name we want, but what did God call him?

God called him trustworthy and faithful, and he blessed him for this. From his birth to his death, God's hand was on this man. Yet he, like all the other biblical personalities, went through a wilderness time of preparation and transformation. We can all learn from the story of Moses. Each of the events in his life can be applied to our own personal journey with the Lord.

The Birth of Moses

As you recall, Joseph had moved Jacob, his father, and the rest of his family to Egypt during the famine. The pharaoh who had shown them favor died, so before Moses was born, the children of Israel were living in slavery in Egypt. The pharaoh was afraid of the numbers and might of the growing Israelites during this time, so he had all of them put under extreme bondage and slavery so he could control them. The Israelites were so fertile that the pharaoh ordered the midwives to kill all of the male children of the Israelites.

It was during this time that Moses was born. Hebrews 11:23 tells us that by faith, his parents hid him for three months so he would not be found and killed by Pharaoh. After three months, his mother then placed him in a basket made out of papyrus and placed him among the reeds along the riverbanks, hoping someone would find him and raise him up safely. It wasn't by coincidence that the daughter of the pharaoh was the one who actually found him as she was getting ready to wash herself in the river.

Moses' sister, who was watching from a distance, asked the pharaoh's daughter, "Shall I go and get one of the Hebrew women to nurse the baby for you?" The pharaoh's daughter said yes, and the girl got Moses' biological mother. Who else but God could have orchestrated this? Once the nursing stage was over, the mother then gave the child back to the pharaoh's daughter, so that she could raise him up as one of her own. Moses was thus raised up in Pharaoh's house. That is divine protection!

I imagine that life in the palace was routine for Moses, prince of Egypt and heir apparent to Egypt's vast wealth—that is, until he killed one of the Egyptians and had to flee the country after Pharaoh found out about it and sought to kill him. At this point, Scripture tells us that Moses fled to the desert, a place called Midian, where he lived for forty years, until God called him out to deliver the Israelites from bondage to the Egyptians. I always wonder what went on in Moses' head for forty years as he looked back at his life in the palace and compared it to his life in the desert.

He had been raised in the palace—a prince among men, with all the wealth that the greatest nation at that time could offer. Now, alone, alienated, and isolated from everything and everyone dear to him, he sat watching sheep day after day, year after year, for forty years. I believe that at the beginning, like many who have experienced great loss, Moses went through a period of grief. He had lost his home, his family, and his life as he knew it. The security he once knew was gone, and he was thrust into the unknown. What Moses had not discovered as yet was that after the grieving period, one day he would wake up and everything would be new. Scriptures tell us that mourning lasts for a night, but joy comes in the morning. His enemies might even say, "How the mighty has fallen." And it would appear so. However, God had a divine purpose for Moses, and he needed to prepare him for his divine mission—to deliver the Israelites from slavery.

Moses had learned royal duties in the palace, but during these forty years in the wilderness, he had to learn how to deal with sheep and shepherds. Since the Israelites were shepherds, it was an extremely important skill to develop. God was preparing him for the task ahead. There may have been times when Moses felt he was wasting his time in the desert, but God had a plan for him, and God's plan is fail-proof.

Question to ponder: Do you think you are wasting your time where God has you now?

Moses' Call as a Deliverer

After Moses spent forty years in the palace and forty years tending sheep in the wilderness, honing the skills he needed, God decided that Moses was prepared to begin his ministry. He was going to have to lead the people out of Egypt because of the covenants that God made with Abraham, Isaac, and Jacob.

Exodus 3:1 tells us that God first made contact with Moses through a burning bush as he was tending his father-in-law's flocks in the desert at Mount Horeb. Moses saw the bush and thought, *This bush is burning with fire, but the bush itself is not being consumed by the fire!* So out of curiosity, Moses said, "I must turn aside now and see this marvelous sight, why the bush is not burned up" (Ex. 3:2–3). And there on Mount Sinai, Moses met the living God for the first time. God called him by name and told him to remove his sandals because he was standing on holy ground. In Exodus 3:7–9, God revealed to Moses his purpose for Israel. He said,

> I have surely seen the affliction of My people who are in Egypt,
> and have given heed to their cry because of their taskmasters,

for I am aware of their sufferings. So I have come down to deliver them from the power of the Egyptians, and to bring them up from that land to a good and spacious land, to a land flowing with milk and honey, to the place of the Canaanite and the Hittite and the Amorite and the Perizzite and the Hivite and the Jebusite. Now, behold, the cry of the sons of Israel has come to Me; furthermore, I have seen the oppression with which the Egyptians are oppressing them.

In this portion of Scripture:

- God identified himself as the "God of your father the God of Abraham, God of Isaac, and the God of Jacob."
- God told Moses the purpose of his visit. He said:
  - ° I am concerned for the people.
  - ° I have heard their cry.
  - ° I will rescue them.
  - ° I will bless them by giving them a new land, one that is flowing with milk and honey.
  - ° I want you, Moses, to go to Pharaoh to bring my people out of Egypt.

It is interesting to note that Moses did not immediately jump at the chance to be God's instrument in delivering Israel. He was very reluctant and expressed it to God. Here is the dialogue between God and Moses:

God: Therefore, come now, and I will send you to Pharaoh, so that you may bring my people, the sons of Israel, out of Egypt.

Moses: Who am I that I should go to Pharaoh?

God: I will be with you.

Moses: What if they do not believe me or listen to me.

God: What is in your hand?

(Here, God performs miracle number one by turning Moses' rod into a snake and back again to a rod.)

God: Put your hand inside your bosom.

(God performs miracle number two by turning his hand leprous and then back to normal.)

Moses: Please, Lord, I have never been eloquent, neither recently nor in time past, nor since you have spoken to your servant; for I am slow of speech and slow of tongue.

God: Who gave man his mouth? Or who makes him deaf or mute? Who gives him sight or makes him blind? Is it not I, the Lord? Now go; I will help you speak, and will teach you what to say.

Moses: Please, Lord, please send someone else to do it.

Does this dialogue ring a bell in your ear?

There is a lot to learn from this dialogue between God and Moses. You have heard the voice of God in your spirit. He wants you to do something. Yet you say, "Lord, I have to look after my family. Lord, I have to work, and I'm too tired at the end of the day. Lord, I'm afraid. Lord, I'm stressed out. Lord, I'm busy. Lord, my health won't stand up to the stress. Lord, I'm wounded and in pain. Lord … Lord …"

God's response is, "Who gives you your family? Who gives you your job? Who sticks closer than a brother? Who gives you peace? Who gives you health? Come unto me those who are weary and heavy burdened …

He says the same thing to you as he said to Moses: "I AM who I AM."

God made this powerful statement to Moses, yet Moses still

questioned God's choice of him and said to God, "O my Lord, please send someone else."

In other words, when we say no to God we say, "God, although you are an all-knowing, all-seeing omniscient God, you don't know me well enough to know how I will fare when I go to Egypt, and I can't trust you to protect me."

If you have been wounded, you have been in your wilderness of pain for a while. What is your response to God? Do you think he can use your scars to help someone going through the same situation?

Life Principle

Let us be careful how we respond to God when he wants to use us as his resource!

At this point, the Bible says that the "anger of the Lord was kindled" as a result of Moses' questioning God's decision to call him out for this task. However, God saw Moses' heart rather than his lack of confidence or lack of trust in him. He told him to take his brother Aaron with him, because Aaron could speak well. God then laid out some simple ground rules for Moses and Aaron:

- Moses was to convey God's message to Aaron.
- God promised them that he would be with both of them, and he would teach them what to say and what to do.
- He told them that Moses would be the prophet to the people.
- Moses would be to Aaron "as God."
- Aaron would be the spokesman to the people.
- God would still deliver the orders and instructions directly to Moses.

Their roles seemed simple enough, but later on as their journey progressed, we see how Aaron listened to someone else's perspective on the situation, forgot his part of the agreement, allowed pride to set in, and got into trouble with God.

Moses Goes into Egypt

When all points of the "discussion" were settled between God and Moses, God imbued Moses with power and sent him off to Egypt. The Bible says that Moses was eighty years old; and his brother Aaron was eighty-three when they went into Egypt to rescue the Israelites from bondage.

God was in charge of the mission, so off they went to Egypt. However, when Moses and Aaron approached Pharaoh and told him that he was to let the people go, so they could go into the wilderness to hold a three-day feast with their God, Pharaoh refused to even consider their request. So God did his first miracle in front of Pharaoh and his court. At Moses' request, Aaron took his rod and threw it to the ground, where it became a serpent. However, in copycat fashion, several of Pharaoh's magicians threw their rods down and those rods also became serpents. God then caused Moses' serpent to devour all the other serpents of Pharaoh's magicians and sorcerers. This was a demonstration of God's power over the magicians and foreshadowed events to come.

Moses was imbued with divine power from the one true God. The expectations were that Pharaoh would recognize this different power and follow instructions. But Pharaoh recognized only his power, and after seeing this display of God's power and his magicians' tricks, Pharaoh chose to believe his own press release. He hardened his heart and refused to let the children of Israel go. It was at this point that Pharaoh got on a collision course with God, and God began his judgment of Pharaoh and the Egyptians by releasing ten powerful plagues that showed his power over all the gods of Egypt. This evidence of God's power would eventually free his people from captivity and set them on a journey they would not quickly forget.

In any case, prior to letting the children of Israel go, Pharaoh's heart became harder and harder. Proudly, he scoffed at God and mocked his deity. He said, "Who is the Lord that I should obey His voice to let Israel go? I do not know the Lord, and besides, I will not let Israel go." He even ordered the taskmasters to withhold the straw the Israelites needed to make bricks, yet they had to supply the same quota of bricks (Ex. 5:10–11).

The Israelites were angry that the taskmasters had said, "You must not reduce your daily amount of bricks," and they were angry as they met Moses and Aaron waiting for them. They said to them, "May the Lord look upon you and judge you, for you have made us a stench to Pharaoh and his officials and have put a sword in their hand to kill us."

Then Moses returned to the Lord and said, "O Lord, why have You brought trouble upon this people? Is this why you sent me? Ever since I went to Pharaoh to speak in your name, he has brought trouble upon this people, and you have not rescued your people at all" (Ex. 5:21–23).

Again, a Foreshadowing

This time, it is a foreshadowing of the relationship that would exist between Moses, the Israelites, and God.

The Israelites and the Wilderness

God's Purpose for the Israelites

As a people, the nation of Israel had been called by God to be his witness to the world. He said to Moses,

> I am the Lord. I appeared to Abraham, to Isaac, and to Jacob, as God Almighty, but by my name, the Lord, I did not make myself known to them.
>
> I also established my covenant with them to give them the land of Canaan, where they lived as aliens.
>
> Moreover, I have heard the groaning of the Israelites, whom the Egyptians are enslaving, and I have remembered my covenant.
>
> Therefore, say to the Israelites: I am the Lord, and I will bring you out from under the yoke of the Egyptians. I will free you from being slaves to them, and I will redeem you with an outstretched arm and with mighty acts of judgment.
>
> I will take you as my own people, and I will be your God; then you will know that I am the Lord your God, who brought you out from under the yoke of the Egyptians.
>
> And I will bring you to the land I swore with uplifted hand to give to Abraham, to Isaac and to Jacob. I will give it to you as a possession: I am the Lord. (Exodus 6:2–8)

What an exciting promise—to have a sovereign God display his power on behalf of the Israelites. After four hundred years of bondage, God, with a sweep of his mighty hand of power, would take control and move them on to a better situation. Yet Scripture tells us that the Israelites did not listen to Moses. I believe that they were so institutionalized from their lengthy time in slavery that they just could not envision being free. God was ready to redeem them, but they weren't ready. The slavery mentality had slowly seeped into their minds and souls.

We sometimes speak badly of the Israelites' lack of faith and lack of vision, but isn't it the same for some modern-day Christians? We have been redeemed. Romans 3:23 says, "For all have sinned and fallen short of the glory of God, and are justified freely by his grace through the redemption that came by Christ Jesus."

Redemption was given to free us from being slaves to sin (Rom. 6:7) and to free us from an empty way of life (1 Pet. 1:18), with the result that we can now live free lives as according to Galatians 5:1, "It is for freedom that Christ has set us free. Stand firm then and do not let yourselves be burdened by a yoke of slavery."

My question therefore is, is there much difference between the Israelites' refusal to behave like freed people, and modern-day Christians who accept freedom from hell through Jesus' death on the cross but who refuse to live like freed people?

The Israelites either *refused* to accept their freedom or were *unable* to accept their freedom. Some Christians accept the freedom of salvation through Christ's redemptive work at Calvary, but sometimes this freedom from the slavery of sin is not evident in their life and lifestyle. It seems, at times, that the message and behavior inside the Christian circle is the same as outside in the world. Yet at the same time, I have met people outside the Christian circle whose philosophy reflects the Christian principles more than actual Christians. How sad!

The week prior to writing this chapter, I was invited to be part of a conference on gender violence. I was also asked to do a book reading from my book, *God's Grace: A Long Night's Journey into Day* and showcase the nonprofit organization I had formed. *God's Grace* is of Christian content and tells of my journey after my thirty-five year marriage ended and how God led me through this journey. The book reading was a privilege that God granted me, because I was able to speak of him in a non-Christian environment. Never underestimate the power of God and what he can do if you make yourself available to speak for him.

Let me give you a bit of background information. On my high school record, it says of me, "painfully shy." So when I got saved, I asked the Lord to give me boldness and to take away my shyness. He did! I have always prayed and asked God to send me to the trenches, send me to speak to people to whom others are afraid to speak, and lead me to places where others are afraid to go. Many Christians are not willing to go to non-Christian events, and there are some that I definitely avoid. Nonetheless, I will go if I believe the Lord tells me to go and if there is an opportunity to talk about my faith or my God.

At the conference on gender violence, I had the opportunity to talk about my book, my faith, and how I was able to go on after my marriage ended after thirty-five years. At the radio interviews, during the presentation and book readings, and afterwards, during the question and answer periods, there was no doubt that it was my faith in God that carried me through this difficult season of my life.

Surprisingly enough, many of the non-Christian men at the conference engaged me and asked many questions about sustaining a relationship. I and the other women there openly discussed with them all the issues they brought up. It was a little sad for me, though, because the message from these non-Christian men echoed the sanctity of God's principles regarding marriage more than some of the Christian men and women I have heard in the past. Why is this so? It would seem that when God took Israel out of Egypt, it was very difficult to take Egypt out of the Israelites. Is it possible that God is having difficulty taking "Egypt" out of the Christian Church?

As I reflected on this thought, I remembered telling a friend that it seemed that I had a target on my forehead for the devil. I told her that when I became a Christian, I told the Lord that I wanted the devil to know my name. This prayer was based on the story in Acts 19:13, where the sons of Sceva tried to cast demons out of a man "in the name of Jesus that Paul talked about." The demons refused to cooperate with the sons of Sceva and replied, "Jesus, I know. Paul, I know, but who are you?" The story goes on to say that the demons beat up the men, tore off their clothes, and sent them running outside the house, naked. I use this story as an illustration, because the only way for the devil to know our name is get "Egypt" out of our life. The devil doesn't care about anyone in his camp. He won't give them any trouble. It is the ones who are invading his territory that he worries about and troubles. So, do you want the devil to know your name?

Complaining in the Wilderness

The devil certainly knew the name "Moses." The Bible tells us that after inflicting ten plagues on Pharaoh and all of Egypt, God released the Israelites from bondage with a "mighty hand." Earlier, God had said, "The Egyptians shall know that I am the Lord, when I stretch out My hand on Egypt and bring out the sons of Israel from their midst" (Ex. 7:5).

The Israelites were now on their way to the Promised Land. Slavery should have been the preparatory stage for the Promised Land. After leaving Egypt and traveling through the wilderness, the Israelites should have been in anticipation of entering the Promised Land, a land described as "flowing with milk and honey." But biblical records show that this was not the case at all. Apparently, milk and honey held little appeal for them. What they craved was the stinky smell of garlic, leeks, and the slave pits of Egypt.

So instead of going on a journey that should have taken a few days, God led them into the wilderness to be tested, because he knew their hearts and their proclivity to sin. Exodus 13:17-18 says,

> When Pharaoh let the people go, God did not lead them on the road through the Philistines country though that was shorter for God said, if they face war, they might change their minds and return to Egypt. So God led the people around by the desert road toward the Red Sea.

During their passage through the wilderness, once the familiar comforts of Egypt were taken away, they were supposed to have learned to depend on God for all their material, emotional, physical, and spiritual needs. However, when things got tough, they wanted to run away from the wilderness experience, because this involved stress and pain. They wanted to go back to the bondage of their former life. After eleven months in the region of Mount Sinai, they soon began to complain about their hardships. But first, they romanticized their past situation.

They said, "If only we had meat to eat! We remember the fish we ate in Egypt at no cost—also the cucumbers, melons, leeks, onions and garlic. But now we have lost our appetite; we never see anything but this manna!" (Num. 11:4–6).

They seemed to minimize the slavery experience. They seemed to have forgotten that they, their parents, and their grandparents were the same ones who had cried out to God for over four hundred years to deliver them from the whips of the Egyptians. They seemed to have forgotten their protection against the ten plagues, the miracle of crossing the Red Sea, and even the miracle of the manna in the desert. The Israelites kept saying, "Did God bring us out here into the wilderness to kill us?" This angered God! In one sense, God did want to kill them. He wanted to kill the old slavery identity of Egypt.

I can only imagine how the constant discontentment with their situation and complaining hurt God. After being spared the horrors of the ten plagues and having been led across the Red Sea, you would think that they would be in awe of God's power. The Bible says that while the Israelites were crossing over, the "waters were a wall to them on their right hand and on their left." Can you visualize this incredible scene? The Bible also tells us that after they had passed through the Red Sea and saw the Egyptians lying dead on the shore, the children of Israel believed Moses and the Lord.

I have three questions:

1. They had seen the ten miracles. Why didn't they believe before?
2. Why didn't they believe, even after the ten plagues?

3. What took them so long to acknowledge the power and might of God?

Food for Thought

- In comparison to the Israelites, do you think there are modern Christians with the spirit of the Israelites in them?
- Are we sometimes so immersed in the world, so "me-centered," that it is difficult to see events and situations spiritually?
- Can we say that their eyes were open, but they were spiritually closed?

The history of the Israelites reminds me of a story I heard years ago about the boiling frog. Apparently, if a frog is placed suddenly in boiling water, it will jump out. But if it is placed in cold water, and the water temperature gradually is raised to the boiling point, it will not perceive the danger and will sit in that boiling water and eventually die. This story is usually used as a metaphor to suggest that many are unable to react to significant changes if the changes occur gradually. In concurrence with our Christianity, if we allow worldly pleasures and personal pursuits to permeate our minds and push out spiritual pursuits, this will result in the same mentality as the Israelites. We will adjust to the situation around us and, like the frog in the story, we might not be able to perceive spiritual danger until it is too late!

Memories are great. I recall a great story a pastor told me. He was in a church, and one of the music pastors made the mistake of moving the piano to the opposite side of the sanctuary. Some of the people complained that they didn't want the piano moved. Some said that they didn't want it on the opposite side. The story goes that the music pastor acquiesced and put it back in its original position. However, every day, without saying anything, the music pastor moved the piano inch by inch in the direction he wanted. The people never noticed the piano's journey to the opposite side of the sanctuary—exactly where the music pastor had suggested it be in the beginning.

Some people are just chronic complainers, like the Israelites. Some just do not like change. I believe that their motto is "Only a wet baby likes change." Others are just like the frog. They cannot perceive the direction they should go or when to jump out of danger, especially spiritual danger. They have allowed themselves to get lost, and their spiritual eyes are so scaled over that they act foolishly and make costly decisions.

I'm not sure why the Israelites complained so much. Was it fear of the unknown? Was it fear of change? Or were they just chronic complainers? Obviously, they complained so much that even God lost patience with them. They had sat in slavery for so long and had probably complained every minute about their lot in life and about the Egyptians; the slavery mentality gradually permeated their minds. Even though they had been "redeemed" from the bondage of slavery and set free to travel to the Promised Land, slavery was still an ingrained part of their being. It was easier for God to get the people out of Egypt than it was for him to get "Egypt" out of the people.

This complaining also had another dimension. During this time, there were murmurings, bickering, and undercurrents of unfaithfulness against Moses and against God.

When Pharaoh and the Egyptian army chased after the Israelites and overtook them by the sea beside Pi-hahiroth, in front of Baal-zephon, the Israelites saw the armies. They were frightened and said to Moses,

> Was it because there were no graves in Egypt that you brought
> us to the desert to die? What have you done to us by bringing
> us out of Egypt? Didn't we say to you in Egypt, leave us alone;
> let us serve the Egyptians? It would have been better for us to
> serve the Egyptians than to die in the desert (Ex. 14:11).

After reading this statement from the Israelites, I went back and re-read the passage. I still can't find it anywhere that they wanted to stay in Egypt. Initially, they were all eager to escape their taskmasters' whips. In addition, when God spoke to Moses from the burning bush, he had said, "I have heard the cries of my people." If they were not frantically calling out to God to free them, why did he say he had heard their cries? God doesn't lie! And the Israelites were back to romanticizing their stay in Egypt again. It would appear that their vision and knowledge of the situation and of God were skewed. They were crying to leave Egypt, not to stay. God finally allowed them to leave because he wanted to take the four hundred years of slavery and Egypt out of them and purify their hearts, so he could be their God and they his people.

Maybe all that free time in the wilderness was too much for the Israelites. They had nothing to do—no bricks to make, no straw to gather—so what better thing to do but what they were accustomed to doing: complain, like a sow going back to mud (2 Pet. 2:22). They complained about the lack of water; God gave them water. They complained that they had no food; God gave them manna. They complained about the manna; God gave them quails. They kept on complaining and testing God until the final assault on God's grace was the golden calf. Moses had gone up to Mount Sinai to receive the Ten Commandments from God and according to their timeline, he had stayed too long. Exodus 32:1 begins with the story of the golden calf.

> Now when the people saw that Moses delayed to come down from the mountain, the people assembled about Aaron and said to him, Come, make us a god who will go before us; as for this Moses, the man who brought us up from the land of Egypt, we do not know what has become of him.

Aaron, who should have known better, took the gold from the people in a weak moment and made it into a golden calf. He proclaimed, "This is your god, O Israel, who brought you up from the land of Egypt." Their slavery mentality had brought them full circle. They were now ready to give God's glory and credit to an idol and to worship one of the Egyptian gods. Similar to Pharaoh's earlier choice, they were on a collision course with God. It was a terrible spiritual state for the Israelites. Even Miriam and Aaron got into serious trouble with God when they too complained about Moses.

"Miriam and Aaron began to talk against Moses because of his Cushite wife, for he had married a Cushite. Has the Lord spoken only through Moses? they asked. Hasn't he also spoken through us?" (Num. 12:1–2).

As an aside, let me say this: I hear many people complaining all the time. Even Christians have gotten into this bad habit. They bad-mouth the pastor, they talk badly about fellow Christians, and they bad-mouth their spouses and complain constantly about their children. Don't people realize that God is listening? At the end of Exodus 12: 2, as plain as day, are the words "And the Lord heard this."

How it must have hurt Moses to have his siblings—the ones he thought he could trust—betray him too. Moses might have been ready to forgive them, in his humility, but God was not going to let that sin go unpunished. They were brought before the tent of God immediately. God said,

> When a prophet of the Lord is among you, I reveal myself to
> him in visions, I speak to him in dreams. But this is not true
> of my servant Moses; he is faithful in all my house. With him
> I speak face to face, clearly and not in riddles; he sees the form
> of the Lord. Why then were you not afraid to speak against my
> servant Moses? (Ex. 12:6–8)

For the sin of complaining against God's servant, Moses, Miriam (the principal offender) became leprous, "as white as snow." She was put out of the community for seven days and had to suffer the pain and humiliation as an outcast for her sin. Moses is the one who begged God for mercy for her and asked that God heal her. God answered his prayers, but God had her stay outside the camp for seven days as a consequence of her sin. The principle here is that even though she was eventually healed and restored to her community, God did not take away the consequences of her sin—a lesson to be learned by modern Christians!

I think I need to address this point again.

We often criticize the Israelites for complaining and murmuring, but if we do some self-reflection, don't we sometimes do the same? How many times do we complain about not being happy with the job we have, the same job that God gave us while so many are unemployed. We are not happy with our spouse, the same spouse that God ordained for us from the beginning of time. We complain about the children, yet there are people who are desperate to have children and cannot conceive. We complain about the house we live in, yet there are many homeless people in our city. We want more money in our bank accounts, we envy others their financial blessings, and on and on we go, just testing God. We forget that God is listening. As a matter fact, if you put some people in the Garden of Eden, they would find something to complain about. How about you? Do you know anyone like that? God does not tolerate complaining for long.

Remember … there are always consequences to a behavior that goes against God's mandate.

Food for Thought

Complaining is very toxic, especially when God has us in the desert for a specific purpose.

The wilderness experience is to get rid of the idols in our lives. In the wilderness, we get a chance to look deeply into our souls, face ourselves honestly, and reverently ask God to cleanse us. Therefore, complaining is cancer to the spirit that needs cleansing.

Psalm 51:7 says, "Cleanse me with hyssop and I will be clean; wash me, and I will be whiter than snow." The Israelites must have been absent from the class when God was teaching that lesson; hence, they were allowed to wander in the wilderness for a period of forty years. We would be very foolish if we did not learn from their history.

Wandering in the Wilderness

Whenever I read the story of the Israelites—their complaining, their disobedience, their rebellion and hardness of heart—I always wonder who the cankerous sores in the camp were. There had to be a few ringleaders who sought every opportunity to stir up discontent in the camp. When the Israelites arrived at Kadesh, the Lord said to Moses,

"Send some men to explore the land of Canaan, which I am giving to the Israelites. From each ancestral tribe, send one of its leaders" (Num. 13:1–2).

So they went up and explored the land. After coming back, they showed Moses the fruits they had picked, confirming that the land was good and that it was indeed flowing with milk and honey. However, some of the men spread a bad report about the land among the Israelites. They said, "The land devours those living in it. The people are powerful and the cities are fortified and very large ... We seemed like grasshoppers in our own eyes and we looked the same to them" (Num.13:33).

If I had been in Moses' shoes, I would have said sarcastically (if God would let me get away with it), "Goodness gracious, mercy me! Four hundred thirty years of protection during slavery—protection from the plagues of bloody water, frogs, gnats, flies, dead livestock, boils, hail, locust, darkness, protection of your firstborn, protection from drowning in the Red Sea, water to drink in the desert, manna rained down from heaven, meat in the desert—and you have the gall to stand before me, talking about powerful men. What about a powerful God?"

Of course, Moses would not have said that, even if he wanted to. He knew God only too well. He knew his God was able to take care of his own business, the Israelites, and he had to let him. But think of it! After the majestic display of God's power thus far, he had to listen to the ten spies telling the story of how they looked around the land and saw the descendants of Anak, the Amalekites, the Hittites, the Jebusites, the Amorites, and the Canaanites.

Following the bad report, we are told that "all the people of the community raised their voices and wept aloud. All the Israelites grumbled against Moses and Aaron." Someone even put forth a motion that they should choose a leader and go back to Egypt.

When I read, I always engage in what I am reading. So at this point in the story, my response to this is always, "Good-bye and good luck crossing that Red Sea without a rod! And you can forget about a pillar of cloud by day and a pillar of fire by night!"

Conversely, of the twelve spies who explored the land, Joshua and

Caleb were the only two who saw the giants for who they were—small in God's eyes! The other ten spies looked around and reacted to their circumstances. But Joshua and Caleb saw the circumstances through the eyes of faith. They said,

> If the Lord is pleased with us, he will lead us into that land, a land flowing with milk and honey, and will give it to us. Only do not rebel against the Lord. And do not be afraid of the people of the land. Their protection is gone, but the Lord is with us. (Num. 14:6–9)

Imagine that! The protection of the enemy was gone—nonexistent! But the Israelites were so blinded that they could not even see that. Is there a lesson here for us?

Joshua and Caleb's words reflected Hebrews 11:1, "Faith is being sure of what we hope for and certain of what we do not see."

"So we fix our eyes not on what is seen, but on what is unseen. For what is seen is temporary, but what is unseen is eternal" (2 Corinthians 4:16).

Numbers 14:10 tells us that the whole assembly talked about stoning Joshua and Caleb, the two faithful spies. What were they thinking? They were on the brink of entering the Promised Land and about to stone the only two of the twelve spies who had a clear vision of God.

> God was fed up with them. He said to Moses, "How long will these people treat me with contempt? How long will they refuse to believe in me? I will strike them down" (Num.14:11).

But Moses interceded for Israel and asked God for forgiveness for the whole community.

As you recall in Numbers 13:1-33, Moses had sent twelve spies to scout out the land of Canaan. Joshua and Caleb brought back a good report that the land was fruitful and that they could claim the land as God had promised. The other ten spies, on the other hand, gave a bad report including that of being small compared to the size of the giants of the land. They said, we seemed like grasshoppers in our own eyes and we looked the same to them.

Can you think of the number of times God makes a promise to us and instead of going on faith, we believe the "bad report" of our friends and family? In addition to disbelieving God's promises, we allow the grasshopper mentality, our smallness in our eyes and others, to get a grip on our minds? When we do take on this kind of mentality, we deny God the opportunity to do what he does best—perform a miracle!

Putting Principles into Action

Let us make a promise to ourselves that from now on, we will not believe the bad reports. The Israelites did just that, and we see the slow erosion and eventual demise of a divine promise.

CHAPTER 24

God's Judgment on the Israelites

Death of a Promise

The Israelites seem to have had a sense of entitlement. They were entitled to food, water, comfort, and anything that contributed to their personal happiness. The motto seemed to be, "If you don't make us happy, we will go wild" or "If we're not happy, nobody else will be happy." After their last act of rebellion and complaining, God was angry and was ready to destroy them as a nation, but Moses interceded for them, and God forgave them. But in response to Moses' prayer, God made this statement:

How long will this wicked community grumble against me? I have heard the complaints of these grumbling Israelites. So tell them, as surely as I live, declares the Lord, I will do to you the very things I heard you say: In this desert your bodies will fall – every one of you twenty years old or more who was counted in the census and who has grumbled against me. Not one of you will enter the land I swore with uplifted hand to make your home, except Caleb son of Jephunneh and Joshua son of Nun.

As for your children that you said would be taken as plunder, I will bring them in to enjoy the land you have rejected. But you – your bodies will fall in this desert. Your children will be shepherds here for forty years, suffering for your unfaithfulness, until the last of your bodies lies in the desert. For forty years – one year for each of the forty days you explored the land – you will suffer for your sins and know what it is like to have me against you. I, the Lord, have spoken, and I will surely do these things to this whole wicked community, which has banded together against me. They will meet their end in this desert; here they will die. (Num. 14:26–35)

Ouch! That hurts! The Israelites complained so often about God's bringing them to die in the wilderness that in the end, after repeatedly testing the Lord and doubting his Word, God decreed that they would die in the wilderness—exactly what they proclaimed with their mouths. Only their children who were under twenty at the time would make it into the Promised Land. The exceptions to this were Joshua and Caleb, who had a different attitude and believed God. What a shameful end to a glorious promise!

Reminder:

"The tongue has the power of life and death, and those who love it will eat its fruit" (Prov. 18:21).

Scripture verses to ponder:

"He who guards his mouth and his tongue keeps himself from calamity" (Prov. 21:23).

"An evil man is trapped by his sinful talk, but a righteous man escapes trouble" (Prov. 12:13).

Jesus said to the Pharisees, who were being their usual unrighteous selves, "For by your words you will be acquitted, and by your words you will be condemned" (Matt. 12:37).

We, as modern Christians, sometimes have the spirit of the Israelites in us—the spirit of discontent! We think we deserve more than what God has provided for us. We always want more of some material object and sometimes not just more but bigger than the next person's. I believe that discontentment is a sin that retards our spiritual growth and leads to other sins. When we become discontented with what God has provided for us, we begin to covet. In other words, we begin to desire things out of God's will. The antidote to covetousness is contentment. Paul the apostle's experience should inspire us to say also,

For I have learned to be content whatever the circumstances. I know what it is to be in need, and I know what it is to have plenty. I have learned the secret of being content in any and every situation, whether well fed or hungry, whether living in plenty or in want. I can do everything through him who gives me strength. (Phil. 4:11–13)

The Israelites focused on their happiness and their bellies. In their discontent, they wanted to go back to Egypt—a place they thought would make them happy. However, the downside to discontent is judgment from God. When we begin to grumble, complain, and become discontented, it is a personal attack on God. We forget that it is God who keeps us alive while we are sleeping. It is through his power that our heart beats through the night. The many stars in the hemisphere stay on course without any assistance from us. Why can't we just wake up and thank God for giving us another day?

Food for Thought:

- Are we so focused on what we do not have that we forget to thank God for what we do have?
- When we focus on our primary happiness, we are treading on dangerous ground and, like Pharaoh, colliding with the living God!

Lessons Learned from the Israelites

1. *Complaining and judgment*

Throughout our life, we need to learn many lessons. First, our complaining is particularly obnoxious to God. When we complain, we are saying that God is not doing right by us and that he is not fair or just. The Israelites learned the hard way that complaining against God, in any form, will bring judgment, not blessings. It is in our human nature to want to be greater than we are or to arrive at our destination in life when we think we're ready, but we must trust the Lord to put us in the right place, at the right time and to give us what we need, not what we want.

2. *Complaining and mistrust*

It is a form of mistrust in God when we complain and compare ourselves to others. God has given everyone gifts and talents that he wants us to use. When we complain about our gifts and envy others, we are saying that God is not treating us fairly. *We are saying that we deserve more!* Let it be a careful reminder that God couldn't bless the Israelites because of their stinking attitude, and he hasn't changed in that respect. A common malady in the church is the constant complaining about others and comparing oneself to others. *"Oh, I wish I could sing like that. Why is she the worship leader? What about me? Why is she a board member? Why is he a deacon? What about me? I don't think she should lead the children's church. I would do a better job."*

For many people, it doesn't register that they don't have a jot of talent in certain areas and wouldn't be suited for certain positions. Envy and discontent with their lot in life will always cause people to complain, compare, and invariably sin against God.

3. *Complaining or usefulness*

If you are a complainer, *stop it!* If we are busy complaining, we cannot be useful to God's kingdom. Many people have a talent for complaining—although complaining is not a talent. Even if we have to dig deep to find a talent, each person has a talent somewhere. In addition, God wants us to use what he has given us. Always aspire to be useful to God. Whether we are a one-talent Christian or a ten-talent Christian, we have to be satisfied with what God gives us. We have to develop and use the talent or talents he gives us for his honor and glory, but the talent has to be used within the framework that he sets. You might not be able to sing, lead worship, or sit on a board, but can you encourage someone? Can you give hope to someone for whom Jesus is the answer to the problems he or she is facing? Can you cook? There are so many young single mothers who need someone to walk alongside them. Why not you? God is gracious to his children. He gives at least one talent to everyone. What is yours?

You do not have to be the "head cook and bottle-washer" in the church. There is always a need for people who were not meant for the spotlight.

4. *Complaining en masse*

I don't know why the group mentality was such in the Israelites' camp, except to say that they had the battle scars of slavery to contend with and possibly, it was a matter of "misery likes company." What do you think?

I would also add that the contagion of complaining, dissatisfaction, and rebellion seemed to have contaminated the majority of adults of the nation of Israel, except Caleb and Joshua, as only those two men and children under twenty were allowed to go across to the Promised Land. This is another lesson we need to learn as modern Christians. Family and friends cannot lead us astray unless we let them. God's words and covenants are sacred. Individuals are the ones held accountable, not groups. *Bad company corrupts good character* (1 Cor. 15:33). We should avoid people, "friends," or groups that encourage us, as believers, to act contrary to God's words. It is our soul that is at stake!

The punishment meted out to the Israelites for rebellion was harsh. We have their history. We can and should hastily learn from it as individuals. Do not allow yourself to be drawn into complaining by a friend, coworker, or even your own family. You are an individual. *Think like an individual.*

5. *Complaining: our wounds—God's filter*

If you are contending with your own battle scars, God understands. He knows your heart and will help you to get to where you need to be. He understood what the Israelites were going through. He was patient and long suffering. He could have "zapped" them at the first complaint, but he provided everything they complained about lacking. We need to remember that God knows our pain; he is patient and long-suffering with us too. However, be reminded that everything has to pass through God's filters; and complaining about our situation is disrespecting God and showing mistrust in his ability to guide us. God only allows what is necessary for our spiritual growth, so we have to trust him. It gives me great comfort to know that God is never taken by surprise at the events in my life.

I have been wounded several times by people I trusted. Was God surprised? Absolutely not! He did not have to come up with a backup plan for my life. My wounds and yours are all included in his original plan for our lives. So was our healing. We might never know the reason why some events take place in our lives, but remember, our past, present, and future is known by God. According to Psalm 31:15, "My times are in his hands."

So do not allow difficult situations to harden your heart and take your focus off God and his plan for your eternal destiny.

6. *Complaining—God's silence*

The Israelites were left in the wilderness because of the hardness of their hearts. As they grumbled and complained, they viewed the lack of comfortable amenities and lack of food and water as a sign that God had abandoned them. They questioned God's motive in putting them in a hard place and even questioned his presence, when in reality, God's presence was visible but beyond their comprehension. God deliberately led them in a difficult situation. Was God being mean? Definitely not! When our challenging situation remains unchanged or becomes more difficult, despite our prayers, is God deaf to our tears or cries? Absolutely not! We learned early in the conversation between God and Moses that God had heard the cries of the Israelites. Even after four hundred years, he was still listening.

Although the Israelites were allowed to remain in slavery for over four hundred years and in the wilderness for much longer than God's original timeframe, note that sometimes we, too, are allowed to stay in the wilderness longer than we think we have to. Also, sometimes when we are faced with a difficult situation, we, too, fail to recognize God's presence and provision. Rather, we tend to think his silence is an absence of his presence and an indication of his disinterest in our personal well-being. The story of the Israelites should encourage us to bow to God's tests, if we feel we are being tested. I would also encourage you to never doubt his presence in a time of personal crisis or stressful situation. In my experience, that's when he is most present, taking care of me like a mother takes care of a newborn baby. There were times in the past when he literally surrounded me with his love, and I could feel his hand rocking me to sleep. Psalm 34:17–19 says,

The righteous cry out, and the Lord hears them, he delivers them from all their troubles. The Lord is close to the brokenhearted and saves those who are crushed in spirit. A righteous man may have many troubles, but the Lord delivers him from them all.

7. *Complaining and a hard heart*

We also need to remember that grumbling was typical of Israel's stubbornness and rebellion against God. It was a persistent problem, not a rare occurrence. When they were finally allowed to enter Canaan, they were referred to as "stiff-necked," to the point that God wanted to destroy them at Horeb (Deut. 9:6–8). As contemporary Christians, this lesson is referenced for us in Hebrews 3:7–11.

Today, if you hear his voice, do not harden your hearts as you did in the rebellion, during the time of testing in the desert, where your fathers tested and tried me, and for forty years saw what I did. That is why I was angry with that generation, and I said, their hearts are always going astray, and they have not known my ways. So I declared on oath in my anger, they shall never enter my rest.

As we discussed earlier, the Israelites' sins increased with every complaint. They were dissatisfied with Moses, Aaron, their situation, and with God. When we, like the Israelites, complain and become unhappy and dissatisfied with where God has placed us, we put God to the test, and we challenge him. That's one challenge and battle we are going to lose. Why fight a battle that is already lost? The forty years that Israel spent in the wilderness wasn't just a punishment for those who rebelled; it was also a learning experience for the nation of Israel—and should be for us too.

8. *Adversity and spiritual maturity*

The Israelites could have developed spiritually, had they been open to God's teaching. But as soon as adversity and a little stress came upon them, they wanted to run away. They started to blame the very ones who could help them grow. When we run away from stress and adversity, we forgo the spiritual growth God intends for us to have as his children. We also forgo the possible ministry opportunity God has ordained for us. My encouragement would be to stay focused on God when stress, difficulties, and adversities come your way. We need to dig deeper into the Word of God, so our spiritual roots get stronger. James advises us,

> Consider it pure joy, my brothers whenever you face trials of many kinds, because you know that the testing of your faith develops perseverance. Perseverance must finish its work so that you may be mature and complete not lacking anything. (James 1:2–3)

In John 15:5, Jesus shows us the only way to survive the trials and tribulations of life. He says,

> I am the vine; you are the branches. If a man remains in me and I in him, he will bear much fruit; apart from me you can do nothing. If anyone does not remain in me, he is like a branch that is thrown away and withers; such branches are picked up, thrown into the fire and burned.

I like the garden analogy that Jesus makes reference to in the above text. Any gardener will tell you that a branch can only receive food if there is life in the tree. As an avid gardener, I can hardly wait to walk around my garden in spring and prune the dead branches. The dead branches are useless to the tree, because they cannot get the food or nourishment that the tree sends out. Healthy branches feed off the tree and receive sustenance. Coupled with light, this allows them to grow and produce beautiful leaves, flowers, or fruits. If the branches are lifeless, they must be pruned.

Pruning is usually beneficial for growth. If we are abiding in the vine that is Jesus, then we should expect God to prune us. It might be that he sends us into the wilderness for pruning, either because we have too many "dead branches," or we need to grow. When he prunes us, he is preparing us for spiritual growth, because spiritual growth allows us to be more useful to him. Whatever form of pruning God allows in your life, remain faithful to his Word. Always trust him and know that he will eventually bring you into the path he has prepared for you. When we are pruned, we face an uncertain time. But the only certainty of which we can be sure is that we will be transformed—and we will never be the same again.

Food for thought

How can we attain spiritual growth if we avoid his pruning by running away?

The Death of Moses

As the Israelites traversed through the wilderness, with one calamity after another assailing them, Moses had disturbing news. God told Moses that he was not going to cross over to the Promised Land. I always feel sorry for Moses, but the Bible says that the reason Moses was not allowed to go into the Promised Land was because he "trespassed against God among the children of Israel at the waters of Meribah Kadesh." I feel sorry for Moses because he had come so close but missed the mark of the Promised Land. The Israelites tried and tested Moses' patience in so many ways that he eventually lost his temper. However, we cannot blame the Israelites for his failure and say that their troublesome behavior caused him to lose his temper and disobey God. He was responsible for his own behavior. And although we should feel sorry for Christians and weep for those who have traveled so far in the Christian life and then are drawn away from everything they once knew, they too are responsible for their own behavior. Where once they were strong and brave, like eagles, flying high for the Lord, now they are like sparrows, scratching and pecking on lower heights as they pursue their own desires. What a sad path!

What happened to Moses? God had told Moses to speak to the rock in the presence of the Israelites, and the rock would bring forth water for the people and their animals. However, Moses struck the rock twice in anger with his rod instead of just speaking to it, as God had instructed. He violated a direct command from God himself.

The Bible does not say why Moses did this. He obviously should have known better. But sometimes we allow our anger to get hold of us, and we act according to the dictates of our emotions instead of relying on the Word of God. As Christians, we do things that directly contravene God's Word, even though we know better. It is easy to sit in judgment of Moses. but I would challenge anyone to say he or she has never done anything wrong or has not acted as Moses did. The good news is that God forgives our mistakes. However, we must learn from Moses' mistake, because the mistakes we make can cost us just as much as it cost Moses. Moses had an incredible relationship and journey with God, and we can too. But God needs to be obeyed and honored totally. Half measures are not acceptable. There is a lot we can learn from Moses' story.

Two Questions to Ponder:

- What was Israel's purpose in the overall scheme of God's plan?
- What do you think your purpose is in the overall scheme of God's plan?

Here are two applications for our lives:

1. When God tells you to do something specific, do not ever question his command. Just do it, or, like Moses, you could end up losing more than you bargained for.
2. We are under the dispensation of grace, but we should be careful not to test God.

David

A man after God's Own Heart
Vignette

We drew closer to our teacher as she took out the storybook. She gathered us more closely as she painted word pictures of the army, the noise, and the confusion. My young mind was the canvas as she painted a tale of a young boy and his daring feats of victory.

"Children, this morning's story is about a young boy who had a big obstacle he had to overcome—a huge giant standing before him. The giant was loud and tough! Many people thought this little wimp of a boy couldn't beat him, but against all odds, he did, and he won not just the battle but the war. His name was David, later known as King David."

As young David lifted up his arm, and twirled the slingshot, and let it loose, in my child's mind it was my arm that swung, my arm that threw the stone that sunk deep into the giant's forehead. In my mind, I heard the huge thud as he fell to the ground. In my mind's eye, I saw the dust flying everywhere as he fell with a heavy *oomph!* I heard his agonizing cry as it echoed along the hillside.

As a child, my elementary school teacher used to read a Bible story to our class every morning—she was a master storyteller. Every inflection in her voice would produce an "ah" or "mmm" from us. She weaved the components of the story so well that everyone loved David.

I remember when she got to the part about David and Bathsheba. Like a pro, she drew us in: "David was a musician and a poet, and he could slay wild animals." Then she said in a sad, whispery voice, "But children, do you know that David did something bad?" In one accord, we all chorused, "Oh no!" I was almost in tears that day as she softly told the story of David and Bathsheba. After the story, she said in a lighter tone, "But, God still had plans for David." A long drawn-out "Oooooh" was her reward.

My early years were spent in a country where, at that time, it was politically correct to have prayers in school and read from the Bible. So when everyone's heroes were pop singers, movie stars, and rock stars, mine was David. I always loved his heart! It is an interesting story how David came to be anointed king over Israel, God's chosen nation.

Samuel, the prophet, had secretly come down to anoint a new king. Therefore, he had to keep the knowledge from Saul, the present king. Samuel invited Jesse, David's father, and David's brothers to a sacrifice, where God told Samuel he would choose the next king. As Samuel inspected all Jesse's sons and waited for the Lord's approval of each one, he kept thinking, *Is this the one? This must be the one.* They were big, strong, tall, and a pleasure to look at. But God continued saying no to each one. Finally, he said to Samuel,

"Do not consider his appearance or his height, for I have rejected him. The Lord does not look at the things man looks at. Man looks at the outward appearance but the Lord looks at the heart." (1 Sam. 16:7)

After God rejected Jesse's seven sons, Samuel asked Jesse, "Are these all the sons you have?" Jesse replied, "There is still the youngest, but he is tending sheep." Here is the scenario: Jesse had an honored guest, Samuel the prophet, in his home, and David was not even invited to dinner, much less to the sacrifice. Eventually, David was called into dinner and was anointed to be the next king of Israel. "From that day on the Spirit of the Lord came upon David in power" (1 Sam. 16:1). David now had a calling upon his life, according to God's plan;

but he had to go on God's timetable. What did David do? He went back to tending sheep until God was ready for him.

Let us see how his story unfolds!

The Philistines had gathered their forces for war at Socoh in Judah. Along with the Philistines were the rabble-rousers, the gawkers, the vultures, and a few righteous prayer warriors. The media had been talking for days about Goliath. He was a giant of a man who stood over nine feet tall—a man of strength. A champion of champions! His very armor weighed five thousand shekels. His spear shaft was a fearsome weapon. Its point alone weighed six hundred shekels.

His taunts terrified even the bravest Israelite soldier. For forty days, his words rang out across the hills. At night, they were every man's nightmare. People were frightened! Were they going to be taken into captivity again? Were the days of slavery upon them again, like the days of their forefathers in Egypt? Many decided they had to go to see this event unfold. Nerves were stretched tightly in the Valley of Elah. The tension was thick in the air. Something had to give eventually.

In the meantime, along the road to the Valley of Elah, the young boy David came whistling. He had a day off! As much as he loved tending his father's sheep, he had an errand today. He had left his sheep with a fellow shepherd so that he could do an errand for his father, Jesse. Little did he know he was on a divine mission for his heavenly Father. He whistled and sang a song in praise to God as he walked. He wished he had his harp as he composed songs of praise to God, but today, his voice was his musical instrument as he shouted to the surrounding hills of the goodness of God.

Oh Lord, our Lord, how majestic is your name in all the earth! You have set your glory above the heavens. From the lips of children and infants you have ordained praise because of your enemies, to silence the foe and the avenger. When I consider your heavens, the work of your fingers, the moon and the stars, which you have set in place, what is man that you are mindful of him, the son of man that you care for him? You made him a little lower than the heavenly beings and crowned him with glory and honor. You made him ruler over the works of your hands; you put everything under his feet: all flocks and herds, and the beasts of the field, the birds of the air, and the fish of the sea, all that swim the paths of the seas. O Lord, our Lord, how majestic is your name in all the earth! (Ps. 8:1–9)

"The heavens declare the glory of God; the skies proclaimed the work of his hands" (Ps. 14:1).

"The Lord is my shepherd; I shall not be in want. He makes me lie down in green pastures, he leads me beside quiet waters, he restores my soul. He guides me in paths of righteousness for his name's sake" (Ps. 23:1–3).

David finally reached his destination. It was a startling contrast for him to leave the tranquility of the hills and his communication with God and to arrive at the battlefield where Goliath, in his usual flamboyant way, was "performing." He was flaunting himself and mocking the nation of Israel. David was offended at this behavior and said, "What will be done for the man who kills this Philistine and removes this disgrace from Israel? Who is this uncircumcised Philistine that he should defy the armies of the Living God?" (1 Sam. 17:26).

As we continue to read the account of David and Goliath, we will see a marked difference between the two:

Goliath	David
adult, giant	youth of medium stature
soldier	shepherd
confidence in self	confidence in God
dependence on strength	dependence on God
support of friends	no support from family
perspective of the world	perspective of God
wrong perception of the situation	right perception of the situation
outwardly dressed for the situation	inwardly dressed for battle

Goliath was a showman who had perfected his showmanship. He was loud, brash, boastful, and feared. He had won quite a few battles and had the trappings of success to prove it. When David stood before him with only his slingshot and his confidence in God, Goliath looked at David and said, disparagingly, "'Am I a dog that you come at me with sticks?' And the Philistine cursed David by his gods. 'Come here,' he said, 'and I'll give your flesh to the birds of the air and the beasts of the field!'" (1 Sam. 17:43–44).

David, on the other hand, was young and untried in battles. He had a slingshot, of all things, but he exuded confidence in the only person who could win this battle and the war—God. He said to Goliath, "You come against me with sword and spear and javelin, but I come against you in the name of the Lord Almighty, the God of the armies of Israel, whom you have defied."

Then he boldly said,

This day the Lord will hand you over to me, and I'll strike you down and cut off your head. Today I will give the carcasses of the Philistine army to the birds of the air and the whole world will know there is a God in Israel. All those gathered here will know that it is not by sword or spear that the Lord saves; for the battle is the Lord's, and he will give all of you into our hands. (1 Sam. 17:45–47)

Don't you love this guy!

Questions to Ponder:
1. Do you have a giant to slay?
2. How are you dressed?
3. What is your weapon of choice?

CHAPTER 27

David: One Down

David's Triumph

David was also a man of contrast, but one constant in his life was his heart toward God. The story of David slaying Goliath is one of the most famous and well-loved stories in the Bible. David's killing of the giant is a symbol of the triumph of good over evil. The story of David sleeping with Bathsheba, Uriah's wife, getting her pregnant, and having Uriah killed afterward represents a moral failure. The biblical account of David, king of Israel and direct ancestor of the Messiah, acclaimed warrior, musician, and poet comes from the books of Samuel, Chronicles, and Kings. After such a courageous beginning, David failed dismally, yet God called him a man after his own heart. He said of David in, 1 Kings 15:5, that David did what was right.

David was anointed king to lead the children of Israel, God's chosen people. Yet he was an adulterer and a murderer. Many people have asked, "Why is the story of David so popular? Why are we gripped by his persona?" And more important, "Why would God call him a man after his own heart after what he did?"

Let's see!

Historically, God had repeatedly demonstrated his power on behalf of the Israelites. But they continually rejected his leadership over them, as did their forefathers in the wilderness. David came on the scene after God rejected Saul as king. Time after time, we see Israel, God's chosen nation, rejecting God, repenting, and then God forgiving them. Prior to David, Saul was chosen to rule as king over Israel because the people had told Samuel, the prophet, that they wanted a king "like the other nations." 1 Samuel 8:4 says,

So all the elders of Israel gathered together and came to Samuel at Ramah. They said to him, you are old, and your sons do not walk in your ways; now appoint a king to lead us, such as all the other nations have.

Samuel was very displeased and went to God in prayer; but God said,

Listen to all that the people are saying to you; it is not you they have rejected, but they have rejected me as their king as they have done from the day I brought them up out of Egypt until this day, forsaking me and serving other gods, so they are doing to you. (1 Sam. 8:4–8)

Samuel described to the people what a human king would do to them. He even warned them that the day would come when they would "cry out for relief from the king" they had chosen, but the people refused to listen to him. They said, "No, we want a king over us. Then we will be like all the other nations, with a king to lead us and go out before us and fight our battles" (1 Sam. 8:18–20).

I always wonder who the Israelites thought had been leading and guiding them since they left Egypt. Exodus 13:20–22 tells us, "After leaving Succoth, they camped at Etham on the edge of the desert. By day the Lord went ahead of them in a pillar of cloud to guide them on their way and by night in a pillar of fire to give them light so they could travel by day or night."

The key verse is: *"Neither the pillar of cloud by day and the pillar of fire by night left its place in front of the people."*

At the time they asked for a king, God had been working through Samuel to protect them and preserve their nation. Now, like their forefathers, they had out rightly rejected God by demanding a king, which constituted a denial of the covenant relationship with God. They asked for a king and got Saul, who didn't quite measure up to his expectations, so God rejected him. Now Samuel had to choose another king. God had found the "right" someone, David, whose heart was soft toward God. God knew David's heart. He was a man, like any other, who made mistakes. But when he did, he was always quick to repent and regain his perspective of God and God's expectations of him. He had never rejected God but always sought his protection, provision, and most of all, God's heart.

Do you think it grieves God when we reject him and turn to the things of the world? As modern-day Christians, we might never say in words, like the Israelites, that we want to be like others in the world. However, sometimes our actions speak louder than our words. We will never know the full extent of God's provision for us and his protection of us until we enter eternity. It is then that we will find out about all the things he saved us from. It is only then that we will also realize the full extent of the things we lost when we failed to seek God's heart. If you are still wondering why God called David *"a man after my own heart,"* read on! David was called by God. He now had to prepare him for his ministry.

After the great victory over Goliath, you would think that David would continue dancing down the streets of his city. However, his life took a decisive turn for the worse—or so it would seem. Saul knew that his days as king of Israel were numbered. By now, he knew that David would be the next king. In addition, Jonathan, his son had committed the biggest "sin," in Saul's eyes. He had formed an alliance with David, his enemy. Saul was jealous, he was angry, and he was afraid. With all those emotions on the boil, Saul sought to kill David at every opportunity he got, which meant that David became a fugitive.

So David and his men, about six hundred in number, left Keilah and kept moving from place to place. When Saul was told that David had escaped from Keilah, he did not go there. David stayed in the desert strongholds and in the hills of the Desert of Ziph. Day after day Saul searched for him, but God did not give David into his hands. While David was at Horesh in the Desert of Ziph, he learned that Saul had come out to take his life. And Saul's son Jonathan went to David at Horesh and helped him find strength in God. Don't be afraid, he said. My father Saul will not lay a hand on you. You will be king over Israel, and I will be second to you. Even my father Saul knows this. (1 Sam. 23:13–17)

For a long time, David had to continue to hide out in the desert of Ziph, because Saul was seeking his life. He knew God had promised that he would be the next king of Israel, but he was on the run like a common criminal. It was during this time that David could have become angry at God for allowing this. But through his wilderness experience, God prepared David for the next stage of his life. He learned about loyalty from Saul's son, Jonathan. Even though Jonathan was the rightful heir to the throne, he was willing to give it up to fulfill God's plan for David's life. David learned compassion, forgiveness, and mercy for an aging King Saul and from his wilderness experience. These were necessary lessons for the future king of Israel. It was in the wilderness that God would mold him into his image and produce a replica fit for his service.

Do you feel like you have been sent into the wilderness through no fault of your own? Do you feel persecuted? Do you have many "Sauls" baying at your heels?

When David was first anointed as king, he had to go back to tending sheep. Many would say that he was wasting his time—he should have been taking courses for "anointed kings in waiting." Some might even venture to say that Samuel the prophet got his heavenly wires crossed. How about you?

Perhaps you feel like you are just spinning your wheels out in the pastures. You have been "anointed" to be in ministry. You want to begin a work for God, but none of the doors are opening up like you want. You feel like you are in a desert far from where you think God wants you to be. Everything you have tried hasn't worked so far. Why not?

Maybe, like Abraham, Moses, Jacob, and all the others, God wants you to spend some time learning new things and unlearning old things. Before we can effectively minister to others, we must be ministered to by God, where he can have all of our attention, in solitude, without lights, fanfare, and distractions. *Allow God to speak to your heart in your wilderness.*

Each one of these great leaders had to spend time in the wilderness.

You and I are no different from any one of them. Even Jesus spent time in the wilderness. We, too, have to be prepared for God's purpose.

God doesn't change. According to Numbers 23:19, "God is not a man, that he should lie, nor a son of man, that he should change his mind. Does he speak and then not act? Does he promise and not fulfill?"

"He who is the Glory of Israel does not lie or change his mind; for he is not a man, that he should change his mind" (1 Sam. 15:29).

God doesn't change! In fact, we are the ones who need to change. Eventually, David was molded into God's image. We are also being molded into the image of God, but we have to stay the course with him.

When I became a Christian, I asked God to help me to become a woman after his own heart, just like my hero, David. I have made mistakes in my life and probably will until I draw my last breath. But like David, my heart has always been turned toward God. I can say with certainty that no matter what difficulty I face—and I have faced many—God and his Word will always be my guidepost, my lodestar.

How about you? What is your lodestar?

Question to Ponder:

What do you think God wants you to learn?

Here are some suggestions to consider:

- God can make a brand-new you.
- God knows how much we can bear.
- Don't run from the crisis hovering around you or your family.
- Do not abandon the faith or family if you are going through a difficult situation. Stay and emerge as a spiritual giant.
- Everything that is happening to you has been permitted by God.

CHAPTER 28

King, Warrior, and Fallen Hero

Looking at David's life, we see his great strengths, such as his physical abilities, his musical abilities that indicated that music has charms to soothe Saul's savage breast, his spiritual awareness of God's sovereignty, and his devotion to God. He had slain Goliath and, in great victory, was paraded through the streets, with women singing songs to him and about him. Heady stuff! Years later, we see a few of his greatest weaknesses exposed. But juxtaposed to his weaknesses were his strengths and the reason why God called him a man after his own heart.

We have discussed some of David's strengths already. As a man of contrast, one of his greatest weaknesses was his inability to lead his family, even though as king, he was one of Israel's greatest leaders. His family fell apart, but he did nothing. One of his sons raped his own sister. Another son committed murder. Another tried to usurp his throne, but there was no indication that David reprimanded or disciplined his sons. Even though he had slain the giant Goliath, you could say that family was a giant that David never quite conquered.

It is difficult to understand why David would allow his family to become so dysfunctional without doing something about it. God gives men the leadership of their homes. There's the possibility that he had been too busy being king and had forgotten that God would hold him accountable for his family responsibility. Everything rises and falls on leadership in the home, and it is no wonder that his home life was in a mess. He provided no leadership! His abdication of the "throne of fatherhood" almost cost him the position of king. This would have given the throne to Absalom, had God not had the final say in the leadership of his people.

One of David's strengths was his ability as a great warrior, yet when his name is mentioned, it is in relationship to Goliath and Bathsheba. I always wonder why he stayed home from battle that fateful day he saw Bathsheba. Maybe he was just plain weary. Whatever the reason, David did stay home, and he made one of the greatest mistakes of his life—and placed himself in another season of his life.

> In the spring, at the time when kings go off to war, David sent Joab out with the king's men and the whole Israelite army. They destroyed the Ammonites and besieged Rabbah. But David remained in Jerusalem.

> One evening David got up from his bed and walked around on the roof of the palace. From the roof he saw a woman bathing. The woman was very beautiful, and David sent someone to find out about her. The man said, "Isn't this Bathsheba, the daughter of Eliam and the wife of Uriah the Hittite?" Then David sent messengers to get her. She came to him, and he slept with her. Then she went back home. The woman conceived and sent word to David, saying, "I am pregnant." (2 Samuel 11:11–5)

David committed adultery with Bathsheba and he, his family and, subsequently, Israel had to pay a heavy price for that catastrophe. David saw Bathsheba and allowed his flesh to take control. Do you ever wonder if Bathsheba knew the king's patio overlooked her bathing area? Everyone knew when the king was home. Do you think she knew? Unfortunately, David's "seeing Bathsheba" went too far—if an affair, pregnancy, and murder can go too far. This relationship shouldn't have started in the first place. David's decision to sleep with Bathsheba, his employee's wife, compromised his reputation and his position with God. I don't know how easy it was to chloroform his conscience about his action; but it wasn't until Nathan the prophet pointed that long, bony finger of accusation and accosted him that David confessed to adultery and thus his affair with Bathsheba was exposed (2 Sam. 12:1–14).

David's first mistake was letting his gaze linger on Bathsheba. Who knows what his thoughts were then? But she must have seemed like an oasis of beauty in the midst of his stress, the disunity in his family, and being king. It was then that he made a fatal decision. He decided to live for the temporal!

Many modern people head down that same treacherous path. Some men say, "My wife doesn't cook. Oh, that she would …" A wife might say, "My husband won't … Oh, that he would …" And Satan pumps his fist and say, "Yes, I got them!" Whatever is being said, we have to remember it is spiritual warfare. As long as those negative thoughts enter our mind, and we allow them to take root, it will lead us to make wrong decisions. Satan doesn't care what happens to us or to our families and our marriages. His only concern is to hurt God, because he knows the family is close to God's heart. He knows his days are numbered, so his only intent is to bring down as many of God's people as he can with him.

If David had been leading his household well and tending his heart and spiritual life diligently, he never would have taken Bathsheba and had Uriah killed. I pray that men will be godly fathers and husbands, that they will be men who hold fast to God and their families. David made many mistakes, but we can learn from him. When we've made mistakes, no matter how big or small, God is always there to dispense mercy, compassion, and forgiveness, because, as is demonstrated in the relationship between David and God, despite David's failings, God forgave him and still called him *"a man after my own heart."* David's moral failures caused grievous wounding to his family and to Uriah and his family. Yet God was able to forgive David when he repented. So why did God continue to call him by this name? The reason is that despite all his failings, David still had a soft heart for God.

If you are the one who did the wounding or the one who initiated the wounding, God still offers forgiveness. Don't hesitate to put things right! Waiting for a "Nathan" is not a good idea. David gave in to his flesh and started on that slippery slope that culminated in his murdering Uriah, Bathsheba's husband. David used murder to cover up his sin and to get rid of his competition. Nowadays, the common weapon of choice is not murder but divorce. I would like to put forth the suggestion that divorce and murder, are one and the same. With the divorce rate the highest it has been in history, there are so many broken homes, so many broken families, and so many fatherless children, as spouses walk out without a thought to God's Word.

In essence, the family structure that God ordained is literally being murdered, thoughtlessly and callously!

One year prior to writing this book, I attended a wedding. While I was standing in the reception line, waiting for the bridal couple, a man and I struck up a conversation, and he began to tell me about his life. Years ago, he said, he had walked out on his wife and family, and decades later, his children still would not talk to him. No sympathy I offered him could eliminate the regrets with which he had had to live. I'm sure he thought he had good reasons for leaving at that time—who knows? Yet decades later, he is still living with the consequences of his decision. This man was experiencing deep regret.

Still, there are some runaway spouses and fathers who continue to live without feelings of guilt or shame. Instead of remorse, confession of sin, and repentance, they seem to shake a fist in the face of God, sin with impunity, and carry on happily, because they have not acknowledged their sin before God. Therefore, it is impossible for them to feel guilty. David, on the contrary, showed concern and contrition in his prayer of confession in Psalm 51. He asked for mercy and pardon. He asked for cleansing; verse 4 is the key to his life: "Against you, you only, have I sinned and done what is evil in your sight."

David was always quick to go to God, acknowledge his sins, and ask for forgiveness. Of course, he sinned against Uriah too, but he knew that when a person sins, it is primarily against God. We know that David asked God for forgiveness, and it was granted. As for poor Uriah, it was too late! He had to pay the price for David and Bathsheba's sin.

On the flip side, when we are wounded, we should not wait for the person who wounded us to acknowledge the sin he or she committed against us. This may never happen, because the people who sin against us might continue to think they are in the right. But whether we are the "wounded" or the "wounder," we should be quick to seek God. Over previous years, I have read Psalm 51 and Psalm 73 many times.

These psalms remind me that God is taking notes; therefore, I don't have to. We, like David, are accountable to God and are responsible for our own behavior, not someone else's.

I've heard so many stories of women who had to work, had to study, were out of town, or were busy with the children, and while they were busy tending to family matters, the husband found a "willing woman" to listen to complaints about his wife. Pretty soon, the willing woman was cooking and offering advice and before you know it, a marriage and a family were destroyed. It is sad that this scenario is so common at present. Jesus talked to such a woman at the well. He said to her, "You have had five husbands and the one you have now is not yours."

The Bible does not elaborate on the character of Bathsheba. Was she a "woman at the well" type? Did she feel neglected while her husband was at war? What were her reasons for giving in to the king? Was it because he was the king? These are questions I would ask her if I were to meet her.

Of David, I would ask, "Other than Bathsheba's obvious beauty, why Bathsheba? Why would you jeopardize your position with God? What on earth were you thinking?"

The "woman-at-the-well" type of woman is a walking wounded. I was in conversation with a counselor some time ago. As we began to discuss several women's issues, the conversation turned to situations involving the woman-at-the-well type of women. She said something I never thought of before. She said that in the past, some of these women might have been betrayed or abandoned by their previous husbands. They might have been the victims, but now, in going out with someone else's husband, they were the victimizers. I pondered long and hard on that. This counselor gave me a new perspective on the woman at the well to whom Jesus spoke.

Have you ever wondered who the victims in the David and Bathsheba story were? In my opinion, they were all victims—David, Bathsheba, Uriah, and even the baby that died. However, I believe that Uriah and the baby were the only *real* victims—the innocent ones. There is no disputing the fact that God was angry. Here were two consenting adults who sought their own pleasure at everyone else's expense. In 2 Samuel 12:7–12, after David tried to cover up Bathsheba's pregnancy by murdering Uriah, Nathan the prophet gave him God's message. He said to David,

> This is what the Lord, the God of Israel, says: I anointed you king over Israel, and I delivered you from the hand of Saul. I gave your master's house to you, and your master's wives into your arms. I gave the house of Israel and Judah. And if all this had been too little, I would have given you even more. Why did you despise the word of the Lord by doing what is evil in his eyes? You struck down Uriah the Hittite with the sword and took his wife to be your own. You killed him with the sword of the Ammonites. Now, therefore, the sword will never depart from your house, because you despised me and took the wife of Uriah the Hittite to be your own.

Sadly, after David committed that sin of murdering Uriah, the Bible tells us that as part of his punishment, "The sword never left his house."

What calamity do we bring upon ourselves and our household by disobeying God's Word?

To New Testament Christians who think that God is sleeping or that God has changed his mind about sin, God doesn't change. He says the same thing to us as he said to David: "All personal pleasure is bought at a price." Many people think that pleasure gained illegitimately is pleasure. But the Bible tells us that the pleasure of the world only lasts for a season. This pleasure is bought at a price—you pay the price at a later date.

Food for Thought

What do you need to change in your life?

CHAPTER 29

Paul the Apostle

Paul the apostle, also known as Saul of Tarsus, is one of the most influential writers of the New Testament. His writings form a large portion of the New Testament and continue to be a source of inspiration to New Testament Christians. Paul's writings were used to spread the gospel across the Roman Empire and to the Gentiles. It changed the religious beliefs of people in many cultures of his time and continues to do so, even in our modern age.

Prior to his conversion as a follower of Jesus, Saul's sole purpose was to persecute the early followers of Jesus and have them put to death because they were heretics. At his conversion, Saul changed his name to Paul, became a Christian, and was himself later a target of persecution. He was proud of who he was. His ancestry was impeccable for that period. He indicated that he was "of the stock of Israel, of the tribe of Benjamin, a Hebrew of the Hebrews; as touching the law, a Pharisee." (Phil. 3:5)

He refers to his father as a "Pharisee, the son of a Pharisee" (Acts. 23:6). Paul was born in Tarsus, hence the term Saul of Tarsus, but was raised in Jerusalem (Acts 26:4) and "sat at the feet" of Gamaliel, the leading authority in the Sanhedrin at that time. Many would call Paul, "the cream of the crop."

Conversion of Paul the Apostle
We first meet Saul as a witness to the stoning of Stephen, the first Christian martyr. He held the clothes of the stoners. Paul says in Galatians 1:13, "I was violently persecuting the church of God and was trying to destroy it." But on his way to Damascus, he was confronted by the risen Jesus in a heavenly vision, and Saul found himself on the

ground, blinded by a bright heavenly light. The directions Jesus gave him were for him to go to his house and wait for someone to come to see him. After the vision, Saul was blinded, so someone had to lead him home. What a contrast! He rode out as the great avenger but was led back, blinded and immensely humbled. I suspect that after three days of blindness, Paul was seeing correctly for the first time in his life. At his meeting on the Damascus road, Jesus gave Paul a commission to "be a light to the Gentiles." After his conversion, Paul, the past religious murderer and self-righteous persecutor, was to propel the new Christian Church into fulfilling the Great Commission by taking the gospel to the Gentiles. What an honor and privilege!

According to Paul, after his conversion, he immediately went to Arabia, where the risen Jesus taught him "by revelation" for the next two to three years (Gal.1:11–18). So instead of sitting at the feet of Gamaliel, Paul sat at the feet of Jesus for three years. Paul's wilderness experience follows the tradition of Abraham, Jacob, Moses, and Joseph: he was called for a purpose, he was prepared, and he was transformed. Paul the apostle was now ready for his mission. Acts 13:2–3 says, "While they were worshiping the Lord and fasting, the Holy Spirit said, set apart for me Barnabas and Saul for the work to which I have called them. So after they had fasted and prayed, they placed their hands on them and set them off."

Paul had aggressively pursued his self-righteous calling as an avenger. Now, he aggressively pursued his calling as an apostle, even though it cost him greatly. He says in Galatians 1:15-18,

> But when God, who set me apart from birth and called me by his grace, was pleased to reveal his Son in me so that I might preach him among the Gentiles, I did not consult any man, nor did I go up to Jerusalem to see those who were apostles before I was, but I went immediately into Arabia and later returned to Damascus. Then after three years, I went up to Jerusalem to get acquainted with Peter and stayed with him fifteen days.

In Galatians 2:9, Paul says that the leadership in Jerusalem recognized this calling and gave him "the right hand of fellowship."

However, in the ensuing years, Paul found out that many were unwilling to give him the right hand of fellowship; not everyone was on his side or even pretended to be. Some of them would have rather given him the boot instead of the hand of fellowship.

I once was nominated to be the women's ministries president of the church I was attending at that time. I had prayed about it and felt that God wanted me to take on this role. As the votes were counted, it ended up to be thirty-nine votes for me being the president and four against me. I remember the pastor saying to me, "Sister Leta, just remember that even though the Israelites crossed over the Red Sea, not everyone was on Moses' side." I found out later that the pastor knew his congregation extremely well. But the Word of God says, "If God is for you, who can be against you?" In later years, amid the trials and tribulations, Paul was to be consoled by this thought.

The Apostle Paul: In Danger from Every Side

Paul's entire ministry was fraught with conflict. Paul and his companions were opposed in almost every city. Many times they were attacked and chased out. In Paul's second letter to the Corinthians, he described the opposition he continually faced in order to fulfill his calling.

> Five times I have received from the Jews the forty lashes minus one. Three times I was beaten with rods. Once I received a stoning ... in danger from bandits, danger from my own people, danger from Gentiles, danger in the city, danger in the wilderness, danger at sea, danger from false brothers and sisters ... many a sleepless night, hungry and thirsty, often without food, cold and naked. (2 Cor. 11:24–27)

Paul's Conflicts—the Personal Paul

When you read the writings of Paul, you get the impression that he was a man who was very forthright, one who did not mince his words for anyone. So in Galatians 2:11, Paul's confronting Peter over his behavior should not come as a surprise to anyone. Peter had been eating and sharing fellowship with Gentile Christians until some of James' men came to visit. Peter then began to give the Gentile believers the cold shoulder. Paul was not slow in taking Peter to task.

Paul definitely had an opinion on various topics. He also had been going in his own direction for a long time, doing things his way, as we are all wont to do. He had been zealously persecuting the church, but at the appointed time, Jesus graciously apprehended him because he had a lot of talents and abilities that God wanted to use. It was time for Paul to answer to his call, but first, God wanted him to go through the process of his purpose, preparation, and transformation. Only then was he ready to minister as the apostle to the Gentiles. His résumé reads as such:

Work Experience—Adversities, Challenges, and Difficulties:

- escaped in a basket when people in Damascus tried to kill me (Acts 9:19–25; 2 Cor. 11:32–33).
- persecuted in Iconium. When I preached, the people of the city were divided. Half of the population believed and the other half plotted to kill me. Barnabas and I had to flee the city (Acts 14:1-7).
- stoned at Lystra (Acts 14:8–20).
- friction with Barnabas over John Mark occurred (Acts 15:36–41).
- imprisoned in Philippi (Acts 16:16–40).
- attacked by Jews (Acts 18:12–17).
- suffered many hardships (2 Cor. 1:3–10).
- riot in Ephesus (Acts 9:23–41).
- attacked and beaten by Jews (Acts 21:27–32).
- arrested by a Roman commander (Acts 21:33–35).
- went on trial before Felix the governor on false charges (Acts 24:1–21).

- went on trial before Festus, where I appealed to Caesar (Acts 25:1–12).
- shipwrecked on my way to Rome, stranded on the island of Malta, bitten by a poisonous snake, and suspected of being a murderer, and then acclaimed as a god (Acts 28:1–10).
- arrived in Rome as a prisoner, was eventually freed, but was imprisoned again and eventually killed.

I'm sure Paul would have preferred to dwell with the Christians and be able to minister to others in Jerusalem and the surrounding areas about the wonderful miracle God had performed in his life. Most of us, if given a choice, would not choose the hard road. But taking the easy way doesn't teach us anything. From my experience, it is when we are, as some say, "between the devil and the deep blue sea" or "between a rock and a hard place" that we seek God fervently. Sometimes we get too complacent on the mountaintop and God has to knock us down into the valley before we remember him. Obviously, God wanted to transform Paul's heart and his mind, and for this, he had to go into the wilderness.

When we go through the wilderness experience, it tests our faith and strengthens our commitment to God. As a Pharisee, Paul probably lived in the lap of luxury in many ways. He certainly had many privileges. Being in the wilderness could not have been a pleasant time for Paul, but he persevered because he knew that the one true God had called him for a divine purpose—he was preparing him in the wilderness, transforming him, and only then would he be ready to minister.

If you are going through a difficult time, try to learn what God is trying to teach you. You may feel that what you are going through is useless, unprofitable, and doesn't quite make sense, but there are benefits to being called into the wilderness. If you are willing to place your full trust in God, you will discover that those times that seem most difficult are actually the times that are most spiritually productive. For it is only then that God is able to prepare you for his work.

Remember there are four stages: the call and purpose, the preparation, the transformation, and the future.

What stage of the process are you? How are you faring?

Embrace each stage and trust God! Great things are ahead!

Even Jesus, the Son of God, had to go through the wilderness. Let us look at how he handled this wilderness experience.

CHAPTER 30

Jesus

Navigating through the Wilderness Successfully

I wish I could put in this book as much as I learned about Jesus since I began to write this book. But it would be impossible! Therefore, I will write just a few pertinent facts.

Jesus, like several of the biblical personalities we've studied, also went through a wilderness experience; but unlike some of these personalities, he showed us how to pass through it successfully. His amazing entrance on earth is covered in the Gospels of the New Testament. His short time on earth shook up royalty, the common people, and nature itself. Take time to read the Gospels and learn about this awesome person, Jesus. His whole life was a process. From the cradle to the grave, his life had a call, a purpose, and preparation and equipped him for his work as the divine human Messiah. Jesus' call was to save a sinful world. He, being without sin and the Son of God, was the only qualified candidate. Despite claims by many human religious leaders, no one else could accomplish this task.

Jesus' Call and Purpose

1. To seek and save the lost (Luke 19:10)
2. To give us eternal life (John 10:10, 28)
3. To give his life as a ransom for many (Mark 10:45)
4. To die for our sins (1 Cor. 15:3; Gal. 1:4; 1 Pet. 3:18)
5. To reconcile us to God (2 Cor. 5:18–19; Eph. 2:14 -17)
6. To rise from the grave for our justification (Romans 4:25)
7. To destroy the works of Satan (Heb. 2:14; 1 John 3:8)

Jesus' Preparation

We have to prepare for every task we have to accomplish. Scripture tells us that when John the Baptist saw Jesus coming toward him, he said, "Look, the Lamb of God, who takes away the sin of the world! This is the one I meant when I said, A man who comes after has surpassed me because he was before me. I myself did not know him, but the reason I came baptizing with water was that he might be revealed to Israel" (John 1:29–31).

Scripture also tell us that when Jesus came from Galilee to the Jordan to be baptized by John, John tried to deter him. He said,

> I need to be baptized by you and do you come to me? Jesus replied, let it be so now; it is proper for us to do this to fulfill all righteousness. Then John consented. As soon as Jesus was baptized, he went up out of the water. At that moment heaven was opened, and he saw the Spirit of God descending like a dove and lighting on him. And a voice from heaven said, this is my Son, whom I love; with him I am well pleased. (Matt. 3:13–17)

Jesus' baptism signified his imminent readiness as the Messiah and the beginning of his Messianic ministry. Several significant factors marked his baptism:

1. It was to fulfill all righteousness.
2. God consecrated and officially approved him, as shown by the descent of the Holy Spirit.
3. God the Father endorsed him.
4. All three persons of the Trinity were present.

There was an eyewitness. John's testimony said,

> I saw the Spirit come down from heaven as a dove and remain on him. I would not have known except that the one who sent me to baptize with water told me, the man on whom you see the Spirit come down and remain is he who will baptize with the Holy Spirit. I have seen and testify that this is the Son of God. (John 1:31–34)

After Jesus was baptized by John and anointed by the Holy Spirit, Scriptures say that Jesus was "led by the Spirit into the wilderness, being tempted for forty days by the devil. And in those days He ate nothing, and afterward, when they had ended, He was hungry" (Luke 4:1–2).

There was nothing in that dry, arid wilderness to eat. There was nothing and nobody to comfort Jesus, except God the Father and the Holy Spirit. Jesus spent his time in the wilderness in intense fasting and prayer, being prepared and empowered by the Holy Spirit. He went into the wilderness as a carpenter and came out as a minister. As a result, Jesus returned to Galilee in the power of the Holy Spirit.

Jesus' Equipment for Ministry

Jesus was sent by his Father; led, prepared, and equipped by the Holy Spirit; and now, he was ready to minister. He explained his task in Luke 4:18. He says,

> The Spirit of the Lord is on me, because he has anointed me to preach good news to the poor. He has sent me to proclaim freedom for the prisoners and recovery of sight for the blind, to release the oppressed, to proclaim the year of the Lord's favor.

Prior to Jesus' birth, Isaiah the prophet had prophesied about the long-awaited Messiah. He said,

> A shoot will come up from the stump of Jesse; from his roots a Branch will bear fruit. The Spirit of the Lord will rest on him – the Spirit of wisdom and of understanding, the Spirit of counsel and of power, the Spirit of knowledge and of the fear of the Lord—and he will delight in the fear of the Lord. He will not judge by what he sees with his eyes, or decide by what he hears with his ears; but with righteousness he will judge the needy, with justice he will give decisions for the poor of the earth. He will strike the earth with the rod of his mouth; with the breath of his lips he will slay the wicked. Righteousness will be his belt and faithfulness the sash around his waist. (Isa. 11:2–5)

It is clear from this prophecy that Jesus would come as a man to fulfill his Father's will, and he would be empowered and equipped by the Holy Spirit to carry out this purpose. Luke 4:1 tells us, "Jesus, was full of the Holy Spirit," and Luke 14:14 confirms: "Jesus returned to Galilee in the power of the Spirit." This clearly indicates that Jesus began his ministry not in his own power but filled with the power of the Holy Spirit.

Conversely, whenever God calls us to ministry, we are also equipped by the Holy Spirit to carry out our calling. However, there are usually obstacles placed before us by the enemy. For example, when Jesus finished his forty days of fasting, sure enough, guess who showed up. After fasting forty days and forty nights, Jesus was in a physically weakened state. He was hungry, thirsty, tired, and parched from being in the desert for such a long period. The tempter came to him and said, "If you are the Son of God, tell these stones to become bread."

Jesus could have used his supernatural powers to fulfill his personal needs, but he didn't. He answered, "It is written; Man does not live on bread alone, but on every word that comes from the mouth of God."

Then the tempter wanted Jesus to throw himself down to prove that God would send his angels to protect him. Once again, Jesus used the Word to rebuke the tempter. Jesus was not in a popularity contest! He did not have to prove anything to anyone. Therefore, he was not going to use his power to win people over to his side. Satan was not going to give up so easily, though. Jesus was at his weakest physically, so Satan paraded "all the kingdoms of the world and their splendors" before Jesus and promised to give them to him if he would worship him. What a joke! Jesus owns a lot more than the kingdoms of the world. It is similar to my threatening to withhold a ride on my bicycle from someone who drives a Lamborghini.

Jesus is our model in these things. He did not compromise with Satan; neither should we if we want the power of the Holy Spirit to help us pass the tests in the wilderness. Jesus navigated the wilderness successfully through the power of the Holy Spirit and by speaking the Word of God. He trusted his Father. He knew him intimately. He knew he would not leave him alone in the wilderness. He also knew the Word of God was power. It has the power to fight against Satan.

The apostle Paul encourages believers to fight the evil one with the Word of God. He says, "Take the helmet of salvation and the sword of the Spirit which is the Word of God. And pray in the Spirit on all occasions with all kinds of prayers and requests" (Eph. 6:17).

James advises us, "Submit yourselves, then, to God. Resist the devil and he will flee from you. Come near to God and he will come near to you" (James 4:7–8).

Isaiah 12:2 says, "Surely God is my salvation; I will trust and not be afraid. The Lord, the Lord, is my strength and my song; he has become my salvation."

Psalm 27:1 says, "The Lord is my light and my salvation—whom shall I fear? The Lord is the stronghold of my life—of whom shall I be afraid?"

There is absolutely nothing to fear from the devil!

The same methods that Jesus used to subdue Satan and pass the test in the wilderness will work for any of us, because the Holy Spirit resides in God's children. This is what makes it possible for us to resist the devil and overcome his wiles!

A Thought to Consider

If we are not God's children, we cannot navigate the wilderness successfully. We have to acknowledge Jesus as the Son of God and accept him as Lord and Savior to be called a child of God.

Another thought: if one does not study the Word and have it in one's heart, that heart is like an open cistern that is vulnerable to spiritual contamination and spiritual infections. This makes it easier to succumb to temptations when they come our way.

Food for Thought

The contents of our heart are what we are able to give out. The Word of God has to be in our heart to make biblical decisions, to resist the Devil, and to be a light to the world.

We cannot give out what we don't have.

CHAPTER 31

Oh Lord, Help! It's My Turn

Growing Ouch by Ouch

So ... you're in the wilderness? We get sent into the wilderness for different reasons, but basically, God sends us there so that:

1. We can put him in exclusive control of our lives.
2. We can learn to trust him no matter what we are facing.
3. We can understand the purpose of being there and his purpose for our lives.
4. He can prepare us and equip us for ministry or the next season of our life.
5. He can prepare us for service and usefulness to him.

When we are sent into the wilderness, some of us are like the Israelites. We have the "grasshopper mentality." We look at the difficulty of our situation, rather than at the power of God. We might seem like grasshoppers in our own eyes, but in God's eyes, we are giants, we are champions, and we are winners!

The grasshopper mentality is Satan's biggest weapon against Christians. It worked on the Israelites, and it is still working on many Christians. We are short-sighted when we bail out of our marriage before we see if God can mend it and use it for his glory. We are short-sighted when we complain about our children walking away from the Lord, instead of praying for them and asking the Lord to turn their face toward him. If your family, business, or life is in disarray, is your vision 20/20 in the situation? God said to Ezekiel, "Can these bones live?" He said to Moses, "What do you have in your hand?" We are short-sighted and blinded when we give up before we see what God has planned for us!

When we cease to put God's promises first and do not focus on who he is, we play into the enemy's hands. We lose such a blessing when we cease to struggle and we give up because we want to live a stress-free life. It is so easy to take the easy path, but let me inform you: only dead men have no stress. So check your pulse. If your heart is beating, you will have stress. Don't let the enemy fool you.

Where is your faith in the difficult times? Jesus says, "I am the true vine and my Father is the gardener. He cuts off every branch in me that bears no fruits, while every branch that does not bear fruit he prunes so that it will be even more fruitful" (John 5:1–2).

If we are true believers, we will grow "ouch by ouch." Sometimes it will be a little snip. Sometimes it will be a big snap. But if we complain about the pruning, we will not ever grow spiritually; we will stay a long time in that wilderness and will probably never reach the heights God has ordained for us. As we are snipped, clipped, and pruned, we will grow spiritually. Our faith will expand and grow as we continue to strive and thrive.

The Israelites wanted to turn back to the so-called pleasure and the fleshpots of Egypt when the path got rocky and difficult. How about you? Do you want go back? Did you turn back from the path God ordained for you? A lesson we can learn from the Israelites is that when they were disobedient to God's directions and focused on their own needs, they were defeated by the Amalakites and all the other *"ites"* on their journey.

Don't be discouraged. We do not have to be defeated by our situation or by our wounds or broken promises. A wilderness period or a period when God seems to be silent may go on forever, but that is the time when God's grace is manifested most powerfully. Those are the times when our faith seems to grow stronger, and we become more spiritually mature. As the old adage goes, "This is when the rubber meets the road," because there are no hindrances.

The Holy Spirit speaks, and we listen. He gives us the strength we need to go on because: "As your day is so your strength shall be" (Deut. 33:25).

The Word of God says, "The Lord is my strength and my shield; my heart trusts in him, and I am helped" (Ps. 28:7).

Isaiah 40:29–30 says,

He gives strength to those who are tired and more power to those who are weak. The people who trust the Lord will become strong again. They will rise up as an eagle in the sky; they will run and not need rest; they will walk and not become tired.

The Holy Spirit gives us the power to resist the temptation of breaking God's word, to speak when we should be quiet, and to break apart when we should build up. On the days when we think we've failed, Paul tells us that we are more than conquerors.

In all these things we are more than conquerors through him who loved us. For I am convinced that neither death nor life, neither angels nor demons, neither the present nor the future, nor any powers, neither height nor depth, nor anything else in all creation, will be able to separate us from the love of God that is in Christ Jesus our Lord. (Rom. 8:37–39)

What a wonderful comfort! God gives us strength when we need it. He protects us, he gives us the power to resist temptations, and he prepares us for the ministry he has planned for us. No matter how many times we have failed, he still loves us. This is the time when we have to depend totally on God's grace. Paul the apostle says that he was given a thorn in the flesh. Many people have given different explanations as to what this thorn was, but the Bible doesn't say specifically. He said that he pleaded with God three times to take away this thorn, but the only answer he got was, "My grace is sufficient for you, for my power is made perfect in weakness" (2 Cor. 12:9).

God's grace has always been and will always be sufficient. Therefore, one of the cries of my heart as a Christian has always been the desire for God to use me in a special way. One skill that I have developed through a painful divorce is being able to listen more carefully to people who are going through difficult relationships. In my previous book, *God's Grace: A Long Night's Journey into Day*, I mentioned how God had changed me and was still in the process of transforming me. I was in this wilderness of desolation for many years. In the wilderness, I learned how to really cry out to God and found that his grace was definitely sufficient for me!

Somehow in the wilderness, truth can be more easily discerned. We see ourselves for who we are and who God is. Going through my experience, I saw that even though I had made many mistakes in my life, I was loved, highly favored, and forgiven. I saw God as my heavenly Father who is perfect yet loves me—this imperfect child of his. That gave me the courage I needed to go on when the foundation of my life shifted. It gave me the anchor of hope to hang my future and the faith to know that he will never leave nor forsake me, no matter what other mistakes I might make in my life. In the wilderness, I had to give God total control over my life and allow him to be God in my life. In the wilderness, I developed a relationship with God that I never had before. *His grace was truly sufficient for me!*

When you have no one else to turn to, you learn absolute trust in God, and you are totally humble before God. This time of despair was the instrument God used to get me past the obstacles to my spiritual growth. He also used this time to allow me discover him in new ways. It was through the most difficult period of my life that I learned to identify with Paul, when he said, "I want to know Christ and the power of his resurrection and the fellowship of sharing in his sufferings, becoming like him in his death, and so, somehow, to attain to the resurrection from the dead" (Phil. 3:10).

As you allow God to prune you and grow you, you too can identify with Paul. As an avid gardener and garden designer, I believe the wilderness experience represents the "winterized" period of a plant. Some plants need to be winterized for spring. To winterize means to fix, gear up, prepare, ready, or "make ready or suitable, equip in advance for a particular purpose." In other words, if some plants are not winterized, you won't get flowers in spring. Likewise, God has placed us in the wilderness for a particular purpose. There will be spring after your winter. So don't run away from the tough times. If you do, you are only cheating yourself.

If you are in a difficult situation or have many challenges, you are in good company. The Bible's elite list consisted of Abraham, who was in the wilderness because he was following God's instructions; Moses, because he failed and ran for his life and then was led back into the wilderness with the children of Israel; and David, because King Saul was trying to kill him. We are not told, specifically, if Paul was forced to go into the wilderness after his encounter with Jesus on the Damascus road, but he said that he went immediately to Arabia. It seems that he went by choice, where he was taught by Jesus himself.

Jesus was led into the wilderness in preparation for his ministry. After the wilderness experience, we are told that Abraham's experience transformed him. Moses spent forty years in the wilderness and was transformed to become God's leader of his chosen people. Moses was so transformed that it is said of him, "Now Moses was a very humble man, more humble than anyone else on the face of the earth" (Num. 12:3). David's transformation made him one of Israel's greatest kings. Jesus' wilderness experience inaugurated his ministry, and after Paul's time in the wilderness, he came back with the majority of the New Testament.

I would suggest that you stay exactly where you are! Don't try to circumvent your transformation!

Although there are times when we want to run away because the children have gone astray, a spouse has abandoned the family, the marriage is falling apart, or the finances are in shambles, trust God! What's the point of having a God who wants to be a Father, who wants to walk with us, talk with us, answer our prayers, and transform us in his image, if we don't trust him to guide us through our difficulties?

So often, instead of facing God and allowing him to be God, we run away and hide. We try to Band-Aid our problems, our inadequacies, and our challenges and shut down, when what we need is to open up to the Great Physician. Do you think God can't see behind the mask we wear? The mask is as transparent as glass to him. One advantage of being in the wilderness is that we have no distractions. It's just us, God, our wounds, and everything that we bring to him. Remember that he is the God who will heal anything that we bring him.

A wilderness experience demands transformation and provides preparation for something special!

Pray that God will help you to learn from the wilderness experience and that the experience will equip you to fulfill your God-given purpose.

CHAPTER 32

Healing

Cleansing the Wound
Vignette

Years ago, I met a young student who was smart, sassy, and always optimistic. She told me that she had completed her university degree in her country, but because English was not her first language, she had to study English. I later learned from some of her friends that she had come to Canada as a refugee after being in a refugee camp for several years. Not only had she had to run and hide for weeks in the jungle, but she also had been sexually assaulted several times during that time. Yet I never saw her angry or downcast. She was completely free from her past. She had forgiven her abusers and had shed the shackles of her past. She had made the decision to allow her wounds to heal. She participated in her healing. The only way she could have done this was to cleanse her wounds through forgiveness.

Have you ever been treated unjustly? Has someone hurt you or betrayed you so badly that it left you reeling in pain? God is the ultimate healer. Here are some elements that play a role in the healing process.

Prayer

James 5:14 says,

Is any one of you in trouble? He should pray. Is anyone happy? Let him sing songs of praise. Is any one of you sick? He should call the elders of the church to pray over him and anoint him with oil in the name of the Lord. And the prayer offered in faith will make the sick person well.

1 Peter 3:12 says, "For the eyes of the Lord are on the righteous and his ears are attentive to their prayer, but the face of the Lord is against those who do evil."

In Psalm 86:5–7, David, the psalmist, is confident that if he prays and calls upon the Lord, he will answer his prayers. He says, "You are forgiving and good, O Lord, abounding in love to all who call to you. Hear my prayer, O Lord; listen to my cry for mercy. In the day of my trouble I will call to you, for you will answer me."

Faith

In Luke 18:35–42, as Jesus was walking by, a blind beggar began to shout his name. The crowds tried to shut him up, but he persisted in his efforts to gain Jesus' attention. Jesus heard him amid the noise of the crowd and stopped. He asked him a crucial question: "What do you want me to do for you?" The man answered, "Lord, I want to see." Jesus responded, "Receive your sight; your faith has healed you."

The apostle Paul reminds us that as believers, we do go through spiritual warfare, and the only way to win against the enemy is to put on the full armor of God. In addition to the belt of truth, the breastplate of righteousness, and the gospel of peace, Paul says, "Take up the shield of faith, with which you can extinguish all the flaming arrows of the evil one" (Eph. 6:16).

Simply put, he says, "We live by faith, not by sight."

Intercession

In Isaiah 62:6–7, the prophet Isaiah says, "I have posted watchmen on your walls, O Jerusalem; they will never be silent day or night. You who call on the Lord, give yourselves no rest, and give him no rest till he establishes Jerusalem and makes her the praise of the earth."

My understanding of Old Testament times is that watchmen were posted on the city walls to look out for danger and to give warning to the residents of the city. The watchmen's responsibility required vigilance, diligence, and fidelity. It was their duty to guard and protect the citizens. You can imagine the catastrophe that would fall on the city and its people if these watchmen failed to do their duties. In the New Testament context, we, as believers, have a mortal enemy of our souls. We are in spiritual warfare for our families, our homes, and our church. We must intercede—watch and pray for them!

In Biblical times, the enemy would try to take the city, its residents, and whole nations captive. In our modern times, there is no difference. Our homes, our families, and our church are under assault by the enemy. We hear of church leaders being taken as spiritual captives; we hear of Christians not honoring God as the head of their homes and succumbing to unbiblical behaviors; we hear of children raised in Christian homes getting involved in drugs and other ungodly practices, even though they have been taught differently. The Devil is at work! Yet many Christians don't recognize that—or rather, they choose to ignore that fact. They have abandoned their duties. Psalm 127 reminds us that the Lord has to be the center of our homes and activities, or we are wasting our time. Verse 1 says, "Unless the Lord builds the house, its builders labour in vain. Unless the Lord watches over the city, the watchmen stand guard in vain."

In Mark 14:22–41, we have an incident in the garden of Gethsemane between Jesus and his disciples. Jesus felt the imminent burden of the cross, and he needed to communicate with his Father. He said to his disciples, "Sit here while I go over there and pray."

Scripture tells us that he began to be sorrowful and troubled, and he said to them, "My soul is overwhelmed with sorrow to the point of death. Stay here and keep watch with me."

Going still further, Jesus fell with his face to the ground and prayed, "My Father, if it is possible, may this cup be taken from me. Yet not as I will, but as you will."

When Jesus returned, he found his disciples sleeping. He asked, "Could you men not keep watch with me for one hour?"

Then he said to them, "Watch and pray so that you will not fall into temptation. The spirit is willing but the body is weak."

How often have you felt that you were abandoned in the hour of your greatest need? Have you also said, "If only I had had someone praying for me, I would have been stronger? I would have been able to resist that spiritual pitfall."

Just remember that God has not given up on you. He has not abandoned you. He is right beside you in your greatest need. He says he will never leave you nor forsake you.

Lately, God has brought to my attention his principles on forgiveness and some things he wants me to do in this season of my life. Out of this communication, I've resolved to do two things totally and under the control of the Holy Spirit:

1. Pray more

Jesus himself teaches us about prayer. He says,

And when you pray, do not be like the hypocrites, for they love to pray standing in the synagogues and on the street corners to be seen by men. I tell you the truth, they have received their reward in full. But when you pray, go into your room, close the door and pray to your Father, who is unseen. Then your Father, who sees what is done in secret, will reward you. And when you pray, do not keep on babbling like pagans, for they think they will be heard because of their many words. Do not be like them, for your Father knows what you need before you ask him. This, then, is how you should pray ... (Matt. 6:5–9)

After that, Jesus taught them the Lord's Prayer.

2. Take the Scripture below to heart.

Jesus said,

You have heard that it was said, love your neighbor and hate your enemy. But I tell you: Love your enemies and pray for those who persecute you, that you may be sons of your Father in heaven. He causes his sun to rise on the evil and the good, and sends rain on the righteous and the unrighteous. If you love those who love you, what reward will you get? Are not even the tax collectors doing that? And if you greet only your brothers, what are you doing more than others? Do not even pagans do that? Be perfect, therefore, as your heavenly Father is perfect. (Matt. 5:43–48)

Food for Thought

Until we forgive the people who have offended us, we remain their prisoners.

CHAPTER 33

The Wilderness: Passing Through or Camping Out

The Biblical Measures of Forgiveness

Most of us stay longer in the wilderness than we ought to because we have not made the decision to forgive the person or persons who have hurt us. So instead of visiting the wilderness, we pitch our tent and camp out—just us and our wounds.

I did not grow up on a farm. I used to proudly describe myself as a city slicker. One day in my teens, I went to visit my cousins in the country. I saw something that totally grossed me out, as the typical teenager would say. I saw a cow eating and chewing. It then started to regurgitate its food. It was totally disgusting to see that. I later read that it was necessary for the cow to chew its cud and regurgitate its food for digestive purposes.

As I was writing this section, I thought that often, we camp out and regurgitate every wound, every pain, every incident, and every cruel word that has ever been done or said to us. I know from experience that "talking out" is part of the healing process. But when does talking it out stop and regurgitation begin? When does praying and healing begin? I know I was finally on my road to recovery when one day, I heard of another lie someone had spread about me, and I just said, "Whatever!" After I said that one word, with the usual tone and attitude of a teenager, it made me realize that this person's words and actions were no longer of significance to me. This was part of my healing.

Each person's healing will take different paths or directions. The main thing we have to think about is, why not forgive the one who has let you down? Is it possible to begin to pray for this person who has caused so much wounding?

I remember being very annoyed when people kept telling me to "move on," right after my marriage ended. I had been left with broken dreams and broken promises and for a while, I found it difficult to pick up the pieces of my life. I know people meant well, but I wished people had just loved me without trying to be "helpful." I had to get to the stage of moving on without anyone pushing me to move or even to forgive. When you are hurt and bleeding, you don't need people to lecture you, just to love you. I had to move on in my time, not when people deemed it so.

As an illustration, when we get a physical cut, it bleeds and then after a while, it begins to heal. The cut heals in stages, not instantly, as we would like it to. Even after the healing, there still remains a bit of tenderness if we push too hard on the spot that was cut. Similarly, when we are emotionally and psychologically wounded, it takes time to heal. We don't heal instantly; we heal in stages, even while making progress.

As we make progress, we will get to the stage where we don't focus on our pain as much as we did in the beginning. The next stage is to intentionally make the decision to forgive. And after more progress, we should begin to pray for the people who hurt us.

Why should we pray for the people who wound us? It is simple. It is a biblical principle, one that God himself practiced when he offered forgiveness to a fallen human race. John 3:16 says, "For God so loved the world that he gave his one and only son that whoever believes in him shall not perish but have eternal life."

Many people who wound us are as happy as a lark, merrily carrying on with life and without a care in the world. But as people who have been wounded, we have to become more sensitive to people who are hurting. As we move on through the various stages of healing and forgiveness, we can be resources who can tell of the grace of God and his work in our life.

CHAPTER 34

Principles of Biblical Forgiveness

Forgiveness does not come easily for most of us. Our natural instinct when we have been wounded is to recoil in self-protection, wrap our "pharisaic" robe tightly across our chest, and stew over the offense. We don't naturally overflow with mercy, grace, and forgiveness when we feel we've been wronged. However, that gown of self-protection will become like a shroud if we are not obedient to God's Word regarding forgiveness.

Is it easy to forgive? No! It is not easy in our natural self.

Is it easy to forgive? Absolutely! It is very easy when we want to please God. I believe forgiveness involves three steps:

1. It is a choice we make through a decision of our will.
2. It is motivated by obedience to God.
3. It is a command of God.

The Elements of Atonement and Forgiveness

Forgiveness carries a price; it is not free. From the beginning of time, sin had a price, and someone always had to pay. When our foreparents, Adam and Eve, sinned, they transgressed against God and needed to be forgiven. God had to kill a sacrificial lamb to atone for their sins, thereby resulting in their forgiveness. In the New Testament, Jesus, as the Lamb of God, gave up his life to atone for our sins, because humankind needed to obtain forgiveness from God.

Element 1—Sin of Humanity

It was quite clear that someone had to pay the price for the sin of humanity, and in John 1:29, the writer says: "The next day John saw

Jesus coming toward him and said, Look, the Lamb of God, who takes away the sin of the world?"

Element 2—Blood Must Be Shed

When Moses had proclaimed every commandment of the law to all the people, he took the blood of calves, together with water, scarlet wool and branches of hyssop, and sprinkled the scroll and all the people. He said, this is the blood of the covenant, which God has commanded you to keep. In the same way, he sprinkled with the blood both the tabernacle and everything used in its ceremonies. In fact, the law requires that nearly everything be cleansed with blood, and without the shedding of blood there is no forgiveness (Heb. 9:19–22).

Element 3—Substitutionary Sacrifice Is Offered

"My dear children, I write this to you so that you not sin. But if anybody does sin, we have one who speaks to the Father in our defense—Jesus Christ, the Righteous One. He is the atoning sacrifice for our sins and not only for ours but also for the sins of the whole world" (1 John 2:1–2).

Element 4—Guilt Is Transferred to the Substitute

"God made him who had no sin to be sin for us, so that in him we might become the righteousness of God" (2 Cor. 5:21).

Element 5—Forgiveness Is Granted

For all have sinned and fall short of the glory of God, and are justified freely by his grace through the redemption that came by Christ Jesus. God presented him as a sacrifice of atonement, through faith in his blood. He did this to demonstrate his justice, because in his forbearance he had left the sins committed beforehand unpunished—he did it to demonstrate his justice at the present time, so as to be just and the one who justifies those who have faith in Jesus. (Rom. 3:23–26)

Here, God made the provision to forgive mankind's sins, not because he took them lightly but because he took them so seriously that only the life of his own Son could suffice.

Forgiveness is the decision on the part of the offended to suffer the penalty due the offender. God offers forgiveness to humanity through the atoning work of the cross by Jesus Christ. Jesus is the one who suffered all the consequences of the "abominable" acts mankind has ever done. Scripture tells us that all men have sinned against God and deserve the penalty of eternal destruction. But John 3:16 says, "God loved us and sent His Son to die for our sins so that we might have eternal life."

Some of the results of Christ's atoning blood are:

1. Our sins are forgiven.

"In him we have redemption through his blood, the forgiveness of sins, in accordance with the riches of God's grace that he lavished on us with all wisdom and understanding" (Eph. 1:7–8).

2. We are redeemed.

"For you know that it was not with perishable things such as silver or gold that you were redeemed from the empty way of life handed down to you from your forefathers, but with the precious blood of Christ, a lamb without blemish or defect" (1 Pet. 1:18–19).

3. We are saved and reconciled with God.

"Since we have now been justified by his blood, how much more shall we be saved from God's wrath through him? For if, when we were God's enemies, we were reconciled to him through the death of his Son, how much more, having been reconciled, shall we be saved through his life?" (Rom. 5:9–10).

4. The power of the Devil is destroyed.

"Since the children have flesh and blood, he too shared in their humanity so that by his death he might destroy him who holds the power of death—that is, the devil—and free those who all their lives were held in slavery by their fear of death" (Heb. 2:14–15).

"And having disarmed the powers and authorities, he made a public spectacle of them, triumphing over them by the cross" (Col. 2:15).

Forgiveness Relative to Christian Believers

As we know, God forgives mankind because of his compassion, love, grace, and mercy. But how does forgiveness pertain to believers, followers of Jesus Christ? Matthew 18:15–17 gives advice on how to treat a brother or sister who sins against you. In addition, in Matthew 18:21–35, Jesus tells a parable of the unmerciful servant after Peter came and inquired about forgiveness.

"Then Peter came to Jesus and asked, Lord, how many times shall I forgive my brother when he sins against me? Up to seven times? Jesus answered, I tell you, not seven times, but seventy times."

Jesus' parable expands on the theme of forgiveness. He says that the kingdom of heaven is like a king who wanted to settle accounts with his servants. A man who owned him ten thousand talents was unable to pay him. He then ordered the man and his whole family to be put in jail. However, the man begged and pleaded for his life and the lives of his family. He asked the master to be patient with him until he paid back what he owed. Not soon after, the master was told that the same servant to whom he had shown mercy had grabbed and choked a fellow servant and had had him thrown in jail because he owned him one hundred denarii. The master was very angry because he had shown the servant mercy, but the servant had not shown his fellow servant mercy. The master then threw the unmerciful servant into jail.

Jesus finished his parable with the words, "This is how my heavenly Father will treat each of you unless you forgive your brother from your heart."

If it takes us until eternity, we have to keep forgiving someone who has wounded us. Why? We forgive because God has forgiven our trespasses. According to Ephesians 4:32: "Be kind and compassionate to one another, forgiving each other, just as in Christ God forgave you."

In general, forgiveness is a conscious decision on the part of the one who was wounded to forgive and release the person who has wounded.

God as Our Example

God is our example of perfect forgiveness. He did not overlook our sins, but he sent Jesus to bear the penalty for them. That is genuine forgiveness! Those who place their trust in Jesus Christ, as the one who died for their sins, will experience this forgiveness. Several times, I've made references to making choices, the call of God, preparation, and transformation. This is a time to make a choice to accept God's forgiveness, if you haven't already done so.

Hebrews 9:27 says, "It is appointed unto man once to die and after that the judgement."

Do you want to enter God's presence, knowing you're forgiven? It is up to us whether we ask and receive God's forgiveness and meet him as forgiver and Savior or we reject his forgiveness and meet him as judge.

Finally, our definition of forgiveness must include the fact that true forgiveness is not earned but given freely by the offended. Therefore, in response to God's example, we should forgive others. You might say, "But you don't know what he [or she] did to me. You don't know the things his friends are saying about me. You don't know … "

My reply is, "Yes, I do know some of those things, because I have been wounded too."

As the cliché goes, "Been there, done that, got the T-shirt."

But when I consider that Jesus is the Son of God, perfect in every way, and he was maligned, mistreated, lied to, spat upon, and crucified—well! My wounds cannot be compared to his, can they?

I concur with the apostle Paul when he says, "Bear with each other and forgive whatever grievances you may have against one another. Forgive as the Lord forgave you" (Col. 3:13).

There is no limit to forgiveness.

Question to Ponder

Even though I have been wounded, can I be a true forgiver and forgive from the heart?

CHAPTER 35

I'm Hurting; Why
Should I Forgive?

Forgive Because It Is Necessary

There are several reasons why we should forgive the people who have
wounded us.

1. It is a command, not a suggestion.

Jesus said: "But when you are praying, first forgive anyone you are
holding a grudge against, so that your Father in heaven will forgive
your sins, too" (Mark 11:25, 26).

2. It restores Christian fellowship.

"Now it is time to forgive him and comfort him. Otherwise he
may become so discouraged that he won't be able to recover. Now
show him that you still love him" (2 Cor. 2:5–10).

3. It is necessary for spiritual cleansing.

James says that the elders of the church should pray over those who
are sick, and the Lord will make them well, adding, "And anyone who
has committed sins will be forgiven" (James 5:15–16) .

Corrie ten Boom, a Christian woman who survived a Nazi
concentration camp during the Holocaust, said, "Forgiveness is to set
a prisoner free, and to realize the prisoner was you."

According to Mark Twain, "Unforgiveness is like drinking poison
and expecting the other person to die."

We may ask, "Why should I forgive the ones who have wounded
me?" The answer is simply that we are the ones who suffer most

when we choose not to forgive. When we do forgive, our hearts are set free from the anger, bitterness, resentment, and hurt that previously imprisoned us.

I also believe we should pray for the person we need to forgive. We can pray for God to intercede in the situation, to deal with the injustices, to judge the person's life, to take away our burden of pain, and then we can leave everything at the altar.

We no longer have to carry the anger or the pain. Although it is normal for us to feel anger toward sin and injustice, it is not our job to judge the other person in his or her sin. I used to pray every psalm of judgment against the people who wounded me, and God let me … until I heard the voice of the Holy Spirit saying, "Let it go."

I finally reached a point where I pinned a cross on my wall and literally pinned the names of the people at the foot of the cross. Sometimes, we have to do things literally to make it work. Pinning the names to the cross worked for me. Do whatever works for you.

So what should our attitude be? Our attitude should be that we choose to let go completely, as soon as we can, of people who have wounded us. How do we do this?

First, we must leave vengeance open to God. Let God be God.

Second, according to Luke 6:37, "Do not judge, and you will not be judged. Do not condemn, and you will not be condemned. Forgive, and you will be forgiven."

CHAPTER 36

Attitude Checkup

Attitude of Forgiveness

Why must I forgive? The best and *only* reason to forgive is because Jesus commanded us to forgive. We learn from Scripture that if we don't forgive, neither will we be forgiven:

"For if you forgive men when they sin against you, your heavenly Father will also forgive you. But if you do not forgive men their sins, your Father will not forgive your sins" (Matt. 6:14–16)

Attitude of Trust

We also forgive so that our prayers will not be hindered. "And when you stand praying, if you hold anything against anyone, forgive him, so that your Father in heaven may forgive you your sins" (Mark 11:25)

Attitude of Joy

I am fearfully and wonderfully made.

We are all wounded, in one form or another. We are all inadequate in many areas, and on our best days, our self-esteem is very fragile. I can recall every feeling and emotion, years ago, when I was rejected and felt abandoned. I felt like an old rag that had been used and tossed in the garbage. These are strong feelings. Some might even ridicule the feelings, but they are real because they are mine. No matter how strong a self-esteem you have, wounds can pierce like an arrow.

These adversarial attacks can completely annihilate us when we forget who we really are—unless we go back and read Psalm 139 and sink those words of love deep into our heart.

Attitude of Identity

Who are we? Our identity is in God—no one else! I remember saying to someone who wounded me, "I am God's child, and he will take care of me." Those words kept me sane each time I remembered the hurting, the obstacles I had to face, the difficulties, the loneliness, and everything that goes with being wounded. Every day I would cry out to God and remind him—and myself—that I was his child, and he promised to take care of me. I would constantly read Psalm 139 and remind myself, "I am fearfully and wonderfully made." Over and over, like a mantra, I would thrust my fist in the air defiantly and shout as loudly as I could, "I am a child of God, and he will take care of me."

Attitude of Gratitude

Rejoice that God knows you, cares for you, and will not let anything happen to you. Psalm 139:1–18 says,

O Lord, you have searched me and you know me. You know when I sit and when I rise; you perceive my thoughts from afar. You discern my going out and my lying down; you are familiar with all my ways. Before a word is on my tongue you know it completely, O Lord. You hem me in—behind and before; you have laid your hand upon me. Such knowledge is too wonderful for me, too lofty for me to attain.

Where can I go from your Spirit? Where can I flee from your presence? If I go up to the heavens, you are there; if I make my bed in the depths, you are there. If I rise on the wings of the dawn, if I settle on the far side of the sea, even there your hand will guide me, your right hand will hold me fast. If I say, surely the darkness will hide me and the light become night around me, even the darkness will not be dark to you; the night will shine like the day, for darkness is as light to you. For you created my inmost being; you knit me together in my mother's womb. I praise you because I am fearfully and wonderfully made; your works are wonderful, I know that full well. My frame was not hidden from you when I was made in the secret place. When I was woven together in the depths of the earth, your eyes saw my unformed body. All the days ordained for me were written in your book before one of them came to be. How precious to me are your thoughts, O God! How vast is the sum of them! Were I to count them, they would outnumber the grains of sand. When I awake, I am still with you.

Wonderful! I am happy to say that God has not failed me. He is still taking care of me. As believers, you and I are forgiven children of God. We have been lovingly adopted into God's family as sons and daughters. Our true worth comes from our relationship in him and with him. If we remember that simple truth, then lies, criticism, and hurtful words will eventually bounce off us like water off a duck's back.

However, the problem is that we sometimes forget that truth of who we are when we are wounded and in pain. The pain seems to take center stage and places God's love and power on the periphery.

God the Father, the King of the universe, has accepted us and as such, we are worth more than an earthly king's ransom. We are now a child of the King of Kings and as such, we can walk and talk like royalty. When I go out now, I hold my head up high and sashay pass the people who have wounded me. I walk with confidence, knowing that my Jesus is right beside me, encouraging me, and cheering me on, knowing that God loves me and gives me the grace to forgive. Therefore, my attitude of gratitude is reinforced by psalms such as Psalm 139. Take the time to read and meditate on that psalm!

Attitude with a New Perspective—God's Perspective

To get an attitude with a new view, we have to look at others from God's perspective.

People who deliberately wound us are not doing well on the inside. You have had the experience of being put down by a nasty remark, being sent a nasty e-mail, being lied about, or anything that was meant to hurt. When that happens, it is easy to forget that those people are broken and wounded themselves.

No one understands the brokenness of people quite like Jesus. He was a "religious" leader who had tax collectors and prostitutes among his followers. His followers were the most colorful in history. Why? He knew the human heart like none other. He knew the weakness of each heart, and he was willing and able to forgive each person. When Jesus was here on earth, he looked at the people others rejected. He did not see what others saw—rejects of society. No, he saw what they would become. He saw each person's potential; he saw his handiwork, his creation. When he looks at us now, he still sees each person's potential, his handiwork, and his creation.

We laughingly call Peter "hoof in mouth" because he was always putting his foot in his mouth and treading where angels feared to tread. He made boasts that he couldn't fulfill, such as saying that he would stay with Jesus despite the danger to his life, but he denied Jesus and ran away like a coward when he was supposed to be by his side. Yet Jesus saw, long before that incident, what Peter would become and called him a "rock." For us, though, it usually doesn't help to know that those who have hurt us are also wounded. All we know is that we are hurting. We want revenge, and sometimes we take revenge.

There are times when we can't seem to get over the hurting, and it seems impossible to forgive. However, Jesus' command in the Lord's Prayer leaves us no room for revenge or unforgiveness. He says, "And forgive us our debts, as we also have forgiven our debtors" (Mark 6:12). Therefore, the more we meditate on the Lord's Prayer, the easier it becomes to forgive the ones who wound us. Eventually, the wounds will seem insignificant. First, in the light of the intimate relationship we have established with God, and second, in the spiritual growth we have experienced.

God's Perspective on Forgiveness

When the old instinct of wanting the other person to "pay" resurfaces, we have to be extremely careful, because we are on dangerous ground, so to speak, as we cross into God's territory. Revenge is not ours to take. Romans 12:19 warns us that revenge belongs to God. We know that Jesus died for our sins. God the Father accepted Jesus' sacrifice on our behalf and forgave us. Therefore, the Holy Spirit will enable us to do those things in the Christian life, such as forgiveness, that we cannot do on our own.

Refusing to forgive leaves an open wound in our soul that festers and turns into resentment, bitterness, and many other underlying emotions of anger. For our own good and the good of the person who hurt us, we simply must forgive. We have to trust God to make things right when we forgive. We have to trust God to heal our wounds so we can move on.

The secret of how to forgive is to trust and obey, like the old hymn writer penned many years ago. If we depend on God's power, instead of our own strength and abilities, it will be a hard decision to forgive but not a complicated one. But it is the only way we can truly be free from our hurts and the only way we can truly live in freedom.

Food for Thought

Understanding and practicing forgiveness from God's perspective leaves us no room to maneuver, and it protects us from harboring that root of bitterness.

Avoiding Bitterness

Often, we don't even realize we have slipped into a bitter attitude. Long-term frustration can lead to resentment and resentment into anger. Anger can degenerate into bitterness and unforgiveness, thereby calcifying our heart. This affects our spiritual life and effectiveness as Christians. It is an impediment we cannot afford. Often, we don't even realize we've slipped into a resentful attitude. If that has happened to you, you may realize it's a quagmire. Get out of that quagmire quickly! Here are three good reasons:

1. Bitterness damages your relationship with God.

The apostle Paul tells us in Hebrews 12:15, "Do not harbor the root of bitterness."

Bitterness can put you in an adversarial relationship with God. You blame him, like the Israelites, for everything that you think has gone wrong with your world, but if you don't see your situation or difficulty as his testing you to move you up to another level of your spirituality, and you fight him—my friend, it is a battle you cannot win. God wants to help you, not hurt you. Every obstacle, difficulty, or stressful situation he allows in your life is meant to move you one step closer to him.

He says: "So do not fear, for I am with you; do not be dismayed, for I am your God. I will strengthen you and help you; I will uphold you with my righteous right hand" (Isaiah 41:10).

An intimate, personal relationship with God is the source of your strength when things are going wrong. In bitterness, there is no hope for the future. Bitterness places our focus on us and the problems we are facing. It doesn't focus on the power and might of God. Don't waste your strength being bitter or fighting God. Use your strength to work with him and for him.

2. Bitterness alienates us.

When bitterness inadvertently builds up, it corrodes the heart and impairs relationships with family and friends. Bitterness pushes people away—no one wants to be around a sourpuss. I certainly don't! The people being pushed away are not to be blamed for the situation or obstacles in our path. They're not the enemy. The real enemy—the one who feeds the lie into our mind that we have every right to be bitter—is Satan. Discouragement and bitterness are two of his favorite ways to draw us away from God and from our family.

There's a bumper sticker that says, "Don't get mad, get even." When I'm driving and I see that on the bumper of a car, my first instinct is to look at the driver and try to determine what kind of person he or she is. I look for hostility in the mannerism and try to see if that person looks angry and might possibly be ready to unload his or her anger on me, a fellow driver. Then I stay clear of that car! It is the same thing in a relationship. If we are of the same ilk as those drivers with nasty bumper stickers, and we have a bitter attitude, people will just steer clear of us. We cannot blame anybody but ourselves if we are left alone or if we do not feel a part of the crowd.

Let me repeat Hebrews 12:12: "See to it that no one misses the grace of God and that no bitter root grows up to cause trouble and defile many."

3. Bitterness is a detour.

According to the *American Heritage Dictionary of the English Language* (4th edition), the word "detour" is a noun, meaning:
1. A roundabout way or course, especially a road used temporarily instead of a main route
2. A deviation from a direct course of action
3. To go or cause to go by a roundabout way

When the Israelites complained while journeying through the wilderness, that root of bitterness began to grow in their heart and within the group. They hit a detour! Many of the Bible personalities hit detours for one reason or another.

More important, when we, as modern-day Christians, hit a detour, we can trace it to a root of bitterness growing in our life. Bitterness is toxic! So many people spend their life looking good on the outside, but on the inside is that toxic root that needs attention. Only a healthy spiritual relationship with God can rectify it. Many of the detours we hit in life are caused by what is in our heart. The many tangled roots of bitterness in the heart have grown to such a gargantuan mess that it chokes out human emotions and leaves behind a hardened heart.

- Why do you think it is possible for people to act so evil toward one another?
- Why is it so easy for spouses to walk away from their families?
- Why do drug dealers find it easy to sell drugs to children?
- Why are nations at war with other nations?

- Why is one religious group at war with other religious groups?

The answer: it is what is in the heart of people. The heart is the center of a human being. Therefore, it controls our emotions and what we put into it. In computer language: garbage in, garbage out.

In Psalm 149:2, the psalmist asks the Lord to protect him from men who devise evil in their hearts. He says, "Rescue me, O Lord, from evil men; protect me from men of violence, who devise evil plans in their hearts and stir up war every day."

Bitterness and Unforgiveness: Two of the Greatest Problems of Our Time

Unfortunately, bitterness and unforgiveness are two of the greatest problems among Christians. There is a direct correlation between the emotions of unforgiveness and bitterness. While forgiveness is not a solution to every instance of anger, it is the answer to much of the physical and emotional pain we experience in life. In addition, besides hurting others, bitterness and or unforgiveness is a malignant cancer to the body and soul. If you have complaints of constant stress, headaches, insomnia, depression, and high blood pressure, what is your forgiveness level? The long-term effects of bitterness and unforgiveness will not only lead to physical death but spiritual as well.

CHAPTER 37

A Forgiving Heart Translated to a Changed Heart

Lord, I Still Don't Feel Like Forgiving!

How do we forgive when we don't feel like it? It is simple. Forgiving has nothing to do with "feelings." Feelings are not reality. Senses and feelings can deceive us. If I were to follow my "feelings," I would not do many things. For instance, if I do not feel like going to work and do not go, the natural consequence of that action is that I would be fired. Therefore, feelings are not reliable. Our feelings are very fickle and can get us into trouble.

When we decide to forgive someone who has hurt us, it is a choice made by our mind, not by our own feelings. It is not easy to forgive. Yet it is extremely easy to forgive. Let me explain the paradox. There's a constant battle between two things:

- love and hate
- good and evil
- commandment and choice
- heart and mind
- emotions (feelings) and reason
- past and future
- free will and consequences

It would be a tragedy for humankind if we were to ask God for forgiveness and he said, "Hey, Peter! What do you think? I don't feel like forgiving them today."

However, God doesn't base his forgiveness on his feelings. He bestows forgiveness based on his character and who he is. Therefore, as we strive to be like him, we should base our forgiveness on his character, not on our feelings. We only have to ask him to do the work in us that needs to be done, so that the grace we need to forgive will be complete. A perfect example of forgiveness in the New Testament is Stephen. In Acts 6:8, we become acquainted with Stephen, "a man full of God's grace and power." Stephen was seized and brought before the religious leaders. Even though false witnesses were used to testify against him, we are told that when everyone looked at him, they saw his face, "like the face of an angel." When Stephen was asked to defend himself, he used the Word of God as his testimony. The religious leaders eventually condemned Stephen, and he was stoned to death for preaching the gospel. Saul, later known as the Paul the apostle, "was there giving his approval to his death" (Acts 7:59).

As Stephen was dying, he prayed, "Lord Jesus, receive my spirit." Then he fell on his knees and cried out, "Lord, do not hold this sin against them."

Even in death, Stephen was a perfect portrayal of God's forgiveness. Saul, as he was first known, had wounded many families. Prior to his conversion, he was on a mission to destroy all Christians. Although he hurt many people, God forgave him and gave him a mission that no one else could accomplish. There were many from whom he needed to ask forgiveness. However, there were also many people who needed his forgiveness. It doesn't matter what your situation is now. Your history might be similar to Stephen's or Saul's, who condoned the killing of Stephen, but if you begin to think of God's perspective of forgiveness and purpose in your heart to forgive the person who has hurt you, God is faithful and will give you the strength to forgive. Begin the process!

Philippians 1:6 says, "And I am certain that God, who began the good work within you, will continue his work until it is finally finished on the day when Christ Jesus returns."

CHAPTER 38

Rewards of Forgiving

Forgiveness and Reconciliation

In every situation related to the Bible personalities we examined, we see where forgiveness led to reconciliation. However, let me caution you: it takes two people to reconcile. Don't be disappointed if the other party does not want to be reconciled. Just do as the Holy Spirit commands. If your heart is opened to the Holy Spirit, he will speak, and you must listen and obey.

Many believers refuse to listen to the Holy Spirit's admonition. But we are only responsible for our behavior and our action. We cannot mandate someone else's behavior. This is the work of the Holy Spirit. Here are some of his responsibilities:

The Holy Spirit

- The Holy Spirit is called God (Luke 1:32, 35).
- He is one part of the Trinity of the Father, Son. and Holy Spirit (Matt. 28:19; 2 Cor. 13:14).
- He has the characteristics of God.
    ○ He is eternal (Heb. 9:14).
    ○ He is all knowing (1 Cor. 2:10–I1).
    ○ He is omnipresent (Ps. 139:7–10).
    ○ He has great power (Acts 1:8; Rom. 15:9).
    ○ He gives spiritual life to us (John 3:3–8).

- He is a person who:
    ○ teaches (John 14:26).
    ○ testifies about Christ (John 15:26).

186

- ○ encourages (Acts 9:31).
- ○ counsels (John 14:16).
- ○ convicts people of sin (John 16:8).
- ○ prays for us (Rom. 8:27).
- ○ can be resisted (Acts 7:51).
- ○ can be tested (Acts 5:9).

- • Some of the work of the Holy Spirit in us as individuals:
  - ○ He dwells in us (Rom. 8:11).
  - ○ He gives us new life (Tit. 3:5; John 3:5–6).
  - ○ He shows us God's love (Rom. 5:5).
  - ○ He keeps us in touch with God (Jude 20).
  - ○ He enables us to find the truth (1 John 4:1–6).
  - ○ He sanctifies us (Rom. 15:16; 2 Thess. 2:13).
  - ○ He works his fruit in us (Gal. 5:16–25).
  - ○ He gives us gifts (1 Cor. 12:4–11).
  - ○ He prays for us in times of trouble (Rom. 8:26).

When we are obedient to the Holy Spirit, we are able forgive without rancor. It is a choice, a decision we have to make. As we forgive, we discover that God's command is for our own good, and we receive the reward of forgiving, which is:

- • restoration of Christian fellowship;
- • spiritual cleansing;
- • the absence of bitterness;
- • reconciliation with God; and
- • freedom from pain and hurt we've suffered.

As the second person of the Trinity, Jesus knew the power of the Holy Spirit. So after working with the disciples for three years, Jesus knew that the time had come for him to be crucified. He wanted to comfort his disciples. He gave to them the promise of the Holy Spirit.

He said, "If you love me, you will obey what I command. And I will ask the Father, and he will give you another Counselor to be with you forever—the Spirit of Truth" (John 14:15–17).

When we face obstacles, the Holy Spirit is the only Counselor we need. When we cooperate with the Holy Spirit in our wilderness experiences, we learn to give up control, and we learn the lessons we need to learn. Ultimately, loss of control and obedience to the Holy Spirit translate into having peace; a peace that dabbling in the world doesn't give and a peace that the world doesn't understand. It is a peace that "surpasses all understanding." One of the names of God is, Jehovah Shalom—the Lord is our peace.

Forgiveness and the Peace of God

The source of our peace is a divine gift that comes from God the Father, God the Son, and God the Holy Spirit. With this divine peace, we acquire a wholeness and well-being in all areas of our life. Here are some Bible verses to ponder:

- peace in relationship with others (Heb. 12:14; 1 Pet. 3:8–11)
- peace in relationships in the church (Rom. 14:19; 2 Cor. 13:11)
- peace in our relationships in the home (Prov. 17:1; Prov. 29:17)
- personal peace (Ps. 4:8; Prov. 14:30; 2 Cor. 2:13)

Jesus is our peace. It was predicted before he came that he would be called the Prince of Peace (Isa. 9:6). The apostle Paul writes of Jesus as our peace. He says, "For he himself is our peace, who has made the two and has destroyed the barrier, the dividing wall of hostility, by abolishing in his flesh the law with its commandments and regulations" (Eph. 2:14).

Jesus left this promise prior to returning to heaven. He said to his disciples,

> But a time is coming, and has come, when you will be scattered, each to his own home. You will leave me all alone. Yet I am not alone, for the Father is with me. I have told you these things, so that in me you may have peace. In this world you will have trouble. But take heart! I have overcome the world. (John 16:32–33)

"Peace I leave with you; my peace I give you. I do not give to you as the world gives. Do not let your hearts be troubled and do not be afraid" (John 14:27).

Jesus demonstrates perfectly how we should behave when someone wounds us. He left the situation in his Father's hands, was obedient to his Father's will, and remained at peace. Further on, we see how he grieved in the garden of Gethsemane. It was not an easy task—dying for lost mankind. He was God, he was perfect, he was sinless, and he was going to take on the sins of mankind. Nonetheless, despite the pain he knew that he was going to suffer, he submitted his will to his Father's. The result was that he had that deep-seated peace that only his Father could give—so much so that prior to his crucifixion, he was able to comfort his disciples, although later they would forget his words and desert him.

The people who crucified Jesus thought they had won the victory. Satan thought he had won the victory over God, Jesus, and mankind. Wrong! When someone wounds us, he or she takes power over us, but only if we allow it. Satan doesn't win unless we let him. We may lose our peace for a while, but when we forgive those who hurt us through the working of the Holy Spirit, we take back the power and we get our peace back. We are the winners! The energy spent in unforgiveness is wasted energy. We cannot allow such waste; when, wounds and all, God wants to use us to minister to others in similar situations. As soon as we are able, we need to harness that energy and power to use for God's kingdom.

Therefore, if we are to talk about the reward of forgiveness, then our "reward" for forgiving the people who wound is freedom from a bitter root growing in us, peace through the Holy Spirit, a stronger and more enduring faith in God, and personal and spiritual power. We don't need much more to survive this life, do we? And that, my friends, is called victorious living.

Forgiveness as a Necessity

Forgiveness is not just a necessity; it's also an essential part of our responsibility toward our self, God, and others—both friends and enemies alike. So how should we go on henceforth?

> Let all bitterness and wrath and anger and clamor and slander be put away from you, along with all malice. And be kind to one another, tender-hearted, forgiving each other, just as God in Christ also has forgiven you. (Eph. 4:31–32)

> Jesus said,
> You have heard that it was said, You shall love your neighbor, and hate your enemy. But I say to you, love your enemies, and pray for those who persecute you; in order that you may be sons of your Father who is in heaven; for He causes His sun to rise on the evil and the good, and sends rain on the righteous and the unrighteous. (Matt. 5:43–45)

Forgiveness and Holiness

Another reward of learning to forgive is holiness. This is very difficult for many people as they live and operate in the natural— what Paul calls the flesh. Holiness requires a change in our basic character, desires, and even thoughts. We have to allow the Holy Spirit to "clean house" in our hearts and minds, removing "Egypt" and making room for those things that God desires to place in us. How do we begin to do this?

When Jesus left his disciples and turned his eye to being crucified, he promised to send another Comforter—the Holy Spirit. He told them that the counselor would be the Spirit of Truth but:

> The world cannot accept him, because it neither sees him nor knows him. But you know him, for he lives with you and will be in you. (John 14:15–18)

When I think of the word "holiness," the first thought that comes to my mind is God. We are told in the Old Testament that he is holy.

The Lord reigns, let the nations tremble;
He sits enthroned between the cherubim, let the earth shake.
Great is the Lord in Zion; he is exalted over all the nations.
Let them praise your great and awesome name—He is holy.
The King is might, he loves justice—
You have established equity; in Jacob you have done what is right.
Exalt the Lord our God and worship at his footstool;
He is holy
Moses and Aaron were among his priests,
Samuel was among those who called on his name;
they called on the Lord and he answered them.
He spoke to them from the pillar of cloud;
they kept his statues and the decrees he gave them.
our Lord our God, you answered them;
you were to Israel a forgiving God, though
you punished their misdeeds.
Exalt the Lord our God and worship at his holy mountain,
for
The Lord our God is holy (Ps. 99).

As a holy God (Matt. 6:9), he sent his Holy Son (Luke 1:35; Acts 4:27, 30) to redeem mankind and reconcile people back to him. Through Jesus' death on the cross, God the Father offered forgiveness. Then, when Jesus had accomplished his work, God sent his Holy Spirit (Acts 2:4; Rom. 1:4) to believers who are called to be a holy people. Look at the chart below.

It would be a good idea, at this point, to find the Bible verses, write them down, as shown in the first two examples and ponder the goodness of God.

Holy people	Col. 3:12 1 Pet. 2:9	Therefore, as God's chosen people, holy and dearly loved, clothe yourselves with compassion, kindness, humility, gentleness and patience.	Personal notes:
Holy temple	Eph. 2:21–22	In him the whole building is joined together and rises to become a holy temple in the Lord. And in him you too are built together to become a dwelling in which God lives by his Spirit.	
Sanctified (made holy)	1 Cor. 6:11		
Chosen to be holy	Eph. 1:4		
Called to a holy life	1 Thess. 4:7		

Living a holy life	Heb. 12:14 1 Pet. 1:15–16		Personal notes:
Serve God in holiness	Luke 1:74–75		
Purified in holiness	2 Cor. 7:1		
Presented to God as holy	Col. 1:22		

CHAPTER 39

Sanctification, Holiness, and Holy Living

One of the responsibilities of the Holy Spirit is to sanctify believers so they can live a life of holiness. The word "sanctification" is sometimes thrown around very liberally in Christian circles, yet there is not much sanctified living going on. Let us look at the term sanctification and its implication for the believer. According to the Bible, sanctification is being holy and becoming holy.

We are sanctified in Christ.

"To the church of God in Corinth, to those sanctified in Christ Jesus and called to be holy, together with all those everywhere who call on the name of our Lord Jesus Christ—their Lord and ours: Grace and peace to you from God our Father and the Lord Jesus Christ" (1 Cor. 1:2–3).

We are sanctified through Christ's blood.

"How much more severely do you think a man deserves to be punished who has trampled the Son of God under foot, who has treated as an unholy thing the blood of the covenant that sanctified him, and who has insulted the Spirit of Grace?" (Heb. 10:29).

We are sanctified by the Holy Spirit.

I have written you quite boldly on some points, as if to remind you of them again, because of the grace God gave me to be a minister of Christ Jesus to the Gentiles with the priestly duty of proclaiming the gospel of God, so that the Gentiles might become an offering acceptable to God, sanctified by the Holy Spirit. (Rom. 15:15–16)

We are sanctified by faith, through the Word of God, through the work of God, and the work of the Holy Spirit. As Christians, we are called God's holy people by Paul the apostle (2 Cor. 1:1; Phil. 1:1). As sanctified people we are supposed to resist sinful living.

It is God's will that you should be sanctified: that you should avoid sexual immorality; that each of you should learn to control his own body in a way that is holy and honorable, not in passionate lust like the heathen, who do not know God; and that in this matter no one should wrong his brother or take advantage of him. The Lord will punish men for all such sins, as we have already told you and warned you. For God did not call us to be impure, but to live a holy life. Therefore, he who rejects this instruction does not reject man but God, who gives you his Holy Spirit. (1 Thess. 4:3–7)

Peter the apostle states quite clearly that Jesus is the living stone, and we, like living stones, are being built into a spiritual house to be a holy priesthood. As a chosen people, chosen by God, we are:

a royal priesthood, a holy nation, a people belonging to God, that you may declare the praises of him who called you out of darkness into his wonderful light. Once you were not a people, but now you are the people of God; once you had not received mercy, but now you have received mercy. (1 Pet. 2:11)

He goes on to state that as believers, we should "live such good lives among the pagans that, though they accuse you of doing wrong, they may see your good deeds and glorify God on the day he visits us" (1 Pet. 2:12).

Living a Life Fully Rooted in Christ

There is a world out there that needs purified vessels firmly rooted in God. Too often, the Christian testimony is compromised beyond recognition. When our world as we know it is badly shaken and our foundation begins to crumble, we need to have our roots so firmly secure in our relationship with God that the effects of the trials and tribulations of life are only temporary.

Jesus told the parable of two builders. One was wise and built his house upon solid foundation. The other was foolish and built his upon a shaky foundation. There are many modern-day Christians that Jesus would address as he did his listeners. He said,

> Why do you call me Lord, Lord, and do not do what I say? I will show you what he is like who comes to me and hears my words and puts them into practice. He is like a man building a house, who dug down deep and laid the foundation on a rock. When a flood came, the torrent struck that house but could not shake it because it was well built. But the one who hears my words and does not put them into practice is like a man who built a house on the ground without a foundation. The moment the torrent struck that house, it collapsed and its destruction was complete. (Luke 6:46–49)

When the storm came, the weak house collapsed, but the well-built house stood firm. Jesus is our rock, our anchor. It is only through a solid relationship with God that we can weather the storms of life. When the challenges of life come—and believe me, they will—our "house" will be shaken, but it should not collapse.

On a personal level, several years ago when my world, as I knew it then, collapsed, it was the Word of God, my faith, and the fact that God loves me unconditionally that kept me sane. My house— my world—was badly shaken, but it has only gotten stronger with adversity, because my foundation was already firmly grounded. There was never any doubt on my part that God would sustain me through all the challenges I had to face. How about you? Can you say the same?

Food for Thought
How strong is your foundation?

CHAPTER 40

Digging and Building a Solid Foundation

Jesus said to his listeners, "I am the vine; you are the branches" (John 15:5). God desires that we send our roots deeply into his Word. If we are solidly grounded in the Word, our life will become a sweet aroma, a wonderful perfume to the nostrils of God. Jeremiah 17:7–8 tells us exactly what getting rooted in God's word can accomplish. It says,

Blessed is the man who trusts in the Lord, whose confidence is in him. He will be like a tree planted by the water that sends out its roots by the stream. It does not fear when heat comes; its leaves are always green. It has no worries in a year of drought and never fails to bear fruit.

In this Scripture, the prophet Jeremiah uses nature as an analogy to depict the spiritual condition of God's people who are rooted in God's Word. Most people are familiar with the root system because we remember that as children, one of the first activities in kindergarten was to plant a seed and monitor the progress of its growth. With that prior knowledge, we know that a tree cannot exist without its roots. The roots:

- absorb water and nutrients;
- distribute the water and nutrients to the tree;
- store extra nutrients and dispense the nutrients when the tree needs it; and
- provide stability to the tree.

Some trees have their roots on top of the soil, while others have their roots under the surface. I grow orchids, and I always know the health of my plants when I see new roots shooting out of the pots and trailing along the plant stand. It doesn't matter how the roots grow—underneath or above the surface. What matters is that when there is a storm, the firmer the root system, the less likelihood there is of the plant or the tree uprooting. When we have storms in our lives, our life has to be firmly rooted and established in the Word of God.

Prior to the storms in our lives, we probably acted independently of God, as if we could accomplish everything and anything on our own merit. We either did not acknowledge God's hand in our life, or we took a large portion of the credit for our accomplishments. However, no man is an island. And God has a way of bringing us to our knees to prove that point.

During challenging times, we often will turn to God in a much deeper way because we are so desperate. When we face adversity and tribulations, we have no one else to depend on but God. We think that no one understands what we are going through, but God does. Even when we think God is not listening or that nothing is happening in our storms, we must keep on praying and talking to him. He is closer than we think.

In our desperation, we should seek more of God and dig our foundation deeper. This allows us to extend the relationship with him and be more useful to him, once the storms have subsided. Once we have a real experience of God in the storms, there can be no turning back to our old ways of independence.

God desires to use all his children to further his kingdom. He has a plan and a purpose for the life of each and every believer. As we grow in maturity through the process of the wilderness and through our storms, we grow in usefulness. A believer who has successfully navigated the storms of life is usually able to do much more when exiting the storms than entering them. We usually go into the storms of life full of ourselves and come out full of God.

On another note, quite often, we try to dictate to God on the merits of ruling our lives. It is usually because independence or "self" raises its ugly head. We think we know where we are going. Big mistake! First, we are limited by human understanding. Second, God says, "For my thoughts are not your thoughts, neither are your ways my ways" (Isa.

55:9). Although God allows storms to develop in our lives, he does not take pleasure in our grief. Lamentations 3:32–33 says, "Though he brings grief, he will show compassion, so great is his unfailing love. For he does not willingly bring affliction or grief to the children of men."

That is why we have to focus on him, not on the storms.

A popular song years ago was "My Way." I enjoyed it for a while—until I really thought about the lyrics. There were two differing worldviews: the way of the world and the way of God. If I am a Bible-believing Christian, I can't be doing things my way. I have to do things God's way. So when the storms come in my life, I have to ask myself, "Did I do things my way or God's way?" and "Why am I in the pickling situation I'm in?"

As his children, God will always correct us and allow us to go through grievous situations. However, he does not do it willingly or joyfully. His purpose is only to mold us into the form he wishes for us. So when we are experiencing difficulties in our life, we shouldn't think that God is out to get us.

When our foundation crumbles under the storms of life, we think it is the "end of the world." When we are treated unfairly, when other bad things happen to us, it seems impossible to see the good in these events. But we can only see each event through our human lenses, while God sees each event through his infinite lenses. We can say, then, that God majors in the things that seem impossible to us. And the word "impossible" is not in his dictionary. In fact, here is how God would like us to view our "difficult" situation. James 1:2–4 tells us, "Consider it pure joy, my brothers, whenever you face trials of many kinds, because you know that the testing of your faith develops perseverance. Perseverance must finish its work so that you may be mature and complete, not lacking anything."

As we experience difficulties, God does not see where we are. He sees where we are going. In addition, he does not just see our potential; he sees the finished product. Therefore, we should not be discouraged when the wilderness of trials and tribulations come to greet us; we just have to stretch forth our hands and embrace each one. I have to confess, though, that I'm not at the "consider it pure joy" stage as yet, but I have learned in past years that when I am faced with trials, tribulations, and wilderness times, it is in the wilderness that I truly find Jesus waiting for me. And if I persevere, as James encourages us to do, it is there that I will gain my spiritual strength. That, my friends, is the greatest reward and one of our greatest blessings!

We need to continue to:

- live a sanctified life;
- live a life of holiness;
- stay rooted in Christ; and
- dig a deep spiritual foundation.

One Final Question

If you go through this wilderness experience of trials and tribulations, will you be able to navigate it successfully?

CHAPTER 41

Completing the Wilderness Plan

Let's review the concept of the wilderness. Everything God allows in our life is planned and has a purpose. We have to get in tune with God's "lesson plan."

The objective of the wilderness experience is to acquaint us with God's plan and his purpose, prepare us for the work he has for us, transform us, and set us on our way to the future. How do we get in tune with God's plan? On a spiritual level, we read the Word, pray, and ask God for his direction. On a physical level, we become a learner. Let me take a scenic path for a minute.

Most of us are accustomed to keeping an agenda, day planner, or calendar. What is the purpose of keeping such an item? We want to be organized! First, we list the activities to be done. Then we categorize the activities and prioritize them, based on two things:

1. How important the activity is
2. The timeline; when it has to done

The next thing we do is to assign a time and date of completion. However, an agenda, day planner, or calendar is useless if we don't bother to fill in the pertinent information or if we don't bother to follow what we have written. After reading this book, I hope all readers will list items to be dealt with by God and set priorities of how and when to take them to God.

Let us go back to the concept of lesson plans and you as a learner. You are in the wilderness, and God has a plan for you to participate in. In other words, God has a lesson plan mapped out. You are the student. He is the teacher. Teachers know the value of lesson plans. It goes beyond keeping a calendar. Lesson plans encapsulate:

• setting goals

- structuring the lesson
- having clear outcomes
- identifying materials and activities
- resources
- worksheets

As the student, we are in the wilderness to learn. There is nothing we can do about it. It's just God and us. As students, we must learn how to proactively seek to ascertain God's lesson plan for our life

Questions to Ponder

1. What do you think his goal is for you?
2. What do you think you can or should learn from the experience?
3. Do you want to come out stronger?

At the beginning of the book, I asked you to list all your wounds. If you did, you may have rehashed them and regurgitated them. They are once again open, gaping, and bleeding. What are your emotions? Are you angry at the situation, angry at God, and angry at the offender? Has reconciliation been denied to you? The prophet Jeremiah reminds us of an important fact about God that we should keep at the forefront of our mind.

> For I know the plans I have for you, declares the Lord, plans to prosper you and not to harm you, plans to give you hope and a future. Then you will call upon me and come and pray to me, and I will listen to you. You will seek me and find me when you seek me with all your heart. (Jer. 29:11–13)

As we read the Old Testament, we see how many times God's people forgot him until they ran into trouble. In our modern times, many of his people still forget him, and it is only when their situations become unbearable that they remember that there is a God. That being said, God has never forgotten his people. He is Jehovah Roi—the Lord my Shepherd. In Psalm 80:1, the psalmist beseeches God to come in his glory and might, as he did of old. He says, "Hear us, O Shepherd of

Israel, you who lead Joseph like a flock; you who sit enthroned between the cherubim, shine forth before Ephraim, Benjamin and Manasseh. Awaken your might; come and save us."

As students, the first lesson we have to learn is who we are and who God is. We are God's sheep, and we need to learn to listen for his voice, hear the different timbre of his voice, feel his love and compassion, and experience his mercy and his goodness. The psalmist says, "Come, let us bow down in worship, let us kneel before the Lord our Maker; for he is our God and we are the people of his pasture, the flock under his care" (Ps. 95:6–7).

Psalm 100:1 reiterates the joy of belonging and gives thanks that God is our Shepherd and that we belong to him. The psalmist says,

Shout for joy to the Lord, all the earth. Worship the Lord with gladness; come before him with joyful songs. Know that the Lord is God. It is he who made us, and we are his; we are his people, the sheep of his pasture. Enter his gates with thanksgiving and his courts with praise; give thanks to him and praise his name. For the Lord is good and his love endures forever; his faithfulness continues through all generations.

Reasons to praise and worship God and celebrate as sheep:

1. The shepherd finds pasture for his flocks (Ezek. 34:2, 13–14).
2. He provides for his sheep (Gen. 29:2–8).
3. He protects his flocks (1 Sam. 17:34–36; Luke 2:8).
4. He seeks lost sheep (Matt. 18:10–13; 12:11).
5. He knows the activities of his sheep (Gen. 31:38–39).

Jesus is referred to as:

1. The Great Shepherd (Heb. 13:20).
2. The chief Shepherd (1 Pet. 5:4).
3. The Shepherd and Overseer (1 Pet. 2:25).

He said,

I am the good shepherd. The good shepherd lays down his life for the sheep. The hired hand is not the shepherd who owns the sheep. So when he sees the wolf coming, he abandons the sheep and runs away. Then the wolf attacks the flock and scatters it. The man runs away because he is a hired hand and cares nothing for the sheep. I am the good shepherd; I know my sheep and my sheep know me—just as the Father knows me and I know the Father—and I lay down my life for the sheep. (John 10:11–15)

Jesus:

1. Died for his sheep (John 10:15).
2. Has compassion for his sheep (Matt. 9:36).
3. Searches for lost or wandering sheep (Matt. 18:12–14; Luke 15:3–7).
4. Will judge like a shepherd (Matt. 25:32).

Food for Thought

- Setting goals
  - What goals does God have for you and your life? What goals do you have for your life?
- Structuring the lesson
  - How does your season of life or your present situation fit into the structure of God's plans?
- Having clear outcomes
  - What are some expected outcomes of your present activities?
- Identifying materials and resources
  - What are some identifying materials from which you need to be reading and learning?
  - Are there available resources you can use to help to understand God's plans for your life?

- Activities
  - What activities do you need to participate in, to activate or to facilitate God's plans for your life?
- Can you hear the Shepherd's call?
- Are you a good student?

You have spent time in the wilderness, you have learned the lessons the Lord has taught, you have forgiven the person who wounded you and handed over thoughts of revenge to God, and you have asked him to take out the root of bitterness from your body, mind, and soul. Once you've learned the lessons in the wilderness, you've wiped the slate clean of all the offenses done to you. Hopefully, you have forgiven yourself for the part you played in the situation. God says, "You are ready to get out of the wilderness. Your preparation is now complete. I can use you now!

SECTION 3—

OPEN HANDS

CHAPTER 42

The Hand

Vignette

I spent some of my younger years in Toronto. One beautiful summer's day, I was walking down Yonge Street, one of Toronto's main streets. I was just enjoying the sun, the crowd, and talking to a friend as I walked. There was a group of people doing the same thing, and I was in front of the crowd of people attempting to cross the street. Just as I was about to step off the curb, a policeman blew his whistle and put his hand up. I stopped abruptly, and several people behind me bumped into my back, but I was determined that the one foot hovering in the air was not going to touch the street. So I teetered on one foot for several minutes, arms outstretched like a ballerina, until I could regain my balance. Not for one moment did I think of disobeying that hand of authority, because I knew that hand could comfort me and protect me from oncoming traffic, but it could also make my life miserable if I disobeyed its message.

In this chapter, we are going to examine the concept of hands in general, and we are going to examine God's hands. Years ago, while traveling in Italy, I got lost. I had taken the train to Rome but had gotten off at the wrong station. I asked a policeman for directions with the aid of sign language and a map. I was intent on looking at the officer's face, so I didn't see what he was doing with his hand. I noticed that he was getting very annoyed. He then started to walk away. It was then that I noticed that he had his hand poker-straight at his side, but his fingers were turned toward his back, and he was using his fingers to beckon us. As a Westerner, that was totally foreign to me, because when we beckon someone, the hand is held closer to the face, bent at the elbow, palm facing us, and then we use the fingers to beckon. I chuckled about that incident with the policeman afterwards, because I almost missed the message he was sending with his hand.

The human hand is a paradox. It can be a tool, a weapon, or a symbol. As human beings, we use our hands constantly. We see babies clutching their mother's breast as they are feeding. Children use their hands as they learn to crawl, walk, skip, and balance. We use our hands in nonverbal language in both the positive and the negative sense. I use my hand to talk all the time.

When I traveled to Paris, I saw the great artwork in the Chateau Versailles. Hands are indispensible in creating art. One year I was able to afford season tickets for the symphony. My delight was watching the baton in the director's hand—a musician is dependent upon his hands. A surgeon is not a surgeon without the use of functioning hands. We applaud for our favorite sports person when he or she does well; and in religion, we raise our hands in praise and worship to God. Our hands can be instruments—they can heal or destroy; comfort or hurt; give pleasure or cause pain.

When I think of hands, I see the symbolism in Shakespeare's Lady Macbeth; and in Matthew 27:24, we see Pontius Pilate, after the crowd kept shouting to crucify Jesus, washing his hand and saying, "I am innocent of this man's blood … It is your responsibility."

We see many references to God's hands in the Bible. First, we will look at the human hand and then we will look at the significance of God's hands and what his hands signify.

The Human Hand

Many people are familiar with the movie *The Ten Commandments* starring Charlton Heston and Yul Bryner—a classic! When I was a young child, my father took me to see this movie for the first time. Since then, I have watched this movie every Easter, and other times during the year, for the last forty years. I know the script word for word. One of my favorite scenes in the movie is when Moses stretches out his hand over the Red Sea, and the sea begins to roll back. Moses raises his hand, but his authority and power come from God.

In Psalm 90:17, the psalmist asks a blessing on the works of his hand. He says, "May the favor of the Lord our God rest upon us; establish the work of our hands for us—yes, establish the work of our hands."

Our hands are used:

to write—Galatians 6:11
to touch—1 John 1:1
to clap—Psalm 47:1
to fight—Psalm 18:34
to bless—Leviticus 9:22
to lift in prayer—1 Timothy 2:8
to lift up in praise—Psalm 134:2
to take oaths before God—Genesis 14:22

When God's hand is lifted up, however, it is a sign of authority, power, and strength. He does not have to depend on anyone for power. His source of power comes from himself.

God's hand	Bible verse	Personal application & comment
saves us	Exodus 6:1	
guides us	Ezra 7:9	
provides for us	Psalm 104:28	
protects us	Psalm 139:10	
receives our spirit	Psalm 31:5	
pleads with us	Isaiah 65:2	
chastises us	Psalm 32:4	
punishes unbelievers	Exodus 7:5	

God's hand	Bible verse	Personal application & comment
	John 10:29	
	1 Peter 3:22	
	Ezra 8:11–23	

God's Hand as a Sign of Power:

One of the first indications of God's power and the power of his hand is in Exodus 6:1. The Israelites had been slaves in Egypt for 430 years. God, in his providence, had decided that it was time for them to leave Egypt. So he made a promise to the Israelites:

"Then the Lord said to Moses, Now you will see what I will do to Pharaoh: Because of my mighty hand he will let them go; because of my mighty hand he will drive them out of his country."

"O Lord, your hand is lifted high, but they do not see it" (Isa. 26:11).

"Your arm is endued with power; your hand is strong, your right hand exalted" (Ps. 89:13).

CHAPTER 43

The Omniscient Hand of God

God's Unseen Hands

Many times when trouble comes into our life, we wonder why. We ask God to show us his good will. And at times, as the situation becomes more difficult, we beg God to take away the pain of the situation. Most importantly, we wonder where God is in the midst of our pain. I would like to draw your attention to two biblical personalities. The first is Joseph, whom we already discussed. Do you ever wonder what thoughts were going around in his head during the years he was in jail? He must have cried out to God so many times. And as the years went by, as we read time and time again, "The Lord was with Joseph and he prospered, and he lived in the house of his Egyptian master" (Gen. 39:2).

"From the time he put him in charge of his household and of all that he owned, the Lord blessed the household of the Egyptian because of Joseph. The blessing of the Lord was on everything Potiphar had, both in the house and in the field" (Gen. 39:5).

It was quite apparent that God's hand was in the unfolding events of Joseph's life. God's sovereign rule is assumed, however, at every point in the book of Esther, as there is a total absence of reference to him. The book of Esther is a beautiful book that describes how the Jews of Persia were saved from destruction through divine providence.

Here are a few of the highlights in the book of Esther:

Esther's story happened during the reign of King Xerxes. The king had a feast. We are told that when he was "in high spirits" from the wine, he demanded that his wife, Queen Vashti, put in an appearance so he could display her beauty to the people and nobles. Queen Vashti refused to make an appearance and was subsequently deposed as queen and banished from the palace.

Later, when the king's anger had subsided, he realized that he needed another queen. On the advice of his nobles, all the beautiful virgins in the land were brought into the harem and beautified for one year. Esther was included in this group. At the time that Esther was taken captive to live in this foreign land, her cousin, Mordecai, was also taken captive. When Mordecai heard about this beauty contest, he convinced Esther to participate, with the stipulation that she did not reveal her nationality and family background. After inspecting all the beautiful potential queens, the king eventually chose Esther to be his new queen to replace Vashti. Unbeknownst to Esther, God was placing her in a position of influence, and she was going to be the instrument God used to save his chosen people.

Of course, every story has to have an evil genius. In the book of Esther, it was Haman. Out of pride and arrogance, Haman was angry with Mordecai for not bowing down to him and honoring him. He conceived a plan to eliminate the Jews. When Mordecai discovered the plot to eliminate the Jews, Mordecai persuaded Esther to help to save her people by going into the king's presence and speaking to him about the situation. Esther was very reluctant because anyone who entered the presence of the king without permission was put to death. There are two key phrases that we should consider carefully. First, Esther wanted to continue her silence because she was afraid, as she should have been, but Mordecai warned her that her royal status would not protect her. Then he said to her, "And who knows but that you have come to royal position for such a time as this" (Est. 4:14).

After three days of fasting and praying, Esther was finally ready to brave the king without his prior permission. She said another key phrase:

"When this is done, I will go to the king, even though it is against the law. And if I perish, I perish" (Est. 5:16).

There is one thing we have to remember when we are wounded, with all the emotional pain that goes with it. I quote the psalmist: "But I trust in you, O Lord; I say, You are my God. My times are in your hands; deliver me from my enemies and from those who pursue me" (Ps. 31:14–15).

Here are some interesting facts:

Haman plotted to destroy the Jewish nation. Had this happened, the existence of God's chosen people would have been eliminated, and there would have been no Messiah. Of course, God could not let this happen!

The fact that there is no direct reference to God is significant. It tells me that there is no such thing as a coincidence. Even though it may appear that God is absent in our most challenging moments, he is ever present in all situations, and his sovereign hand controls the reins of our life. Let us look at the verses that point directly to God's hand in the book of Esther.

Esther's entry into the harem wins favor with the keepers:
Esther also was taken to the king's palace and entrusted to Hegai, who had charge of the harem. The girl pleased him and won his favor. Immediately he provided her with her beauty treatments and special food. He assigned to her seven maids selected from the king's palace and move her and her maids into the best place in the harem. (Est. 2:8–9).

Esther wins favor with others:
"And Esther won the favor of everyone who saw her" (Est. 2:15).

Esther wins favor with the king:
"Now the king was attracted to Esther more than to any of the other women, and she won his favor and approval more than

any of the other virgins. So he set a royal crown on her head and made her queen instead of Vashti" (verse 17).

Esther's presence wins favor with the king:
"When he saw Queen Esther standing in the court, he was pleased with her and held out to her the gold scepter that was in his hand" (Est. 5:2)

Mordecai wins favor and is honored:
That night the king could not sleep so he ordered the book of the chronicles, the record of his reign, to be brought in and read to him. It was found recorded there that Mordecai had exposed Bibthana and Teresh, two of the king's officers who guarded the doorway, who had conspired to assassinate King Xerxes. What honor and recognition has Mordecai received for this? The king asked. (Est. 6:1–2)

Haman is hanged, and Esther gains financially:
Then Queen Esther answered, if I have found favor with you, O king, and if it pleases your majesty, grant me my life— this is my petition. And spare my people—this is my request. (Est. 7:3)

That same day King Xerxes gave Queen Esther the estate of Haman, the enemy of the Jews. And Mordecai came into the presence of the king, for Esther had told how he was related to her. The king took off his signet ring, which he had reclaimed from Haman, and presented it to Mordecai. And Esther appointed him over Haman's estate. (Est. 8:1–2)

I have only summarized a portion of the book of Esther, but I hope you take the time to read the full story of how God's hand was actively involved in Mordecai's life, Esther's life, and the nation of Israel. This book serves to remind us that God is in the midst of our pain. He cares what happens to his children, and his hand is ever present to soothe our pain, to protect us, and when necessary, to raise his hand of power to defeat the enemy.

Initially, Esther was very afraid of the real and perceived enemies. But her cousin Mordecai was there to direct and help her. She took the first step when she decided to face her "enemy." If you notice, it was only after she fasted and prayed that she was ready to face the king. Esther knew how she could be victorious.

The Word of God says, "Not by might nor by power, but by my Spirit" (Zech. 4:6). Esther might not have understood everything that was happening in her life—why she was taken into captivity, why she had to go through everything she was going through—but we are told, "She continued to follow Mordecai's instructions as had done when he was bringing her up" (Est. 2:19).

Esther listened to good advice and eventually was able to see the hand of God move to save a whole nation. Sometimes, we are unable to see God's hand in our life, not because it is not there, actively working on our behalf, but because we are blinded by that ever-looming giant of fear. Esther was afraid, but when she listened to good advice, fasted, and prayed for the spiritual power that she needed, stepped out in faith and said, "If I perish, I perish," she trusted God with her fears. Instead of that fear conquering her, she conquered it by trusting God with the outcome of the situation.

Food for Thought

Fear is one of the main giants that can prevent us from accessing God's power and enjoying the privileges of his hands.

CHAPTER 44

Slaying the Giants That Hinder Us

Vignette

I taught English at a university in Tokyo for two years. It was an extremely fulfilling experience, career-wise. But imagine the loneliness of being in a country where culturally, you're chalk to their cheese, and you don't speak the language. At my organization, each teacher was scheduled to work late one night each week. This meant that every Friday, when I should have been ensconced on my tatami mat, relaxing, I was the one to finish at 7:00 p.m., thereby getting home around 8:30. After many missed trains, I finally learned my route. Even so, one night I must have been over-tired when I got on the train because I didn't pay much attention to where I was going. Just when I thought I should be getting off the train, it began to gather speed. I then began to panic, because as the train traveled faster and faster, I noticed the buildings were getting fewer and fewer. We were heading somewhere out into the countryside. Not only had I taken an express train, I had no idea where it was going. At that moment, all I could hear was the loud thumping of my heart beating in my ears.

As soon as I was able to get off, I jumped off the train and stepped onto the platform ... into absolute and utter blackness. I had never felt so much fear in all my life. There was no light, no sign of life. and I had no idea where I was. I remember standing on the platform, too petrified to even move. I remember saying,

"Oh God! Help me! Help me!" I don't know how long I stood there, frozen in fear, but all of a sudden, I saw a little man in a transit uniform walking slowly along the platform. I can't remember how I communicated to him that I was lost, but I did—or the Lord did—and he gave me directions how to get home. I stood in the darkness and waited for the next train to come along. Two hours and an eternity later, I was back at the same station where I had initially boarded the train.

Have you ever felt that hopeless, helpless sense of fear that replicates itself physically, mentally, and spiritually?

Let's address the giant of fear and some of the other giants that can hinder us.

CHAPTER 45

Slaying the Giant of Fear

Many of us share a common experience with the patriarchs we've discussed. They were in a physical wilderness—no greenery, no trees, no water, nothing but dust, sun, dirt, insects, parched throats, and unquenchable thirst. They were also in an emotional wilderness, as have we all. We all have been wounded at one time or another. Unquestionably, being in the wilderness is the ideal time and place to learn faith and endurance and slay the giants that hinder us from progressing spiritually.

One of our greatest obstacles in life is fear. For example, there is the fear of the unknown, fear for our family, fear of being alone, fear of growing old, fear of getting sick, fear that we won't have enough money when we grow old, and so many others. Without a doubt, the wilderness is a place to hear God and a place to get rid of the fears. I had many fears during my wilderness experience of pain and emotional turmoil. I was suddenly single. I had never lived alone, so there was the fear of being alone. As you can imagine, there was the fear of the unknown, the fear of failing, and the fear of further rejection. In addition, I was always second-guessing my decisions, because I was afraid of making a mistake.

Prior to this period of my life, I always trusted God. I was always confident that he would guide me in all my activities. But when I became single, I found I was fearful about so many things. That is when I decided to do what I needed to do—kick my fear out the door and not allow my challenges to overshadow God.

I knew in my heart and mind that God was real, but it wasn't until I was in that emotional wilderness of pain, and I made the decision to give God my fears that he was able to get rid of the things that had a stranglehold on my spiritual life. One strategy that the Holy Spirit used to do this was to encourage me to bring to my memory some faith-building incidents I had experienced in the early days of my Christian walk.

First Memory

I was a new Christian and was just learning the Word. One day I went shopping for groceries. As I was choosing the meat for the family, something led me to pick up a very nice roast. Later, I asked someone for a ride to take the roast to a couple who attended my church. When I knocked on the door and presented the roast, I couldn't believe the reaction. The couple told us that the husband had been looking for work but to no avail, and the wife, a stay-at-home mom, had been cooking macaroni and cheese for the last couple of weeks for their meals. Apparently, the husband had prayed that day and told the Lord that he was tired of eating macaroni and cheese and how much he would love a big juicy steak. You can imagine the reaction when I showed up at the door with this roast. They were also new Christians.

Second Memory

I worked most of my life, except when I took the time off to have my children, but my income was always the smaller one. There was a workers' strike, which meant that the larger income in the household was gone. One evening, I was cooking spaghetti and was trying to stretch it as far as it could go, but I had a problem. I had no spaghetti sauce. As I was standing in the kitchen, the doorbell rang and in walked a friend. He had three bags of groceries and then he said, "I don't know why I picked up just spaghetti sauce, but here it is." You can just imagine the praises in that small apartment when I told him that I had been praying for spaghetti sauce.

Over and over again, God brought back memory after memory of how he took care of me, and even as I was writing this section, I was completely overwhelmed again by the goodness of God, how much he loves me, and how much he has taken care of me all these years.

When the writer of Deuteronomy spoke to the Israelites, he wanted them to remember the past. He reminded them of how God provided for them, protected them, and was ever present in their everyday life. He says in Deuteronomy 8:2–3,

> Remember how the Lord your God led you all the way in the desert these forty years, to humble you and to test you in order to know what was in your heart, whether or not you would keep his commands. He humbled you, causing you to hunger and then feeding you with manna, which neither you nor your fathers had known, to teach you that man does not live on bread alone but on every word that comes from the mouth of the Lord.

Similarly, these words are a reminder to us. Deuteronomy 8:2–3 is there to encourage us to remember the Lord and his Word in our life. So then, if God was able to take care of the Israelites for forty years, especially the fact that they didn't have to change their clothes and shoes for that long a period, isn't he able to take care of us? Why wouldn't we give our fears to him?

A few of my favorite verses that have given me a lot of comfort over the years are found in Isaiah.

> Fear not, for I have redeemed you; I have summoned you by name; you are mine. When you pass through the waters, I will be with you; and when you pass through the rivers, they will not sweep over you. When you walk through the fire, you will not be burned; the flames will not set you ablaze. For I am the Lord, your God, the Holy One of Israel, your Saviour. (Isa. 43:1–3)

"So do not fear, for I am with you; do not be dismayed, for I am your God. I will strengthen you and help you; I will uphold you with my righteous right hand" (Isa. 41:10).

Abraham must have been fearful many times. Do you think that it was out of fear that he wanted Sarah to lie and say that he was her brother? Moses must have experienced fear when he realized that he had to go back to Egypt. Why do you think that he was arguing with

God? When he left, he was branded a criminal. We are told that Jacob was fearful of meeting Esau after twenty years. Hagar was fearful and alone in the desert. David could face a bragging Goliath, yet I imagine he was fearful when Nathan pointed that long, bony finger at him and said, "You're the man." Try to imagine the fear Joseph felt in that Egyptian prison. He went from being a pampered teenager to a slave. Could you have survived if you had been placed in his situation? We all have fears—how do you handle yours? Isaiah 53:5 says,

> Surely he took up our infirmities and carried our sorrows, yet we considered him stricken by God, smitten by him, and afflicted. But he was pierced for our transgressions, he was crushed for our iniquities; the punishment that brought us peace was upon him, and by his wounds we are healed.

When we focus on our fears, we lose sight of God and his power. In Romans 8:35, the apostle Paul asked a very important question: "Who shall separate us from the love of Christ? Shall trouble or hardship or persecution or famine or nakedness or danger or sword?"

He answered his question in verses 36–39.

> It is written; for your sake we face death all day long; we are considered as sheep to be slaughtered. No, in all these things we are more than conquerors through him who loved us. For I am convinced that neither death nor life, neither angels nor demons, neither the present nor the future, not any powers, neither height nor depth, nor anything else in all creation, will be able to separate us from the love of God that is in Christ Jesus our Lord.

God has given us the power to defeat fear. Be encouraged by the words of the psalmist:

"You, O Lord, keep my lamp burning; my God turns darkness into light. With your help I can advance against a troop; with my God I can scale a wall" (Ps. 18:28).

"The Lord is my light and my salvation, whom shall I fear?" (Ps. 27:1)

223

Slaying the Other Giants in Your Life

There are many other giants that we can name, such as discouragement, improper mind-set, indifference, worldliness, guilt, fear of the future, fear of growing old, health fears, financial fears, apathy, among others.

Years ago, I read C. S. Lewis' book *The Screwtape Letters*. This book is written allegorically from a demon's perspective. It depicts what Lewis sees as the basic philosophy of the Christian worldview. In this book, the main character is a senior devil, Screwtape, who tutors his nephew, Wormwood, on the fine distinctions and techniques of tempting humans. In the uncle's viewpoint, the objective of his tutelage is to make people indifferent to the things of God, rather than making them wicked. Wormwood's main goal was to turn the human, called the Patient, and other humans away from the enemy, God, and toward their ruler, Satan.

Screwtape's instruction to Wormwood is to keep the Patient comfortable and let him think about his comfort and other things, such as his lunch, if he begins to think about anything important. Screwtape's strategy is twofold: he will always see to it that there are bad people, and Wormwood will provide him with people who do not care; in essence, apathetic people. The problem of apathy seems to have invaded the modern Christian Church with a vengeance. Many Christians want to just go to church, listen to the sermon, and go home to their lunch without considering that there is a world out there that needs to hear the good news of salvation.

As I've read and reread *The Screwtape Letters*, I'm reminded that not only is the enemy of our soul real but that he works with the giants in our lives. The list of giants above is a miniscule one. It is only my opinion, but apathy and self-centeredness are two of the greatest enemies of the Christian Church today. Not only are they harmful to the church, but they are harmful to our spiritual health and will keep us from the destiny that God has in store for us.

Maybe there are other giants that you need to slay in order to get closer to God. Make a list and find Scripture verses that will help you to counteract the giants that plague you. Look at the examples below.

Giants to slay	Bible verse	Strategy to overcome
discouragement	Heb. 10:35–36	
worldliness	Col. 3:2–3; James 4:4; 1 John 2:15–17	
temptation		
guilt		
apathy		
indifference		
improper mind-set		

When we have to face challenges or ongoing giants that need to be put to rest, I believe we need to exercise our faith, be patient, and trust the Lord. One strategy I use is the power of speaking, singing, or praying God's Word. Learn a lesson from God. The Word says, "God spoke and the universe was formed." When Satan tempted Jesus in the wilderness, Jesus spoke the Word and said, "It is written …" When you speak God's Word out loud, in the name of Jesus, the Devil will be forced to flee. James 4:7–8 says, "Submit yourselves, then, to God. Resist the devil and he will flee from you. Come near to God and he will come near to you."

"The righteous cry out, and the Lord hears them; he delivers them from all their troubles. The Lord is close to the broken-hearted and saves those who are crushed in spirit. A righteous man may have many troubles, but the Lord delivers him from them all" (Ps. 34:18–19).

As you learn to speak, pray, and sing the Word of God, your faith will grow, and it will withstand the tests that have befallen you. In fact, as you learn to put God first, to submit to him, and to praise him, he will reveal his Word to you, and you will begin to see things that you could not have seen before. Every revelation in the Word of God has value and potential to enhance your spiritual success. Therefore, when you think of your wounds, your fears, and your wilderness period, think of them as opportunities to get rid of the giant of fear and any other giants in your life. Every situation in your life is also an opportunity to get to know God in every way you can and to experience his power in your life and your heart. Don't waste these opportunities. Give God the maximum opportunity to be God.

Once God dispenses with the giants in your life, he will be better able to use you for his kingdom. This means that you will get out of that wilderness period of your life. When you get out of the wilderness, you will appreciate the times you had getting to know God. Don't be surprised if the enemy tries to discourage you. Jesus was accosted by Satan as soon as he was out of the wilderness. Paul had adversity right through his ministry, even to the point of having a "thorn in the flesh." However, don't give up in the midst of trials or testing. It is necessary to pass through seasons of trials, but God is there for you, to strengthen you, and to hold you up. Remember, he is there to prepare you for future work in his kingdom. To quote a line of a well-known Southern gospel song, "The God on the mountain is still God in the valley."

CHAPTER 46

The End of the Wilderness Experience

At Last!

In a previous vignette, I told the story of getting lost late at night in a foreign country. It was one of the most horrifying experiences of my life. The contrast in that experience, though, is that of arriving at my correct station and seeing people, lights, and my correct train on the platform. Obviously, my joy was boundless!

In the same way, once we get over the challenges of our life or get out of the difficult situation we are in—out of the wilderness, that is—we can see the light of God and begin to enjoy it. However, sometimes there is the danger of becoming apathetic from the sheer exhaustion of all the physical and emotional turmoil of the trauma we faced. Do not give in to that temptation! Continue to read, meditate on God's Word, grow spiritually, and prepare yourself for the ministry God has in store for you. If you don't do that, you will be back where you started.

Let me remind you that the wilderness is only meant to be for a season, to change and transform you. But if you do backslide, like the Israelites, and lapse back into previous behavior or fail to continue your spiritual growth, be prepared to take another lap in the wilderness. In the wilderness, you gave up all the baggage of your wounds, pain, unforgiveness, resentment, anger, and fears, and everything else that you needed to unpack. Don't let that time go to waste. Continue to grow. Continue to trust God.

It would be sad if we allowed ourselves to be like many Christians who never come into a mature attitude of faith, because at the first

227

sign of testing or when a difficult situation arises, they either embrace a carnal, worldly lifestyle, or they become old and bitter through hoarding their wounds. Either way, they never learn to trust God enough or to give thanks to him in times of testing. At the first sign of testing, they bail out on him, with the result that his promises are not manifested in their lives.

If we don't learn to speak God's Word, thank, praise, worship, and honor him in our wilderness experiences, God knows we are not ready for the blessings or even the ministry he has prepared for us. It is easy to think that we have accomplished things all on our own merit when life is going well and forget the God who gave us the blessings, as well as the blessings of the people he put in our life. The wilderness is a great corrector of such erroneous thoughts. Job uttered a warning that should be taken into serious consideration. He said, "The Lord giveth and the Lord taketh away."

Are there some other giants you need to slay?

The Bible says that only Jesus Christ can set you free.

Is there something in your life that you know God wants you to do, but you have not proceeded to do it because of fear, lack of faith, or other factors?

Let us examine the lives of some women who put their faith into action, despite the odds stacked against them.

CHAPTER 47

Faith That Moves Mountain

Five Exceptional Women and Job

The woman at the well

Let us continue our journey!

You have to travel through the wilderness to get to the Promised Land.

In John 4:1–44, we see Jesus talking to a Samaritan woman. It says, Now Jesus learned that the Pharisees had heard that he was gaining and baptizing more disciples than John although in fact it was not Jesus who baptized, but his disciples. So he left Judea and went back once more to Galilee.

Now he had to go through Samaria. So he came to a town in Samaria called Sychar, near the plot of ground Jacob had given to his son Joseph. Jacob's well was there, and Jesus, tired as he was from the journey, sat down by the well. It was about noon.

When a Samaritan woman came to draw water, Jesus said to her, "Will you give me a drink?" (His disciples had gone into the town to buy food.)

The Samaritan woman said to him, "You are a Jew and I am a Samaritan woman. How can you ask me for a drink?" (For Jews do not associate with Samaritans).

Jesus answered her, "If you knew the gift of God and who it is that asks you for a drink, you would have asked him and he would have given you living water."

"Sir," the woman said, "you have nothing to draw with and the well is deep. Where can you get this living water? Are you greater than our father Jacob, who gave us the well and drank from it himself, as did also his sons and his livestock?"

Jesus answered, "Everyone who drinks this water will be thirsty again, but whoever drinks the water I give them will never thirst. Indeed, the water I gave them will become in them a spring of water welling up to eternal life."

The woman said to him, "Sir, give me this water so that I won't get thirsty and have to keep coming here to draw water."

He told her, "Go, call your husband and come back."

"I have no husband," she replied.

Jesus said to her, "You are right when you say you have no husband. The fact is, you have had five husbands, and the man you now have is not your husband. What you have just said is quite true."

"Sir," the woman said, "I can see that you are a prophet. Our ancestors worshiped on this mountain, but you Jews claim that the place where we must worship is in Jerusalem."

"Woman," Jesus replied, "believe me, a time is coming when you will worship the Father neither on this mountain nor in Jerusalem. You Samaritans worship what you do not know; we worship what we do know, for salvation is from the Jews. Yet a time is coming and has now come when the true worshipers will worship the Father in the Spirit and in truth, for they are the kind of worshipers the Father seeks. God is Spirit, and his worshipers must worship in the Spirit and in truth."

The woman said, "I know that Messiah (called Christ) is coming. When he comes, he will explain everything to us."

Then Jesus declared, "I, the one speaking to you—I am he."

Just then his disciples returned and were surprised to find him talking with a woman. But no one asked, "What do you want" or "Why are you talking with her?"

Then, leaving her water jar, the woman went back to the town and said to the people, "Come, see a man who told me everything I ever did. Could this be the Messiah?" They came out of the town and made their way toward him.

I always get excited when I read this dialogue between Jesus and the woman at the well. We are told that the disciples later joined Jesus and were very surprised at the scene they came upon. This woman was a societal disaster; she was an outcast. We talked about Hagar and the position and role of women in that society. This woman's position was probably lower than Hagar's. Can you imagine how low her self-worth was? She had to go to the well at noon, in the heat of the day, when no one else was around. She could not even be in the company of the other women at the well because of her low character, because they probably distrusted her around their men. I would surmise that she was also open to ridicule because of her loose lifestyle.

Nonetheless, in the dialogue between her and Jesus, I hear an articulate woman who is not afraid to confront Jesus about talking to her, a Samaritan. She also debates the Scriptures with him, although she recognizes him as a rabbi. I believe she is a smart and attractive woman. How else could she have captured the attention of five "husbands"? She is certainly not stupid, as she knows the Scriptures regarding the coming of the Messiah. But she was living a lie.

When Jesus confronted her with the truth and exposed her life for what it was, her faith was activated. She had been in the wilderness for a long time, but despite all her pain and trauma of rejection and abandonment of four other "husbands," she finally encountered the one man she could depend on not to use her for his own purposes. Jesus was the only man she was able to believe in and trust. In talking to Jesus, she caught a glimpse of the Promised Land and all the blessings it offered—a place where she was respected, a place where she was no longer a discard at the whim of a husband, a place where there was peace, and a place where she was no longer an outcast.

The Unknown Woman

Similarly, the woman known only as the woman with an issue of blood was considered by society to be discarded. Luke 8:43–48 tells the story of an unknown woman.

> And a woman was there who had been subject to bleeding for twelve years, but no one could heal her. She came up behind him and touched the edge of his cloak, and immediately her bleeding stopped.

> "Who touched me?" Jesus asked. When they all denied it, Peter said, "Master, the people are crowding and pressing against you." But Jesus said, "Someone touched me; I know that power has gone out from me." Then the woman, seeing that she could not go unnoticed, came trembling and fell at his feet. In the presence of all the people, she told why she had touched him and how she had been instantly healed. Then he said to her, "Daughter, your faith has healed you. Go in peace."

I love this story because it has so many lessons for us! Unknown and ashamed, here is a woman whose name was never mentioned in the Scriptures. She suffered for twelve years with a physical problem and was determined to use Jesus' powers to become well. As a woman, an issue of blood for twelve years is unimaginable. As a woman, she was low on the totem pole. As a woman who had been bleeding for twelve years, she was a social outcast!

Leviticus 15:19–30 outlines the laws regarding bodily discharges in conjunction with uncleanness. As an unclean woman, she was unwelcomed in society. Sexual relations would have made her bed and anything she touched unclean. She would be unclean for as long as she had that bleeding. Even her husband would have been ceremonially unclean, so she probably would have been divorced by her husband after twelve years. According to the law, she was not allowed to worship in the synagogue and would have been barred from going to the synagogue.

> When she is cleansed from her discharge, she must count off seven days, and after that she will be ceremonially clean. On the eighth day she must take two doves or two young pigeons and bring them to the priest at the entrance to the Tent of Meeting. The priest is to sacrifice one for a sin offering and the other for a burnt offering. In this way he will make atonement for her before the Lord for the uncleanness of her discharge. (Lev. 15:28–30)

Physically, she is unwell. Religiously, she is unclean. Some people might believe that these are one and the same factors. Clearly, she was at the end of her rope. She wanted healing and that was it! Mark 5:27–34 says she had heard about Jesus. The physicians had taken all her money and had not provided any cure. She had found out the source of her healing; she had heard how Jesus had healed the man with the demonic spirit, (Mark 5:8), the blind, the lame, and the crippled. "Why not me?" she asked herself. I imagined that as she set out on the road to find Jesus, she did her self-talk. She probably said, "Today! Today is my day. I don't care what anyone says. I don't care who says I'm unclean. I am going to touch his clothes, because his power is so great that even touching the hem of his garments will heal me. Twelve years is too long!"

I can also imagine that as she furtively walked or maybe even skulked amid the crowd of people, hoping that no one would recognize her, her heart pounded and her head was bent low. Her determined steps drew her nearer and nearer to the voice of Jesus. Finally, she was near enough, and she stooped down at the feet of Jesus.

Whenever I get to this part of the story, I always want to shout a hallelujah! She was willing to break social taboos. As a woman, she was restricted from touching a man in public. As an unclean woman, if she touched Jesus, she would make him ceremonially unclean. Yet she said, "If I just touch his clothes, I'll be healed" (Mark 5:28).

How determined are we to touch Jesus? At the beginning of the year, after hearing of all the lies someone was spreading about me, and after being bombarded with cruelty for some time, I finally shouted in the air, "Enough! God, I have had enough! I am not going to fight them! I am not going to defend myself! I am not going to listen to them! God," I said, "you are my redeemer, you are my defender, and you are my vindicator. I lay my weapons down. I will not fight in my own strength anymore. I will only pray."

Since that time, I have spent more time praising, praying, and worshiping than worrying about what people are saying. I'm not saying that it doesn't hurt when people wound you, especially when it comes from people you trusted to watch your back. I'm saying that we can only be accountable for our own behavior. God will do the rest. I know he will take care of my reputation. I have had God's peace since that day. This unknown woman finally knew the peace that touching Jesus brings.

Lessons to Be Learned from This Woman's Faith

- She found the source of her healing.
- She was determined to access that source.
- Despite the obstacles facing her, possibly an angry mob at being touched by an unclean woman, she was determined to touch Jesus.
- She wasn't the only one in the crowd who needed healing, but Jesus said that she was healed because of her faith.
- When Jesus asked, "Who touched me?" she was able to testify of the healing.
- The woman's healing and testimony glorified God.

Let us look at a snapshot of her life from her perspective.

All the doctors had failed her. Her community and family members had mocked, rejected, and shunned her. As for the religious leaders, they had no answer, except to say she was unclean and couldn't come to the synagogue. And here she was—her last chance. At some point, she made the decision and said, "I am going to touch Jesus. What more do I have to lose? I lost my money; I lost my friends; I lost my family. I have nothing else to lose. Yet I haven't lost this tiny pebble of hope. If I can only touch him, I have everything to gain."

The second part of this story is her determination. I believe she said, "Enough! Lord, I have had enough! I am tired of this. Today is the day."

I also believe that at this point, if all the hounds of hell had tried to stop her, she would have turned and stared them down with one steely glance from tired but determined eyes. She was on a mission to get her healing and nothing was going to stop her.

What about you? How determined are you to touch the hem of Jesus' garment?

That day was her day. Are you determined enough to make today your day?

When Jesus called her out to reveal what she had done, I believe he called her out to commend her for her tenacity and faith. Not only was it a teachable moment for the disciples and the bystanders, but Jesus was also showing them, by his actions, that he sees the unknown, faceless people in our society—people we consider discards and of no value.

Jesus said to her, "Daughter, your faith has healed you. Go in peace and be freed from your suffering" (Mark 5:34). Also, an important factor in the story is that when she was confronted, she threw herself down at his feet and humbly admitted what she had done. What better way to glorify God than to tell what he has done for us? After twelve years of wilderness wasteland, she had entered the Promised Land of freedom—freedom from pain, shame, and desolation.

Food for Thought
You cannot enter the Promised Land ... without faith!

Tamar
Tamar was a widow who obtained a child for herself and an heir for her dead husband's inheritance. She risked everything—her life and her reputation—to get what was rightfully hers.

In Genesis 38:1–11, we are told that she married into the family of Judah. First, she married Er, Judah's son, and he died and left her childless. Then she married Onan, his brother. By Jewish law, if the man dies and his wife is left childless, then she has the right to go to the next brother and demand that he marries her and produces a child (Deut. 25:1–10).

So, after Er's death, under Levirate law, Er's younger brother Onan was obligated to marry Tamar and give her a child. However, Onan did not give her the child to which she was entitled. Genesis 38:8–11 says,

> Then Judah said to Onan, lie with your brother's wife and fulfill your duty as a brother-in-law to produce offspring for your brother. But Onan knew that the offspring would not be his; so whenever he lay with his brother's wife, he spilled his semen on the ground to keep from producing offspring for his brother. What he did was wicked in the Lord's sight; so he put him to death also.

Onan failed to carry out his obligation to Tamar and disregarded his father's command. Deuteronomy 25:8–10 describes the punishment of not fulfilling the duty of a brother-in-law.

> Then the elders of his town shall summon him and talk to him. If he persists in saying, I do not want to marry her, his brother's widow shall go up to him in the presence of the elders, take off one of her sandals, spit in his face and say, this is what is done to the man who will not build up his brother's family line. That man's line shall be known in Israel as the Family of the Unsandaled.

Onan's sin was not that he refused to marry Tamar. He married her, but he practiced his own form of birth control by spilling his semen on the ground. The act was so heinous in God's sight that he put him to death. Judah, her father-in-law, then promised to give Shelah, the third son to Tamar when he grew up; but Judah did not keep his promise. Poor Tamar!

Tamar was not to be deterred from her goal of obtaining a child. Genesis 38:12–19 describes how Tamar tricked Judah, her father-in-law, and claimed her right to obtain a child. After the death of Judah's wife, Tamar heard that he was going into another town to shear sheep. In the ensuing events, Tamar disguised herself by veiling her face and dressing as a prostitute. She then waited for Judah,

"And then sat down at the entrance to Enaim, which is on the road to Timnah. For she saw that, though Shelah had now grown up, she had not been given to him as a wife" (verse 14).

Judah did not recognize his daughter-in-law. He thought she was really a prostitute. In any event, Tamar's dalliance with Judah caused her to become pregnant. When the news spread throughout the community, there was a big scandal, and she was accused of promiscuity. First, she did not have a husband and was pregnant; and second, she would not name the father of her child.

Genesis 38:24–26 says,

About three months later Judah was told, your daughter-in-law Tamar is guilty of prostitution, and as a result she is now pregnant. Judah said, bring her out and have her burned to death!

As she was being brought out, she sent a message to her father-in-law. I am pregnant by the man who owns these, she said. And she added, see if you recognize whose seal and cord and staff these are.

Judah recognized them and said, she is more righteous than I since I wouldn't give her my son Shelah.

Tamar was righteous because she was trying to follow the law.

Several times she was treated unfairly by Judah and his sons, but she outwitted Judah by having him sleep with her, secured his own cord and seal that would guarantee her life, and then became pregnant by him. Tamar's actions rewarded her with twin boys.

Genesis 38:27–30 says,

As she was giving birth, one of them put out his hand; so the midwife took a scarlet thread and tied it on his wrist and said, This one came out first. But when he drew back his hand, his brother came out, and she said, so this is how you have broken out! And he was named Perez. Then his brother, who had the scarlet thread on his wrist, came out and he was given the name Zerah.

Perez later became an ancestor of King David, who is an ancestor of Jesus. In a similar fashion to Joseph's story, despite human interference, God's plan continued to unfold.

Rahab

We've traveled with the Israelites on their journey, from their entry into Egypt to their exit over four hundred years later via the Red Sea. We've tarried with them in the wilderness and listened to them complain their way out of the Promised Land. All the complainers were now dead, and their surviving children, along with Joshua and Caleb, were ready to enter the Promised Land.

Prior to crossing the Jordan River to enter the Promised Land, the Bible tells us in Joshua 2:1 that Joshua, the son of Nun, sent two men to secretly spy out the land of Jericho in order to judge the strength of the opposing forces of the land. "Go, look over the land, he said, especially Jericho. So they went and entered the house of a prostitute named Rahab and stayed there."

When the King of Jericho was told that Israelite spies were scouting out his land, he was perturbed. So he sent messengers to Rahab to deliver the men to his messengers. Rahab denied having them in her house but said, "Yes, the men came to me, but I did not know where they had come from. At dusk, when it was time to close the city gate, the men left. I don't know which way they went. Go after them quickly. You may catch up with them" (Jos. 2:4–5).

Rahab sent the king's messengers on a wild goose chase and then made her way up to the roof where she had hidden the spies. She had placed her life and her family's lives on the line to save these men, little knowing that she had also set her destiny into motion. Now, she needed to cement the plans and decisions she had made in her mind. She said to the spies,

> I know that the Lord has given this land to you and that a great fear of you has fallen on us, so that all who live in this country are melting in fear because of you. We have heard how the Lord dried up the water of the Red Sea for you when you came out of Egypt, and what you did to Sihon and Og, the two kings of the Amorites east of the Jordan, whom you completely destroyed. When we heard of it, our hearts melted and everyone's courage failed because of you, for the Lord your God is God in heaven above and on the earth below. Now then, please swear to me by the Lord that you will show kindness to my family, because I have shown kindness to you. Give me a sure sign that you will spare the lives of my father and mother, my brothers and sisters, and all who belong to them, and that you will save us from death. (Jos. 2:9–13)

Rahab had only heard of the happenings between the Israelites, their God, and other nations. She had not witnessed them herself. Yet she was ready to put her life in jeopardy for an unseen, unknown God. I have to interject here that many Christians have seen the miracles of God. They know God, yet they make no effort to live for God or do anything for him.

In our modern world you can turn on your radio or television and hear Christian broadcasts every day, sometimes twenty-four-hours a day. Yet Christians are still bent on seeking their own happiness and putting their own "needs" ahead of God's business.

God could shout in a megaphone, and his voice and his presence would go undetected by Christians who are indulging in worldly affairs. But Rahab, a citizen of a sinful nation, recognized God for who he was—she heard the news of how God had foiled the attempts of the other nations to capture the Israelites, and she decided to abandon the gods of Canaan to seek refuge with the God of Israel.

Her action demonstrated an active faith, and despite her past lifestyle, she is considered to be the epitome of faith. Once a prostitute, she later was considered and numbered among the faithful and righteous.

By faith the people passed through the Red Sea as on dry land; but when the Egyptians tried to do so, they were drowned. By faith the walls of Jericho fell, after the people had marched around them for seven days. By faith the prostitute Rahab, because she welcomed the spies, was not killed with those who were disobedient. (Heb. 11:29–31)

She later married an Israelite, Salmon, and later became an ancestor of Jesus Christ through the line of King David.

"And Salmon the father of Boaz by Rahab, and Boaz the father of Obed by Ruth and Obed the father of Jesse, and Jesse the father of David the king" (Matt.1:5–6).

Here is a woman people would call the "dregs" of society—a woman used and discarded by men, a woman of no value. Yet I see a smart woman—an independent-thinking woman and a cunning woman who knows what she wants and goes after it. When the king sent his messengers to inquire about her nocturnal visitors, who in her right mind would blatantly lie to the king without blinking an eye? It would take nerves of steel to lie to the king's messengers.

I love this woman! Rahab obviously had her pulse on the activities of the community. She was well informed and consciously made her decision when she asked for mercy for herself, her father, mother, brothers, sisters, and all her family members. She and the spies came to an agreement that they would save her and her family if she kept her promises to protect their lives.

The terms of the pledge made by the spies echoed Rahab's request. Based on the history of the Israelites, Rahab knew that God would give the land of Canaan to the Israelites. Rahab gave the spies crucial information regarding the people and the land of Canaan.

She said,

"I know that the Lord has given this land to you and a great fear of you has fallen on us, so that all who live in this country are melting in fear because of you. We have heard how the Lord dried up the water of the Red Sea for you when you came out of Egypt and what you did to Sihon and Og, the two kings of the Amorites east of the Jordan, whom you completely destroyed. When we heard of it, our hearts melted and everyone's courage failed because of you, for the Lord your God is God in heaven above and on the earth below" (Josh. 2:9-11).

Rahab's words confirmed the inevitability of God giving the city of Jericho to the Israelites. Therefore, the spies said to her, "Our lives for your lives! If you don't tell what we are doing, we will treat you kindly and faithfully when the Lord gives us the land."

The promise was made to save Rahab and her family, and we are told in Joshua 6:20–25 that

When the trumpets sounded, the people shouted, and at the sound of the trumpet, when the people gave a loud shout, the wall collapsed; so every man charged straight in, and they took the city. They devoted the city to the Lord and destroyed with the sword every living thing in it—men and women, young and old, cattle, sheep and donkeys.

Joshua said to the two men who had spied out the land, Go into the prostitute's house and bring her out and all who belong to her, in accordance with your oath to her. So the young men who had done the spying went in and brought out Rahab, her father and mother and brothers and all who belonged to her. They brought out her entire family and put them in a place outside the camp of Israel.

Then they burned the whole city and everything in it ... Joshua spared Rahab the prostitute with her family and all who belonged to her, because she hid the men Joshua had sent as spies to Jericho – and she lives among the Israelites to this day.

Food for Thought

Despite our past occupations or our history, God's offer of salvation is still available to all people, all nations, and all ethnicity, providing they repent and come to him (Acts 26:19–20).

Deborah

After the death of Joshua we see a period of Israel's history that bespoke of apostasy, disloyalty to God, and frequent cries for help when they were in trouble. Joshua had secured the Promised Land for them and they were now to "enter rest."

However, they settled in the land of Canaan and adopted the lifestyle of the people of the land. Prior to Joshua's death, he had summoned all Israel—the elders, leaders, judges, and officials and warned them about the nations they would encounter in the Promised Land.

He said,

Be very strong; be careful to obey all that is written in the Book of the Law of Moses, without turning aside to the right or to the left. Do not associate with these nations that remain among you; do not invoke the names of their gods or swear by them. You must not serve them or bow down to them. But you are to hold fast to the Lord your God, as you have until now. (Jos. 23:6–8)

Further into the story, Joshua summoned all the leaders again and renewed the covenant at Schechem (Jos. 24:1–27. A key verse is verse 19. Joshua said to the people,

You are not able to serve the Lord. He is a holy God; he is a jealous God. He will not forgive your rebellion and your sins. If you forsake the Lord and serve foreign gods, he will turn and bring disaster on you and make an end of you, after he has been good to you. But the people said to Joshua, No! We will serve the Lord.

Then Joshua said, "You are witnesses against yourselves that you have chosen to serve the Lord."

He also took a stone, set it up under the oak near the holy place of the Lord, and said, "See! This stone will be a witness against us. It has heard all the words the Lord has said to us. It will be a witness against you if you are untrue to your God (Jos. 24:27).

After that, the children of Israel began to spiral into spiritual defeat. In Judges 2:10–13, we are told that there arose a new generation who did not know the Lord and what he had done for Israel.

Then they did evil in the eyes of the Lord and served the Baals. They forsook the Lord, the God of their fathers, who had brought them out of Egypt. They followed and worshipped various gods of the peoples around them. They provoked the Lord to anger because they forsook him and served Baals and the Ashroreths.

In his anger against Israel, the Lord handed them over to raiders who plundered them. He sold them to their enemies all around, whom they were no longer able to resist.

The last sentence of this Scripture says, "They were in great distress."

Apparently, they were not in so much distress that they curtailed their wicked activities, because Judges 2:16 says, "Then the Lord raised up judges, who saved them out of the hands of these raiders. Yet they would not listen to their judges but prostituted themselves to other gods and worshiped them."

This is the era to which Deborah was born; she was married, a prophetess and leader of Israel, and she dispensed justice under a tree labeled the Palm of Deborah. She is noted for providing wise counsel to Barak, who was supposed to deliver Israel from the hands of Sisera, the commander of Jabin's army. He failed to provide the military leadership, and she had to stand in the gap for his failings. Deborah was an exceptional servant of God. She stood for everything that is lacking in today's society, especially in some circles. She stood for courage, decency, wisdom, and a heart keenly focused on God.

Deborah is another of the personalities in the Bible that intrigues me. She lived in a culture where women were treated like second-class citizens. They were disposable, and their role in society was far below a man's. Yet Deborah was a judge in Israel, God's chosen nation. She lived in a period when, we are told, "Every man did what was right in his own eyes." She is truly an exceptional woman. For God to have chosen her, she had to have stood for godly wisdom, not what was right in her own eyes.

Sometime ago, I completed a research project. I wanted to explore the question, "Why do some long-term marriages end in divorce?" I examined literally pages and pages of information based on interviews, blogs, and books on this phenomenon. I was very surprised at the results and the reasons given for the breakdown of the relationships.

One common theme was "I." Every case I studied, "I" was the center of the relationship breakdown. The most surprising information was the phenomenon in the Christian Church today, where many supposedly "Christian" spouses walk away from their families. As a believer in Jesus Christ, we have the truth; we have the answers to life's difficulties. Yet the divorce rate among Christians, depending on the statistics you read, is higher than that in secular circles. Why is this so?

It would appear that similar to the historical period of the judges where everyone did what was right in their own eyes, so too modern Christians are doing what seems right in their own eyes, not what God's Word says. I am reminded by the apostle Paul's words that in the last days prior to Jesus' return that even the very elect will be deceived. He warns us,

> People will become lovers of themselves, lovers of money, boastful, loud, abusive, disobedient to their parents, ungrateful, unholy, without love, unforgiving, slanderous, without self control, brutal, not lovers of the good, treacherous, rash, conceited, lovers of pleasure rather than lovers of God—having a form of godliness but denying its power. (2 Tim. 3:2–5)

I am also reminded of the parable that Jesus told about the ten virgins. Five were wise and prepared for the Lord's return, and the other five were foolish and unprepared. I believe that the main point of this parable is to keep watch and be prepared in the event that Jesus returns when we least expect him. Jesus is on his Father's timetable, not ours. If we get impatient after serving for a long period, we may fall into the trap of believing that he won't return.

Years ago at my workplace, I heard a frustrated colleague shout to someone from behind his little cubicle. I did not know what his problem was, but he said, "This is as slow as the second coming of Christ." Of course, I couldn't pass up the opportunity! I shouted back, even though I was not part of the conversation, "His coming might be slow, but it is sure." I chuckled to myself, even as I write this, because my answer did not elicit any response from either colleague. I think they were both in shock at my audacity at butting into their conversation.

God's plan for Jesus' return is sure. But before he returns, he has a plan for everyone. He had a plan for the woman at the well, the unknown woman with a sickness, Tamar, Rehab, and Deborah. He also has a plan for you and me. All five women in the illustration were exceptional women who demonstrated exceptional faith in God. Could this be you?

I believe that the story of Job is a fitting conclusion to this section. All the personalities—from Abraham to Paul—were not perfect, except for Jesus. They were either wounded greatly, or they did the wounding. However, as their story unfolded, we were privileged to see the purpose of their calling, their preparation, their transformation, and the reason why they are included in the biblical Hall of Fame. They are portrayed as real people, "warts and all," but God, who saw their future, took their potential and turned it into reality for his honor and glory.

Throughout their journey, we saw the call. Some answered readily, some reluctantly. Their preparatory stages were painful, as we see their sins exposed to reveal ordinary human beings like you and me, who aren't perfect but who have a heart for God. These are the people God used, as they allowed God to take what they had to offer and changed it into what he wanted them to have.

Job's Dilemma

Job's story is different from the others. It may be perceived as the epicenter of great injustices, suffering, and even mistaken identity. Here is a man who, by all accounts, is a righteous man, because Job 1:1–3 says,

In the land of Uz there lived a man whose name was Job. This man was blameless and upright; he feared God and shunned evil. He had seven sons and three daughters, and he owned seven thousand sheep, three thousand camels, five hundred yoke of oxen and five hundred donkeys and had a large number of servants. He was the greatest man among all the people of the East.

Job was so righteous that when his children had feasts, he would offer sacrifices up to God for them, just in case they had sinned against God during the feast. This, I imagine, would be similar to interceding or standing in the gap for our loved ones. Job didn't want to take a chance on his children sinning against God, even unconsciously. Things were going very well for Job, but then his sorrows began after God drew attention to his righteousness. One day when the angels came to present themselves before the Lord in heaven, Satan also came with them.

The Lord said to Satan, "Where have you come from?"

Satan answered the Lord, "From roaming through the earth and going back and forth in it."

Then the Lord said to Satan, "Have you considered my servant Job? There is no one on earth like him; he is blameless and upright, a man who fears God and shuns evil."

Satan replied, "Does Job fear God for nothing? Have you not put a hedge around him and his household and everything he has? You have blessed the work of his hands, so that his flocks and herds are spread throughout the land. But stretch out your hand and strike everything he has, and he will surely curse you to your face."

The Lord said, "Very well, then, everything he has is in your hands, but on the man himself, do not lay a finger."

In the previous dialogue between God and Satan, we note several things happening. First, it is not a fairy tale that the Devil roams around, trying to find a small foot into our lives. Peter refers to "the devil roaming around seeking whom to devour" (1 Pet. 5:8). If we give him an opening, he is going to take it.

Second, Satan is also the accuser of the brethren, God's faithful servants (Rev. 12:10). When people wound you, tell lies about you, and do all sorts of evil to you, who do you think is orchestrating this?

Third, it was God who drew Satan's attention to Job. Job was doing all the right things to please God—living a righteous life, making sure his children were living right, and "minding his own spiritual business." Yet God gave Satan permission to test Job. Many people might groan when they see God doing this and may also ask why.

Fourth, Satan's power is limited. He can only do what God allows him to do.

I recently had a conversation with a friend and told her that in 1981, when I became a Christian, I prayed a special prayer. I had read the story of the seven sons of Sceva and how they tried to cast out demons from a man, "in the name of Jesus whom Paul talks about." The demons beat them up so badly that they ran out of the house naked. The demons said to them, "Jesus I know and Paul I know, but who are you?" When I read that story, I said to the Lord, "I want the devil to know my name."

During this conversation with my friend, I said to her, "If the devil has us in his camp, he doesn't care. We won't have any troubles. But if we are living right and invading his territory for God, he will definitely take notice and go after us. It seems that in the last few years, I have had a target on my forehead for the Devil. He's been taking pot-shots at me for a while."

Food for Thought:

If you are serving God, Satan should know your name!

In the analysis of the book of Job, the overall themes ask many questions but sometimes do not offer answers. For example, the book dares to ask the hard questions: (1) Why do the righteous suffer? (2) Where is God in all of mankind's suffering?

You may be asking, "Why did God allow this person to hurt me when I've been trying to live a godly life?" or "Why didn't God answer when I prayed? Doesn't he care?"

The overall themes of Job show the following:

1. The justice and character of God being discussed by Job and his friends
2. There is knowledge and wisdom (Job 5:2; 8:8–10; 11:6; 15:7; 28:12–28).
3. Friendship and loyalty (Job 4:5; 16:2, 14; 19:13–22; 26:1–4).
4. The wisdom of the young, namely Elihu, who decides in his wisdom to straighten out everyone, especially when he chastises Job for justifying himself and being righteous in his own eyes.

All of Job's comforters were acting like great men of wisdom who had all the answers. They heatedly debated and discussed Job's problems with the wisdom of the human mind until the One with the greatest wisdom, God, joined the debate. According to Job's wishes, he was granted his day in court.

When we are wounded, we tend to rub our spiritual bottle because we want God to pop up like a genie when we call his name. We beg for answers and fire up requests faster than a missile. When God does "appear," we expect a benevolent pat on the head and an explanation as to why we are suffering. We say, "Lord, here I am, working for you. I am using my God-given gifts and talents to do ministry that will glorify your name. But look at what is happening. Someone is bad-mouthing me. Someone else is spreading lies about me. And Lord, you will never believe some of the people in that church. Lord, where you place me, I don't know."

Whenever I get to whining and complaining, I always imagine God saying to Peter, "Peter, here we go again."

A few key verses are in Job 38:1–13. Read the rest of God's response to Job and his friends when he answered Job out of the storm.

He said,

Who is this that darkens my counsel with words without knowledge? Brace yourself like a man; I will question you, and you shall answer me.

Where were you when I laid the earth's foundation? Tell me, if you understand. Who marked off its dimensions? Surely you know! Who stretched a measuring line across it?

On what were its footings set, or who laid its cornerstone – while the morning stars sang together and all the angels shouted for joy? Who shut up the sea behind doors when it burst forth from the womb, when I made the clouds its garment and wrapped it in thick darkness, when I fixed limits for it and set its doors and bars in place, when I said, this far you may come and no farther; here is where your proud waves halt?

Have you ever given orders to the morning, or shown the dawn its place, that it might take the earth by the edges and shake the wicked out of it?

At this point, I would have run for cover if I were a part of this conversation. We speak so foolishly sometimes when we think God is not listening! Job's friends kept talking but forgot that God was listening. God has infinite knowledge, wisdom, and power, while man, as a created being, is finite and has limited knowledge and wisdom. Therefore, in the midst of the suffering and wilderness experience, never be tempted to blame God and quarrel with him about his silence, his lack of action on your behalf, or the injustices done to you.

There are lessons we can learn from the book of Job:

- We should never presume to know why a person is suffering or why someone has to go through a difficult time. We don't have the answers.

- God is not black-and-white. Do not place God into a box of your own making.
- Elihu felt he had to defend God. As modern Christians, we feel we have to lawyer-up to defend God. Believe me; he doesn't need us to defend him! He does very well on his own. God is our advocate, not the other way around.
- People who are suffering need comfort, not our opinions or sage advice. Many people like to preface their comforting remarks with, "If I were you, I would ..." My response is usually, "But you're not me," or I just nod, smile, and tune them out.

Many modern thinkers are quick to question God's sovereignty. They ask, "Why are the children in third-world countries suffering? Why should the innocent suffer? Why should I suffer when I didn't do anything wrong? Is this justice?"

At the beginning of Job's story, God's sovereignty is challenged by Satan, and Job's friends questioned God in many ways. In the end, Satan and Job's friends were silenced. The lesson for us is apparent. Despite the philosophical discussions between Job and his friends, several points are evident:

1. There was no reason given as to why God allowed righteous Job to suffer. All his afflictions and indignities were never explained by God.
2. Our faith in God must endure when there's no reason or understanding.
3. Satan is the accuser and is allowed to test our faith. Be reminded that in Job 1:6, Satan is the adversary, playing the role of prosecutor in the heavenly court. His history goes as far back as to the serpent that tempted Adam and Eve in the garden of Eden.
4. Paul calls him the god of this world and the prince of the powers of the air (2 Cor. 4:4; Eph. 2:2). We need to be on guard all the time. Although he cannot conduct any acts against us

unless God approves, he is a liar and the author of all evil (Luke 10:19) and the prince of this world (John 13:31; 14:30; 16:11).

5. The true character of a person is revealed under stress or duress.

6. As gold is heated and melded to produce a finer substance, so is suffering used to build and fine-tune our character and test our faith.

7. In life, suffering and tragedies are never as simple as outsiders perceive. There is never a shortage of opinions on why good children go bad, or why a spouse abandons his family. These opinions are usually given by people who have never been in the situation they are talking about. When you look at Job's emotional turmoil, his false comforters gave simplistic answers and superficial opinions to these most painful questions.

Job went through a terrible suffering. Similarly, you might be suffering now. We might not be sure why God allows us to suffer, but we can be sure that in the midst of his silence is when he speaks the loudest.

We have to continue to trust in him. God loves us. I have experienced God's love more in the years of suffering than I have in the years prior to that. Not that he loved me more but that I learned, in my suffering, to lay everything at his feet and to trust totally in him. Romans 8:28 has become more real to me.

It says, "And we know in all things God works for the good of those who love him, who have been called according to his purpose."

Paul goes on to say,

Who shall separate us from the love of Christ? Shall trouble or hardship or persecution or famine or nakedness or danger or sword?" For your sake we face death all day long; we are considered as sheep to be slaughtered. No, in all these things we are more than conquerors through him who loved us. For I am convinced that neither death nor life, neither angels nor demons, neither the present nor the future, nor any powers, neither height no depth nor anything else in all creation, will be able to separate us from the love of God that is in Christ Jesus our Lord." (Rom. 8:28–39)

Food for Thought

God needs exceptional people of faith in his kingdom. Are you an exceptional person that God can use?

CHAPTER 48

Entering the Promised Land

With the examination of the five exceptional women of faith and Job, we should now be armed with the knowledge of what will take us into the place of rest—faith and total trust. Three questions to ask at this point are:

- How can we accomplish this?
- How can we get to the Promised Land?
- What does the Promised Land represent for the modern Christian?

The Promised Land symbolizes the place of ultimate blessing in the presence of God. As Christian, how do we enter into the Promised Land or God's rest? You cannot enter the Promised Land without leaving the enslavement of "Egypt."

Referring to Israel's wilderness experience, the apostle Paul wrote, "These things happened to them as examples and were written down as warnings for us, on whom the fulfillment of the ages has come" (1 Cor. 10:11).

Modern-Day Application

Many of our modern-day Christians are deceived about a life entrusted to God. The enemy has deceived many into thinking that:

- Life is about the physical.
- It's about money.
- Life is about seeking happiness at all costs.
- The fulfillment of life is found in pleasure
- Our security lies in how many material possessions we own.

In Hebrews 3:7–19, the apostle Paul warns against unbelief. He discusses the time of testing of the Israelites in the wilderness, their hardening of heart, and subsequent rebellion. The heart of the people of Israel was always going astray from God and eventually, God said that they would never enter his rest. Paul warns Christian believers to "see to it, brothers, that none of you has a sinful, unbelieving heart that turns away from the living God. But encourage one another daily, as long as it is called Today, so that none of you may be hardened by sin's deceitfulness" (Heb. 3:12-13).

Applying the Word of God

In finding God's rest, we must learn how to apply God's Word to any given situation. The Bible is the guidebook for our lives. Yet for many, it is only a book that sits and gathers dust. God desires that we learn to apply his Word to our relationships, to our marriage, and to any given situation. If you are under stress, how much of the Word have you read lately?

In applying the Word, God wants us to be the light to the world around us. If we are reading and meditating on the Word, then the light of God will shine through us for the world to see. There were times, before I became a Christian, when I would meet people, and it seemed there was something about them that I couldn't figure out." As a Christian, I now know that it was the Spirit of God shining through them.

In applying God's Word, we have to begin to declare his Word. His Word is truth, and it is a light into the darkness. Every time we speak the Word, we are speaking life and bringing life to those who need it. Psalm 119:105 reminds us, "It is a light unto my path and lamp unto my feet."

However, we cannot be a light if we are living in the darkness of the world. God delights in us when we walk in his Word and follow his light. Here are several Scriptures on which we can meditate:

Do your best to present yourself to God as one approved, a workman who does not need to be ashamed and who correctly handles the word of truth. (2 Tim. 2:15)

I have hidden your word in my heart that I might not sin against you. Praise be to you, O Lord; teach me your decrees. With my lips I recount all the laws that come from your mouth.

I rejoice in following your statues as one rejoices in great riches. I meditate on our precepts and consider your ways. I delight in your decrees; I will not neglect your word. (Ps. 119:11–16)

Let the word of Christ dwell in you rightly as you teach and admonish one another with all wisdom, and as you sing psalms, hymns and spiritual songs with gratitude in your hearts to God. And whatever you do, whether in word or deed, do it all in the name of the Lord Jesus, giving thanks to God the Father through him. (Col. 3:16–17)

If we apply God's Word, not only can we move mountains with the mustard seed of our faith, the Word can lead others to faith through us. The apostle Paul writes in Romans 5:1–4, "Therefore, since we have been justified through faith, we have peace with God through our Lord Jesus Christ, through whom we have gained access by faith into this grace in which we now stand. And we rejoice in the hope of the glory of God."

"Know that a man is not justified by observing the law, but by faith in Jesus Christ. So we too, have put our faith in Christ Jesus that we may be justified by faith in Christ and not by observing the law, because by observing the law no one will be justified" (Gal. 3:26).

Here are some other Scripture verses you might want to read and meditate upon:

What happens when we believe?	Bible verse	Personal comments after meditation
We receive forgiveness of sin.	Acts 10:43	
We are saved.	Romans 10:9	
We receive eternal life.	John 3:14–16	
We gain access to God.	Ephesians 3:12	

What happens when we believe?	Bible verse	Personal comments after meditation
The Word of God begins to work in us.	1 Thessalonians 2:13	
We become children of light.	John 12:36	
We enter God's rest.	Hebrew 4:3	
We receive peace with God.	Roman 5:1	
We gain security in God's power.	1 Peter 1:5	

The Holy Spirit directly empowers us for all situations through the Word. We are also empowered to do battle with our mortal enemy, Satan. How can we become empowered?

In Ephesians 6:10, the apostle Paul encourages us as he says, "Finally, be strong in the Lord and in his mighty power. Put on the whole armour of God so that you can take your stand against the devil's schemes."

The Holy Spirit is very involved in a person's life when that person begins a faith walk with God. He

- teaches us (John 14:26)
- hears and speaks (John 16:13)
- experiences grief (Eph. 4:30)
- can be resisted (Acts 7:51)
- can be tested (Acts 5:9)

In every moment of our lives, we need to involve the Holy Spirit. Why? Simply because he enables us to live the Christian life!

Those who live according to the sinful nature have their minds set on what that nature desires; but those who live in accordance with the Sprit have their minds set on what the Spirit desires. The mind of sinful man is death, but the mind controlled by the Sprit is life and peace; the sinful mind is hostile to God. It does not submit to God's law, nor can it do

256

so. Those controlled by the sinful nature cannot please God. You, however, are controlled not by the sinful nature but by the Spirit, if the Spirit of God lives in you. And if anyone does not have the Spirit of Christ, he does not belong to Christ. (Rom. 8:5–9)

As we learn to apply God's Word to any situation, we also learn how to slay the many giants assailing us. Paul reminds us, "Our struggles are not against flesh and blood, but against the rulers, against the authorities, against the powers of this dark world and against the spiritual forces of evil in the heavenly realms."

In order to apply God's Word, we have to learn God's heart. God desires to create a depth in his Word within our hearts in every stage of our life, especially in the valleys of life. In addition, reading Christian books and commentaries are good, but we can only attain intimacy with God by spending time with him, talking to him, and applying his Word. To have this type of depth requires that we receive the teaching directly from the greatest teacher of all time, the Holy Spirit. As wounded individuals in the wilderness, we must dig into God's Word. Seek God first!

Jesus instructs us in Matthew 6:33, "Seek ye first the kingdom of God and all his righteousness and all other things will be granted unto you."

Jesus instructs us to seek God and not worry about our life—what we will eat, what we will drink, or what we will wear. He used the examples of the birds of the air that are constantly fed by the heavenly Father and the lilies of the field that are so beautiful that even Solomon "in all his splendor" was not as well dressed.

Therefore, it is the Word—not our actions, not our efforts, and not the world—that will sustain us. Although at times it may seem like we are alone, and God is either not there or not listening, I have found that it is those times when he seems most absent that he is most present. He is constantly providing for our every need. He is Jehovah-Jireh—the Lord provides. Call upon him!

Applying the Word means that it is all about God. Sometimes we think it's about us, but it isn't about us or anybody else. Yes, we have to do our part; our part is to get into the Word of God, get into prayer, and be willing to receive what he has to offer. God issues an invitation to anyone who has a spiritual thirst. He says,

> Come, all you who are thirsty, come to the waters; and you who have no money, come, buy and eat! Come, buy wine and milk without money and without cost. Why spend money on what is not bread, and your labor on what does not satisfy? Listen, listen to me, and eat what is good, and your soul will delight in the richest of fare. Give ear and come to me; hear me, that your soul may live. (Isa. 55:1–3)

In Isaiah 55:11, he says, "So is my word that goes out from my mouth: It will not return to me empty, but will accomplish what I desire and achieve the purpose for which I sent it."

God's part, through the Holy Spirit, is to draw us closer to him to strengthen our faith, fight our daily battles, and bring healing so we can live victoriously. Our response should reflect the psalmist's when he says,

"As the deer pants for streams of water, so my soul pants for you, O God. My soul thirst for God, for the living God. When can I go and meet with God?" (Ps. 42:1–2).

In modern times, there are too many believers who stumble or just die spiritually in their walk with the Lord, because they are not applying the Word of God to their lives. They have "head knowledge" of God, but their relationship with God does not have a solid foundation. Oh, they look fine in church—nice suit and all—but at home, work, and among their friends, the Lord is the farthest thing from their mind. They are the "unseen Christian," because their behavior is no different from the people they are hanging out with.

When I was a teenager, my mother used an expression when she suspected that I was inching toward the wrong type of people: "Show me your friends, and I'll tell you who you are." But I believe this goes a step further. It is, "Show me your friends, and I'll show you your future."

It's really time to get rid of the "Sunday Christian" costume. The second reason for the faulty walk among Christians is reflected in the high divorce rate among Christians. Some statistics have placed the divorce rate higher among Christians than in the secular world. Why do you think spouses are abandoning their families instead of staying and working out problems according to the Word of God? Do you think there is a spiritual problem?

- As believers, God desires that we live our lives holy and blameless. It doesn't mean we are perfect. It doesn't mean we won't make mistakes. The word "holy" means to be set apart or separated. That is what he wants for us. He doesn't want any opportunity for sin to enter into us and cause decay. Neither does he want sin to derail us from our eternal destiny. Can you take time to think about these questions?
- Do you think that the reason for the record number of divorces among departing Christians is unholy living?
- Can the Word of God that provides a depth to our faith domicile together with unholy living?
- Is the Word of God enough for the various situations we face?

The writer of Hebrews puts it simply, saying "without faith, it is impossible to please Him [God]" (Heb 11:6). True faith is unshakeable; true faith doesn't waver; true faith is what gets you through the rough times. Faith isn't to get you out of problems; it's to get you through them victoriously.

When rough times come into our lives, James says,
Consider it pure joy, my brothers, whenever you face trials of many kinds, because you know that the testing of your faith develops perseverance. Perseverance must finish its work so that you may be mature and complete, not lacking anything. (James 1:2–4)

He goes on to say,
If any of you lacks wisdom, he should ask God, who gives generously to all without finding fault, and it will be given to him. But when he asks, he must believe and not doubt, because

he who doubts is like a wave of the sea, blown and tossed by the wind. That man should not think he will receive anything from the Lord; he is a double-minded man, unstable in all he does. (James 1:5–8)

CHAPTER 49

The Transformation

Returning Our Gifts to God
Vignette

I keep going back to my mother and her faith.

As a child, I remember lying in bed and listening to my mama sing. She has the most beautiful voice. If she was happy, she sang. If she was sad, she sang. Even when the neighbors bothered her, she sang. Years later, I realized that my mother had the right attitude. She would just sing and cook; sing and clean; sing and exercise her God-given gifts.

My mother had many gifts, but the one I want to mention is the gift of hospitality, as I seem to have been gifted similarly. Let's look at what the Bible says about gifts. Some primary gifts mentioned in 1 Peter 4:10-11 are:

Each one should use whatever gift he has received to serve others, faithfully administering God's grace in its various forms. If anyone speaks, he should do it as one speaking the very words of God. If anyone serves, he should do it with the strength God provides, so that in all things God may be praised through Jesus Christ. To him be the glory and the power forever and ever. Amen.

It would appear that every believer has been given at least one gift. When God created us, we were endowed with gifts and were commanded to use them. I Corinthians 12:7–10 says,

Now to each one the manifestation of the Spirit is given for the common good. To one is given through the Spirit the message of wisdom, to another the message of knowledge by means of the same Spirit, to another faith by the same Spirit, to another gifts of healing by that one Spirit, to another miraculous powers, to another prophecy, to another distinguishing between spirits, to another speaking in different kinds of tongues, and to still another the interpretation of tongues. All these are the work of one and the same Spirit, and he gives them to each one, just as he determines.

Nine gifts are listed:

- the word of wisdom
- the word of knowledge
- faith
- gifts of healing
- working of miracles
- prophecy
- discerning of spirits
- various kinds of tongues
- interpretation of tongues

A second listing of gifts is found in Ephesians 4:11. These gifts are for the "equipping" of the saints.

It was he who gave some to be apostles, some to be prophets, some to be evangelists, and some to be pastors and teachers, to prepare God's people for works of service, so that the body of Christ may be built up until we all reach unity in the faith and in the knowledge of the Son of God and become mature, attaining to the whole measure of the fullness of Christ.

In Romans 12:6–8, the apostle Paul states that we were created with various talents and qualities built into our personalities. Although they are undeserved, they were given to us through grace. Therefore, our gifts and talents are to be used for the benefit of others. These grace gifts are perceiver, server, teacher, exhorter, giver, administrator, and being a compassionate person.

If you think you don't have any gifts, read Psalm 139 especially verses 13–16. As discussed in previous chapters, we have been called, prepared, and transformed. Now we are ready for the ministry or purpose we were created for!

What is your gift? What talents has God given you that you can identify?

Remember that you are unique and most times, we will see through the lens of our gifts. In Luke 10:38–42, we are told of an incident that happened between two sisters.

As Jesus and his disciples were on their way, he came to a village where a woman named Martha opened her home to him. She had a sister called Mary, who sat at the Lord's feet listening to what he said. But Martha was distracted by all the preparations that had to be made. She came to him and said, "Lord, don't you care that my sister has left me to do the work myself? Tell her to help me!"

"Martha, Martha," the Lord answered, "you are worried and upset about many things. But only one thing is needed. Mary has chosen what is better, and it will not be taken away from her."

Here we have two sisters with different gifts. Martha was always busy serving and exercising her gift of hospitality, while Mary preferred to sit at Jesus' feet and learn from him. I believe that sometimes people are too tough on Martha, because when Jesus spoke to her, he wasn't demeaning her gift of hospitality; he was just correcting her attitude. She was always getting "bent out of shape," always anxious. It might be that the Master was in the house, and she wanted the best for him. The gift of hospitality is a very important gift, as both apostles Paul and Peter seem to think it worthwhile to mention it. The apostle Paul later talked about practicing hospitality (in Romans 12:13). Peter admonishes us to offer hospitality to one another in 1 Peter 4:9.

I understand Martha because I inherited my mother's love of serving people. I love to have people over to my home. Growing up, I saw firsthand how people reacted to my mom's hospitality.

Seen through childlike eyes, my mother had the biggest pots in the neighborhood. If you stopped by our house, you could always get a refreshing drink or something to eat. There were seven siblings, including me, but at any given time, there were thirteen children living at our house. God had blessed my parents financially, and they gave back to anyone who needed help. There were always, cousins, uncles, and children of friends living with us; and we were not allowed to treat anyone differently. The Bible says to bring up a child in the way he should go and when he is old, he will not depart from it. That gift of hospitality was created in my being by God and honed by my mother's skillful hand.

Last December, I was feeling a little depressed because someone who wanted to wound me told me that when I entertained people, I did it only to show off my "nice things." It was depressing, because I know that that was never my motive in inviting people to my home. So I did what I always do. I went to the Lord and asked him to reveal things, especially my heart, to me.

I didn't tell anyone about what this person had accused me of. But one day, not too long after, a friend of mine called me. Without any prompting, she said, "I was just thinking about all the times you used to invite me and the children over to your house for Christmas—how you used to make sure that anyone who had no family came to your place. Anyone who had nowhere to go came to your place. I remember how you used to cook for everyone, for so many people … You would feed us and make us feel so welcomed. It was so enjoyable. I miss that."

This was almost twenty years later that this lady expressed her thanks to me. God is faithful to us if we are faithful to him in using our gifts. He is also a loving God who cares for his children. Time after time, God has had people say things to me to reinforce what this lady said to me.

When I went to a conference, someone came up from behind and held me tightly. I suddenly felt my feet lifted off the ground, and the person spun me around and around. My back was turned to this person, so I couldn't see who it was. When I was allowed to stand, dizzy and wobbly, I turned around and saw a young man I hadn't seen in twenty two years—he'd been a preteen the last time I'd seen him. We talked for a long time, and I laughingly said to him, "I remember you. Every morning, as soon as I woke up—and I'm an early riser—you were on my doorstep. At nights, I always had to ask you if you weren't going home."

It was then that he told me that my home had been a safe haven for him, a refuge. As a child, his father used to abuse his mother and the family. My home was the place he used for his escape. He also reminded me of the many times I would have birthday parties for my sons and would invite up to fifteen of their friends to the party. My response to him was, "I wasn't having parties; I was making memories." He said to me, "Some of my best memories are from the times I spent at your house."

I have one more story of how God encouraged me.

I used to teach the high school Sunday school class, and over the years, I've seen several of my students who are now university students and beyond. All of them have said to me that they can still remember when once a month I would have the class over to my house for a pancake breakfast. It was a tradition I started when I took over the class. I would always make that day special for them. It was a day I took to serve them.

I would make homemade pancakes, topped with lots of homemade syrup of various flavors, add whipped cream, and top it with strawberries. Twenty or more years later, they still remember and tell me about the monthly breakfasts. One student, now an adult, told me that it was the highlight of his month. I later found out that he was being physically abused at home by his father.

God will always have an encouraging word for us when we need to be lifted up. I cannot tell you to forget the people who have wounded you or are trying to wound you. Neither can I tell you to ignore them. It would be too easy to say.

What I can say, as a way of encouragement, is to use the gifts and talents that God has given you, even among your wounds and pain. When you are serving God, the Devil, the enemy of your soul, will try to discourage you. He is there only to kill, steal, and destroy. There are many people who are the Devil's compatriots. Don't let them steal the talent God has given you or the joy you receive in exercising your gift. If your motives for serving or exercising your gift are selfish, God, through the Holy Spirit, will speak to your heart and set you on the right path. God is faithful to give you his gifts; he is also faithful to preserve them.

When I was hurt by this person's cruel words, God sent me someone to encourage my heart. As I was being transformed, he sent the encouragement I needed at the right time.

As part of the transformation stage, you are now ready for God to use you. Don't let the bad report, bad situation, or bad people get you down. Galatians 6:9 reminds us not to become weary in doing good. God has your back! Stay focused! Let God take care of the people wanting to hurt you. I know it hurts when people deliberately hurt you out of jealousy, pain, resentment, and bitterness. But let God take care of it. Just focus on finding out what your gifts are and use them.

The apostle Paul says, "All things are passed away, behold all things have become new."

We are new people in Christ! You were wounded; you are now out of the wilderness. Find a good book on spiritual gifts, one that teaches about the characteristics of each gift. Begin to serve as Jesus would serve. You will know you have the gift of serving if some of your characteristics are the following:

- You find a need and are quick to meet it.
- You are very orderly and meticulous.
- You enjoy showing hospitality.
- You usually show love for others in deeds and actions rather than in words.
- You probably hate things or places to be in disorder.

Part of this gift is that you hate loose ends and clutter, so your finger might be on the pulse of things too much. Lift that finger sometimes! Some years ago, one of my supervisors at work laughed and asked me if my house was as organized as I had organized the workplace. I told him that my organizing skills had paid off, because previous to my working there, their audit result was 30 percent. After one of my "organizational frenzies," the office audit's score went up to 85 percent. I told him that the reason I was always organizing is that I like to have a sense of order.

My point for telling all the stories is for you to get to know yourself. Some people see gifts and talents in us that we are not aware of. Ask your friends to help you to discover your gifts and talents if you are not sure. Then list the characteristics. See where your gifts are. Pray about them, and ask the Holy Spirit to guide you into using them.

You have been transformed, so begin to show it. Work at developing the gifts God gave you and honor Him with them.

Food for Thought

Since you have been transformed, use this stage of your journey for several purposes:

- Find out what your gifts are.
- Use this season of your life to do God's work.
- Praise him for all that he has done and all that he has taken you through.

267

CHAPTER 50

A Season of Praise

There is a Southern gospel song that I listen to all the time. Part of the chorus goes:

"I have so much to thank him for, so much to praise him for."

Vignettes

After returning from teaching abroad, I felt I had reached a stage in my life where I could begin a career, because I had finished raising my children. I had put my career on hold in order to do this, and the children were independent adults. Going abroad to get some international experience in my field was a way of kick-starting a career. I had a degree in linguistics, but prior to going abroad, I had worked at lower-level jobs so my time would be more flexible, and I would be more available to the children.

When I returned to Canada, I felt that my time had come to do something for myself. I was excited! I got a job teaching at a college, and it paid me a good salary, but it was on a contract basis. This meant that I was never sure if I was going to get a contract for the next session. Once, a session started on the Monday, and I did not sign a contract until the Friday afternoon at 4:00 p.m. It was very stressful, especially when I had bills to pay. This caused many problems. It was at this time I became single.

Amid all the stress and uncertainty at work and the personal stress, I struggled through the summer to the fall. In October, the manager at work asked the staff to let her know if we wanted to attend a teachers' conference in Banff. Of course, my hand was up in a jiffy. The school paid for the conference, other expenses, and gave each person a per diem.

The conference was excellent, and on the last night, they had a banquet. A colleague of mine called me over to sit at his table with some of his friends. When I sat down, there was an empty chair on either side of me. About half an hour later, a man sat down on my left. I introduced myself and, as usual, began to socialize. We talked about my travels, his travels, my teaching experience, and my opinion on teaching English as a second language (ESL). Eventually, I asked him where he was presently teaching.

He told me that he wasn't a teacher; he was an administrator with a certain public school. You could have knocked me over with a feather—I had been trying to find out the name of the principal of that school for six months, and here, the Lord had placed me beside this administrator—and had even given me my own private interview.

After the conference, I went home and forgot about the meeting with the administrator. Five months later, as I was heading home from work, I saw a sign advertising a job fair at the coliseum. I quickly swung around and changed lanes, thinking maybe I should just check it out. I wasn't really looking for a job, but I felt the urge to go to this job fair.

The administrator I'd met at the conference was at one of the booths. He remembered me, and we bantered back and forth and also discussed government funding, the cuts they were making to ESL programs, and the lay-offs of ESL teachers. I joked to him, "If I don't have a job, can I call you?" He replied, "If I have a position, you would be one of the first persons I would call."

About three weeks later, I heard that six teaching positions would be cut and one would be mine. I made the decision to send my résumé to the administrator I had met. I was not expecting any reply. My trust factor was low because of recent broken promises, but two days later, I got an e-mail from the administrator, inviting me for an interview.

The next event I'm going to relate is incredible. This was the second time in my life this has happened to me.

About halfway through the interview, the administrator stopped the interview process and offered me a job. He then got up to leave and told me that the program manager would give me all forms that go along with being a new employee. Then he said something very curious. As he was leaving, he said, "This was ordained." I looked at him, thinking, *That's a Christian word. Is he a Christian?*

I was in a daze at the speed of which things had transpired, and thought, like *Alice in Wonderland*, it was, "curiousier and curiousier." The program manager said to me—and note very carefully what she said—"The position has been open for a while but he [the administrator] had said that he wanted to hire the right person for the position."

Apparently, after he met me, he had come back to the office and had said to the program manager, "I found the person I would love to hire for the position." And the reason he said it was "ordained," I later learned, was because after he first met me, he had called my workplace to talk to me but I had not received the message that he'd called.

Isn't it just like God! No matter the human interferences and manipulations, God's plan will never fail. I now have a job that I enjoy very much!

Thoughts to Meditate On

- No matter how difficult the situation, God is always working on our behalf.
- His work does not begin when we have a difficult situation; his work begins long before that. (God was working on my behalf long before I even knew I would need a job.)

The next stage of praise is that I was suddenly single, had only $161 in my bank account and had to begin a new life. I made resolutions then and there: no matter what happens, as the Lord blesses me, I will always tithe 10 percent or more of my income. I will always put God first and trust him for my needs, and I won't forget that my happiness lies in Christ. Nobody else can make me happy

The first month I was single, I did a budget. I needed $1,500 to cover my expenses. It was amazing how God worked it out. One person sent me $500. Two people lent me $500 each (which I have since repaid). When I had to pay for my parking at school, I had to scrape up $45 in change to pay for it by the deadline. I wrote in my book, *God's Grace: A Long Night's Journey into Day* how I needed groceries and had no money, but then I got a rebate check in the mail. This kept on and on, and God still keeps on providing for me.

The next thing I needed was additional income to cover my monthly expenses. One Friday evening after a monthly meeting for professional teachers of ESL, I happened to be in the same elevator as my administrator. I asked him what credentials I needed to teach a certain evening program that my school offered. He said to me, "Leta, you are qualified to teach any program," and he said he would keep me in mind if something opened up.

About three months later, when I had completely forgotten the conversation, I got an e-mail from the program manager. She said that a position had opened up in the evening program—something that rarely happened—and the job was mine if I still wanted it. Over and above my getting paid for the evening classes, I was also asked to be the site coordinator for the evening program and received extra pay for that. God is good and is still looking out for me!

God is blessing my career. At a monthly professional meeting, one of the attendees said to me, "Maybe you should consider presenting at a conference." I insisted I could never do something like that—but she had planted a seed. When the next conference came up, I e-mailed my administrator, who is very supportive, and told him I was thinking of sending off a proposal to be a presenter. He thought it was a great idea and gave me some ideas of what I could possibly present. I put it together and sent it off. The next day, I was talking to two colleagues, and they wanted to present too. So we brainstormed, and I sent that off too. To my surprise, both proposals were accepted.

I give all credit to God, because it is very difficult to be accepted as first-time presenters at conferences such as these. I presented individually and my two other colleagues and I presented as a group. We had great feedback from our peers. I later found out that the lady who had encouraged me to present at the teachers' conference is an associate professor for the ESL master's program at one of the top five universities in Canada. I sent her a thank-you e-mail for planting the seed. You never know who God will use to carry out his plan for your life.

I am blessed financially. The nature of many ESL positions is that they are contract positions. This means that sometimes we have to wait five to six weeks for a paycheck until the new contract takes effect. I got a paycheck mid-December and my next was going to be at the end of January. I had no idea how I was going to get through Christmas, as well as pay the mortgage and bills. Since I made my resolution to trust God implicitly, I prayed and went to bed. I woke up on payday, and as I was heading to my computer to check my bank account, I kept praying, "Lord, if I can get even X amount, it would be sufficient to pay some bills." When I checked my bank account, I just about passed out. I blinked several times, rubbed my eyes, and blinked again, before I could believe what I was seeing. It was three times the amount I had anticipated. Everything, including my vacation pay, had been deposited. I had not expected that to happen.

Another time I needed $618 to cover a bill when I got a call from my life insurance company. They informed me that they had recalculated my policy and sent me a check for $744. God gives me over and above what I need; always at the right time and always when I need it.

I am blessed physically. When I became single, I felt like garbage. I felt old and worn out. I felt like nothing. I couldn't sleep and had constant headaches. However, with God's help, I decided to get back into exercising to reduce the stress. I signed up at the gym and even though it was very expensive, I got a personal fitness trainer. After nine weeks, I lost ten pounds and felt a lot better, physically, mentally, and psychologically. I'm still losing weight and, up to this point, have lost forty pounds naturally and have gone down four dress sizes. I will be getting back into competitive sports, which I had abandoned after my family life got busy and after my knees began to bother me. My knees had begun to bother me a few years earlier, and the only exercise I could do was walking.

At first, it was difficult for me to accept that I could not play tennis or enjoy the sports I had played since I was in elementary school.

The issue of my knees and my weight was always a catch-22. I couldn't lose the weight because I couldn't walk, and I couldn't walk because of my knees. My walking partner would complain about my pace, and it was emotionally distressful to hear the complaints, so many times I would go out by myself, listen to gospel music, and pray and cry as I walked. But God has been so good to me!

Now, every day when I am able to work out at the gym, I give him thanks. I am even training to run a marathon in the summer. I know God will give me the strength that I need. So, marathon here I come!

God is also blessing me mentally. My mental wellness took a turn for the worse at the onset. I was completing my master's degree when I became single. I found that I couldn't focus long enough to study, so I finally went to see my doctor. I then e-mailed my professor and told him what had happened. He advised me to e-mail the director, and he would also write a letter to the director explaining the situation. As it turned out, the university allowed me to take time off without penalty, but I was determined to scale this mountain that had been placed in my path.

It was almost six months before I was finally able to resume my studies and finish the course. I struggled through every month, but I became mentally well again. This was through studying the Word of God more intensely.

This phase was extremely painful for me. I am a lifelong learner. I love to study and learn new things, and I always thank God for the good brain he gave me. When I couldn't function mentally, it was painful. But praise God! My mental acumen resumed, and I was able to complete my program.

God's Transforming Power

The non-profit group, L. M. Empowered Women of Hope Association, which was born out of my pain is growing under God's hand. Being alone and single can be a blessing spiritually. I have taken the opportunity to get even closer to God, and he has been so faithful in sheltering, comforting, and blessing me. I have discovered more about God and his grace, prior to and while writing this book, than I have in almost thirty years.

I could write several pages, over and over again, of how God has blessed me financially, physically, spiritually, mentally, and emotionally. After living in constant pain from a knee injury, I am now pain-free—unless, of course, I forget my age and go prancing around as if I'm a spring chicken. God has been so good to me!

Jesus says, "Come unto me, all who are weary and heavy laden and I will give you rest." I can honestly say that I am at peace. I am content with the Lord. He gives me happy days. I am using this time of singleness to regain my emotional, mental, and physical strength. God has been very gracious to me.

Principle

Staying thankful in all circumstances honors God!

CHAPTER 51

Last Word

It's All About Perspective
Vignette

As I waited impatiently at the travel agent's desk in the Toronto airport during spring break, I began to visualize myself getting disorderly and being led away by security. I was not a happy flyer. I had paid an exorbitant amount of money for my ticket and now ... let me go back a little.

"Excuse me," I said politely to the stewardess. "Is it possible to get an aisle seat?"

The stewardess calmly looked into my sleep-deprived eyes and said, "It's not about an aisle seat; it's about a seat."

They had overbooked the flight and I, despite buying my ticket at an early date, had no seat.

"Are you telling me that I cannot get on that airplane?" I demanded, pointing to the plane sitting outside.

"Have a seat," she said.

I shuffled a few inches to the side but refused to sit down. After about ten minutes, I was joined by another passenger who, *sotto voce*, said to me, "I paid a lot of money for my ticket, and do or die, I'm getting on that plane. I have to get back to work."

"Me, too!" I replied, glad to have the support of an equally disgruntled flyer at my side.

Eventually, the seating was sorted out, and after finally getting on the plane and sitting with a satisfied smile on my face, I decided to examine the experience from another angle. I decided that it was all about perspective!

As I reflected on my return trip from Toronto, my thought was, *Nothing in life is guaranteed.* I had done everything I was supposed to do in order to get on that airplane but there were obstacles. I finally got on the plane, but as I was ascending, my thoughts centered on the only guarantees in life:

- salvation
- a place in heaven at death

Provisions have been made for us to access the guarantees, so we just have to make a choice.

Making a Choice

We have two choices. We can live for ourselves now and pursue our own ambitions, or we can pursue eternal things—things that will last for eternity. We are guaranteed results either way. We just have to choose our outcome—instant gratification or delayed delight.

Where are the guarantees in life?

In the previous years, the storms in my life have buffeted me. Being suddenly single, trying to hold together what's left of the family, and dealing with my grief and the grief of my children and grandchildren hasn't been easy. Sometimes I kept that stiff upper lip when all I wanted to do was give in to my emotions. There were a couple of times when I had a complete meltdown in front of one of the children, but all the time I let them know how much I depended on God to get me through. A quote accredited to Charles Dickens makes me hope that this quote can describe me. It goes like this:

"Suffering has been stronger than all other teaching, and has taught me to understand what my heart used to be. I have been bent and broken but I hope—into a better shape."

There are no guarantees that parts of our life won't be painful. However, there is a guarantee that we will have someone—God—to help us walk through those painful times.

Once again, I quote the apostle Paul who reinforces my belief in God when he says,

Who shall separate us from the love of Christ? Shall trouble or hardship or persecution or famine or nakedness or danger or sword? As it is written for your sake we face death all day long; we are considered as sheep to be slaughtered.

No, in all these things we are more than conquerors through him who loved us. For I am convinced that neither death nor life, neither angels nor demons, neither the resent nor the future, nor any powers, neither height nor depth, not anything else in all creation, will be able to separate us from the love of God that is in Christ Jesus our Lord.

We rejoice in the hope of the glory of God. Not only so, but we also rejoice in our sufferings, because we know that suffering produces perseverance; perseverance, character; and character, hope. And hope does not disappoint us, because God has out his love into our hearts by the Holy Spirit, whom he has given us. (Rom. 5:2–5)

We don't have to have a morbid outlook on life, our wounds, our pain, and our sufferings. But we can be joyous and triumphant, because we know that as God walks with us, his purpose is to produce character in us. When he allows us to go through the wilderness, there is a purpose. Maybe there's just too much of the "Egypt" in us that he needs to remove. Remember: nothing is meaningless with God.

Jesus says,

"In this world you will suffer tribulations but be of good cheer, for I have overcome the world."

Many of us are familiar with Helen Keller and all the trials and tribulations she suffered. According to her, "Character cannot be developed in ease and quiet. Only through experience of trial and suffering can the soul be strengthened, ambition inspired and success achieved."

Each of the Bible personalities we looked at suffered either by their own hand and their own mistakes or at the hand of others. The most important lesson we learn from all the stories is how they got to a place where they had to surrender their pain, dreams, aspirations, fears, and happiness to God.

Being wounded means we have suffered. I have had to give up many dreams. Many of you have had to do the same. You might have had to give up the dream of spending your golden years as part of a couple after raising your children. One verse that comes to mind is Romans 8:28:

"And we know that in all things God works for the good of those who love him, who have been called according to his purpose."

Even though we have suffered, the apostle Paul, who has suffered greatly by anyone's standards, assures, "Our present sufferings are not worth comparing with the glory that will be revealed in us" (Rom. 8:18). Be assured that in this dark and foggy period of your life, God loves you. Take time for cleansing your soul. You have God's abiding love. You have his promises! Now take his hand!

I have come full circle—you will too!

CHAPTER 52

The Legacy of Life

As I've gone through my wilderness period, I think about my mom and the lessons I learned from her and the lessons I want my family to learn from me when life threatens to pull them down. What legacy do I want to leave behind for my children and grandchildren?

Here are a few:

1. Faith: I want my children and grandchildren to say, "She has the faith of Abraham. She believed God."
2. Heart: She has the capacity to forgive from the heart like Joseph.
3. Strength: Her strength comes from the Lord. Her key verse is, "I can do all things through Christ who strengthens me" (Phil. 4:16).
4. Joy: The joy of the Lord is her strength. Her joy doesn't come from her situation; it comes from the Lord.
5. Prayer: Prayer is the key to her success.
6. Happy: She was happy because her happiness was in the Lord.
7. Love: She loved her family.
8. Love: She loved the unlovely.
9. Giving: She gave, even when she had very little.
10. Strives: She was always striving to grow spiritually.
11. Sorrows: When pain, pressure, stress, and sorrows came, she never ran away.
12. Victory: She was victorious because she trusts in the Lord, the God of her childhood.

My Mother's Dream

Vignette

Mama: Hi, Rits. I had a dream last night.

Rits: Mama, you're always dreaming.

Mama: This dream was about you.

Rits: Yeah, right!

Mama: Last night, I dreamed that I was running through a field. I was younger, and my mother was with me. She looked the same, just like she was before she died. She had on a white dress and her long, flowing, waist-length black hair was flowing out behind her as she ran.

Rits: (groans and mentally rolls her eyes)

Mama: She kept calling my name, and she said to me, "Who will go with me to preach the gospel? Who will go with me?"

    I answered her and said, "I will go with you." I joined her and started to run with her, and I started to call, "Who will go with me? Who will go and preach the gospel with me?"

As I was running, I saw you, and I said, "Rits, come with me. Come preach the gospel with me." You then said, "I will go and preach the gospel with you."

Rits: "Me!" (squealing in a high-pitched voice)

Mama: Yes, you!

Rits: That's just a dream. Don't hold your breath.

I was eighteen when my mother told me her dream. I had just gotten my first job, was partying with my friends, and I was enjoying the pleasures of the world. The last thing on my mind was preaching the gospel, although at twelve years, I had had a dream in which the Lord had spoken to me and told me that he wanted me to become a missionary. In the dream, I had told him I was shy and too afraid to speak. I never told anyone, especially my mom, about this dream, yet here she was, telling me about her dream.

In 1981, my younger brother was killed. I subsequently became a Christian through that tragedy. I immediately got involved in the church, and even though I was home in my own country, the Lord gave me a "missionary" heart. Thirty-one years after my mother told me her dream of my "preaching" the gospel, I called her and told her that I had had a dream. Here's how the conversation went:

Rits: I had a dream last night. You'd never believe me.

Mama: Try me.

Rits: I dreamed that the Lord wants me to go into the ministry. So I spoke to the pastor and I'm going to begin my studies.

Mama? Mama! Are you there?

(I could hear laughter at the other end of the line.)

Mama: And you told me not to hold my breath.

Well, I did. I held my breath and prayed.

We both had a good laugh at my expense and the "foolish" words I had said to her when I was eighteen years old. She held her breath and prayed. It was a running joke between us, and every time after that, when I had to do any public speaking or preaching, I would call her and discuss my notes with her. She never underestimated the power of prayer.

As for you, my readers, never underestimate the power of prayer, God's power, and the hand of God as he leads you unto your destiny.

CHAPTER 54
The Board Meeting

"Well, gentlemen? Shall we continue with the search for a candidate for the firm?

"Yes, sir," the board members answered, rather meekly. They all seem afraid to speak.

"Sir," one said, clearing his throat.

"What is the matter?"

"Sir, I believe we have a bigger problem.

"What is it?" the gentleman asked.

"It would appear that all the candidates are more than qualified for the position."

"Well said!"

CPSIA information can be obtained at www.ICGtesting.com
Printed in the USA
LVOW13s0501260214

375150LV00002B/9/P